SCIENCE
FUSION

fusion [FYOO • zhuhn] a combination of two or more things that releases energy

This **Interactive Student Edition** belongs to

_____

Teacher/Room

_____

HOLT McDOUGAL

HOUGHTON MIFFLIN HARCOURT

Consulting Authors

Michael A. DiSpezio

Global Educator
North Falmouth, Massachusetts

Michael DiSpezio is a renaissance educator who moved from the research laboratory of a Nobel Prize winner to the K–12 science classroom. He has authored or co-authored numerous textbooks and written more than 25 trade books. For nearly a decade he worked with the JASON Project, under the auspices of the National Geographic Society, where he designed curriculum, wrote lessons, and hosted dozens of studio and location broadcasts. Over the past two decades, he has developed supplementary material for organizations and shows that include PBS *Scientific American Frontiers, Discover* magazine, and the Discovery Channel. He has extended his reach outside the United States and into topics of crucial importance today. To all his projects, he brings his extensive background in science and his expertise in classroom teaching at the elementary, middle, and high school levels.

Marjorie Frank

Science Writer and Content-Area Reading Specialist
Brooklyn, New York

An educator and linguist by training, a writer and poet by nature, Marjorie Frank has authored and designed a generation of instructional materials in all subject areas, including past HMH Science programs. Her other credits include authoring science issues of an award-winning children's magazine; writing game-based digital assessments in math, reading, and language arts; and serving as instructional designer and co-author of pioneering school-to-work software for Classroom Inc., a nonprofit organization dedicated to improving reading and math skills for middle and high school learners. She wrote lyrics and music for *SCIENCE SONGS,* which was an American Library Association nominee for notable recording. In addition, she has served on the adjunct faculty of Hunter, Manhattan, and Brooklyn Colleges, teaching courses in science methods, literacy, and writing.

Acknowledgments for Covers

Front cover: *Rice fields* (bg) ©Keren Su/Corbis; *false color X-rays on hand* (l) ©Lester Lefkowitz/Getty Images; *primate* (cl) ©Bruno Morandi/The Image Bank/Getty Images; *red cells* (cr) ©Todd Davidson/Getty Images; *fossils* (r) ©Yoshihi Tanaka/amana images/Getty Images

Michael R. Heithaus

Director, School of Environment and Society
Associate Professor, Department of Biological Sciences
Florida International University
North Miami, Florida

Mike Heithaus joined the Florida International University Biology Department in 2003. He has served as Director of the Marine Sciences Program and is now Director of the School of Environment and Society, which brings together the natural and social sciences and humanities to develop solutions to today's environmental challenges. While earning his doctorate, he began the research that grew into the Shark Bay Ecosystem Project in Western Australia, with which he still works. Back in the United States, he served as a Research Fellow with National Geographic, using remote imaging in his research and hosting a 13-part *Crittercam* television series on the National Geographic Channel. His current research centers on predator-prey interactions among vertebrates, such as tiger sharks, dolphins, dugongs, sea turtles, and cormorants.

Donna M. Ogle

Professor of Reading and Language
National-Louis University
Chicago, Illinois

Creator of the well-known KWL strategy, Donna Ogle has directed many staff development projects translating theory and research into school practice in middle and secondary schools throughout the United States. She is a past president of the International Reading Association and has served as a consultant on literacy projects worldwide. Her extensive international experience includes coordinating the Reading and Writing for Critical Thinking Project in Eastern Europe, developing an integrated curriculum for a USAID Afghan Education Project, and speaking and consulting on projects in several Latin American countries and in Asia. Her books include *Coming Together as Readers; Reading Comprehension: Strategies for Independent Learners; All Children Read;* and *Literacy for a Democratic Society.*

Program Reviewers

Content Reviewers

Paul D. Asimow, PhD
Professor of Geology and Geochemistry
Division of Geological and Planetary Sciences
California Institute of Technology
Pasadena, CA

Laura K. Baumgartner, PhD
Postdoctoral Researcher
Molecular, Cellular, and Developmental Biology
University of Colorado
Boulder, CO

Eileen Cashman, PhD
Professor
Department of Environmental Resources Engineering
Humboldt State University
Arcata, CA

Hilary Clement Olson, PhD
Research Scientist Associate V
Institute for Geophysics, Jackson School of Geosciences
The University of Texas at Austin
Austin, TX

Joe W. Crim, PhD
Professor Emeritus
Department of Cellular Biology
The University of Georgia
Athens, GA

Elizabeth A. De Stasio, PhD
Raymond H. Herzog Professor of Science
Professor of Biology
Department of Biology
Lawrence University
Appleton, WI

Dan Franck, PhD
Botany Education Consultant
Chatham, NY

Julia R. Greer, PhD
Assistant Professor of Materials Science and Mechanics
Division of Engineering and Applied Science
California Institute of Technology
Pasadena, CA

John E. Hoover, PhD
Professor
Department of Biology
Millersville University
Millersville, PA

William H. Ingham, PhD
Professor (Emeritus)
Department of Physics and Astronomy
James Madison University
Harrisonburg, VA

Charles W. Johnson, PhD
Chairman, Division of Natural Sciences, Mathematics, and Physical Education
Associate Professor of Physics
South Georgia College
Douglas, GA

Program Reviewers *(continued)*

Tatiana A. Krivosheev, PhD
Associate Professor of Physics
Department of Natural Sciences
Clayton State University
Morrow, GA

Joseph A. McClure, PhD
Associate Professor Emeritus
Department of Physics
Georgetown University
Washington, DC

Mark Moldwin, PhD
Professor of Space Sciences
Atmospheric, Oceanic, and
Space Sciences
University of Michigan
Ann Arbor, MI

Russell Patrick, PhD
Professor of Physics
Department of Biology,
Chemistry, and Physics
Southern Polytechnic State
University
Marietta, GA

Patricia M. Pauley, PhD
*Meteorologist, Data Assimilation
Group*
Naval Research Laboratory
Monterey, CA

Stephen F. Pavkovic, PhD
Professor Emeritus
Department of Chemistry
Loyola University of Chicago
Chicago, IL

L. Jeanne Perry, PhD
Director (Retired)
Protein Expression Technology
Center
Institute for Genomics and
Proteomics
University of California, Los
Angeles
Los Angeles, CA

Kenneth H. Rubin, PhD
Professor
Department of Geology and
Geophysics
University of Hawaii
Honolulu, HI

Brandon E. Schwab, PhD
Associate Professor
Department of Geology
Humboldt State University
Arcata, CA

Marllin L. Simon, Ph.D.
Associate Professor
Department of Physics
Auburn University
Auburn, AL

Larry Stookey, PE
Upper Iowa University
Wausau, WI

Kim Withers, PhD
Associate Research Scientist
Center for Coastal Studies
Texas A&M University-Corpus
Christi
Corpus Christi, TX

Matthew A. Wood, PhD
Professor
Department of Physics & Space
Sciences
Florida Institute of Technology
Melbourne, FL

Adam D. Woods, PhD
Associate Professor
Department of Geological
Sciences
California State University,
Fullerton
Fullerton, CA

Natalie Zayas, MS, EdD
Lecturer
Division of Science and
Environmental Policy
California State University,
Monterey Bay
Seaside, CA

Teacher Reviewers

Ann Barrette, MST
Whitman Middle School
Wauwatosa, WI

Barbara Brege
Crestwood Middle School
Kentwood, MI

**Katherine Eaton Campbell,
M Ed**
Chicago Public Schools-Area 2
Office
Chicago, IL

**Karen Cavalluzzi, M Ed,
NBCT**
Sunny Vale Middle School
Blue Springs, MO

Katie Demorest, MA Ed Tech
Marshall Middle School
Marshall, MI

Jennifer Eddy, M Ed
Lindale Middle School
Linthicum, MD

Tully Fenner
George Fox Middle School
Pasadena, MD

Dave Grabski, MS Ed
PJ Jacobs Junior High School
Stevens Point, WI

Amelia C. Holm, M Ed
McKinley Middle School
Kenosha, WI

Ben Hondorp
Creekside Middle School
Zeeland, MI

George E. Hunkele, M Ed
Harborside Middle School
Milford, CT

Jude Kesl
Science Teaching Specialist 6–8
Milwaukee Public Schools
Milwaukee, WI

Joe Kubasta, M Ed
Rockwood Valley Middle School
St. Louis, MO

Mary Larsen
Science Instructional Coach
Helena Public Schools
Helena, MT

Angie Larson
Bernard Campbell Middle School
Lee's Summit, MO

Christy Leier
Horizon Middle School
Moorhead, MN

Helen Mihm, NBCT
Crofton Middle School
Crofton, MD

Jeff Moravec, Sr., MS Ed
Teaching Specialist
Milwaukee Public Schools
Milwaukee, WI

**Nancy Kawecki Nega, MST,
NBCT, PAESMT**
Churchville Middle School
Elmhurst, IL

Mark E. Poggensee, MS Ed
Elkhorn Middle School
Elkhorn, WI

Sherry Rich
Bernard Campbell Middle School
Lee's Summit, MO

Mike Szydlowski, M Ed
Science Coordinator
Columbia Public Schools
Columbia, MO

Nichole Trzasko, M Ed
Clarkston Junior High School
Clarkston, MI

Heather Wares, M Ed
Traverse City West Middle School
Traverse City, MI

Contents
in Brief

The water hole is a great place to see all kinds of interactions as animals gather to drink water.

Contents

Talons are very useful in snatching fish right out of the water. To prey, the sharp talons of an eagle are deadly weapons!

Assignments:

_____

_____

_____

_____

_____

_____

_____

Although the coral animal is tiny, some corals help build reefs that support millions of organisms. The Great Barrier Reef is so large that it can be seen from space.

© Houghton Mifflin Harcourt Publishing Company • Image Credits: ©Digital Vision/Getty Images

Contents (continued)

Careful management of renewable resources, such as trees and fish, will help maintain their populations for the future.

© Houghton Mifflin Harcourt Publishing Company • Image Credits: ©David R. Frazier/Photo Researchers, Inc.; ©Jeff Rotman/The Image Bank/Getty Images

Assigned   Due

Protecting our resources helps us and all of the other organisms that rely on the same resources.

Assignments:

© Houghton Mifflin Harcourt Publishing Company • Image Credits: ©artpartner-images/Photographer's Choice/Getty Images; ©NASA image by Marit Jentoft-Nilsen, based on data from NOAA GOES. Blue Marble Imagery by NASA's Earth Observatory Team; ©Tyrone Turner/National Geographic/Getty Images

Contents   **ix**

Power up with Science Fusion!

Your program fuses...

e-Learning and Virtual Labs

Labs and Activities

Write-In Student Edition

... to generate energy for today's science learner — *you*.

Write-In Student Edition

Be an active reader and make this book your own!

You can answer questions, ask questions, create graphs, make notes, write your own ideas, and highlight information right in your book.

Learn science concepts and skills by interacting with every page.

Labs and Activities

ScienceFusion includes lots of exciting hands-on inquiry labs and activities, each one designed to bring science skills and concepts to life and get you involved.

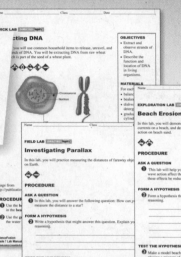

By asking questions, testing your ideas, organizing and analyzing data, drawing conclusions, and sharing what you learn...

You are the scientist!

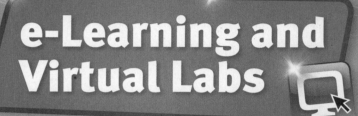

e-Learning and Virtual Labs

Digital lessons and virtual labs provide e-learning options for every lesson of Science Fusion.

On your own or with a group, explore science concepts in a digital world.

360° of Inquiry

Interactions of Living Things

Harcourt Publishing Company • Image Credits: (bkgd) ©Comstock/age fotostock; (br) ©Millard H. Sharp/Photo Researchers, Inc.

Big Idea

Organisms interact with each other and with the nonliving parts of their environment.

Fish and sponges in a coral reef.

What do you think?

Ecosystems consist of living things that depend on each other to survive. How might these fish depend on a coral reef? How might this bird depend on a dragonfly population?

Eastern bluebirds feed on insects.

Interactions of Living Things

CITIZEN SCIENCE

Sharing Spaces

Wetlands provide living space for many kinds of birds. Ospreys are large birds of prey that eat mostly fish. They often nest on telephone poles and other man-made structures. Yellow-rumped warblers are small birds that live in trees and eat insects and berries.

1 Ask A Question

How can organisms affect each other and a whole ecosystem?

An ecosystem is made up of all the living and nonliving things in an environment. Ospreys and yellow-rumped warblers are part of the same ecosystem. With your teacher and your classmates, brainstorm ways in which ospreys and yellow-rumped warblers might affect each other.

Yellow-rumped Warbler

② Think About It

A Look at the photos of the ospreys in their environment. List at least two resources they need to survive and explain how the ospreys get them.

_____

_____

_____

B What are two ways nonliving things could affect yellow-rumped warblers?

_____

_____

_____

Osprey nest

③ Apply Your Knowledge

A List the ways in which yellow-rumped warblers and ospreys share resources.

_____

_____

_____

B Yellow-rumped warblers have a diet that consists mainly, of insects and berries. Make a list of other organisms you know that might compete with the warblers for these same food resources.

_____

_____

_____

_____

C Describe a situation that could negatively affect both the osprey population and the yellow-rumped warbler population.

_____

_____

_____

Take It Home

Are ecologists looking for people to report observations in your community? Contact a university near your community to see if you can help gather information about plants, flowers, birds, or invasive species. Then, share your results with your class.

Introduction to Ecology

ESSENTIAL QUESTION

How are different parts of the environment connected?

By the end of this lesson, you should be able to analyze the parts of an environment.

This rain forest is an ecosystem. Hornbills are organisms in the ecosystem that use the trees for shelter.

✋ **Lesson Labs**

Quick Labs
• Which Abiotic and Biotic Factors Are Found in an Ecosystem?
• Which Biome?

Field Lab
• What's in an Ecosystem?

Engage Your Brain

1 Describe In your own words, write a list of living or nonliving things that are in your neighborhood.

_____

_____

_____

_____

_____

_____

_____

_____

2 Relate Write a photo caption that compares the ecosystem shown below and the ecosystem shown on the previous page.

_____

_____

_____

_____

Active Reading

3 Synthesize You can often define an unknown word or term if you know the meaning of its word parts. Use the word parts and sentence below to make an educated guess about the meaning of the term *abiotic factor*.

Word part	Meaning
a-	without
bio-	life

Example sentence
In an ecosystem, rocks are an example of an <u>abiotic factor</u> since they are not a living part of the environment.

abiotic factor:

_____

_____

Vocabulary Terms
- ecology
- biotic factor
- abiotic factor
- population
- species
- community
- ecosystem
- biome
- habitat
- niche

4 Apply As you learn the definition of each vocabulary term in this lesson, create your own definition or sketch to help you remember the meaning of the term.

The Web of Life

How are all living things connected?

Organisms need energy and matter to live. Interactions between organisms cause an exchange of energy and matter. This exchange creates a web of life in which all organisms are connected to each other and to their environment. **Ecology** is the study of how organisms interact with one another and with the environment.

Through the Living Environment

Each individual organism has a role to play in the flow of energy and matter. In this way, organisms are connected to all other organisms. Relationships among organisms affect each one's growth and survival. A **biotic factor** is an interaction between organisms in an area. Competition is one way that organisms interact. For example, different kinds of plants might compete for water in the desert.

This desert includes all of the organisms that live there, and all of the living and nonliving things that they need to survive.

This horse is a part of the living environment.

Through the Nonliving Environment

All organisms rely on the nonliving environment for survival. An **abiotic factor** is a nonliving part of an environment, such as water, nutrients, soil, sunlight, rainfall, or temperature. Some of these are resources that organisms need to grow and survive. For example, plants use sunlight, water, and soil nutrients to make food. Similarly, some organisms rely on soil or rocks for shelter.

Abiotic factors influence where organisms can survive. In a terrestrial environment, temperature and rainfall are important abiotic factors. In aquatic environments, the water's temperature, salt, and oxygen content are important abiotic factors. Changes in these basic abiotic factors affect where organisms can live and how many individuals are able to survive in the environment.

Active Reading **5 Infer** How does the environment determine where an organism can survive? Explain your answer.

_____

_____

_____

_____

_____

_____

The rocks and air are parts of the nonliving environment.

Visualize It!

6 Categorize List the abiotic factors that are present in the photo.

_____   _____

_____   _____

7 Relate Choose one abiotic factor that you listed above and explain how the horse interacts with it.

_____

_____

_____

_____

Stay Organized!

What are the levels of organization in the environment?

The environment can be organized into different levels. These levels range from a single organism to all of the organisms and their surroundings in an area. The levels of organization get more complex as more of the environment is considered.

Active Reading 8 **Identify** As you read, underline the characteristics of each of the following levels of organization.

Populations

A **population** is a group of individuals of the same species that live in the same place at the same time. A **species** includes organisms that are closely related and can mate to produce fertile offspring. The alligators that live in the Everglades form a population. Individuals within a population often compete with each other for resources.

Population

Individual

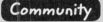

Ecosystems

An **ecosystem** is a community of organisms and their nonliving environment. In an ecosystem, organisms and the environment exchange energy and other resources. For example, alligators need to live near a body of water such as a marsh or a pond. They eat animals, such as birds, that wade near the shoreline. The water also helps alligators keep a stable body temperature. All abiotic and biotic factors make up an ecosystem. Examples of ecosystems include salt marshes, ponds, and forests.

Community

Communities

A **community** is made up of all the populations of different species that live and interact in an area. The species in a community depend on each other for many things, such as shelter and food. For example, the herons shown here get energy and nutrients by eating other organisms. But organisms in a community also compete with each other for resources just as members of a population do.

Visualize It!

9 Identify This osprey is a predatory bird that is part of the Florida Everglades ecosystem. Identify individuals of one other population that you see.

_____

10 Apply How does the osprey interact with the population that you just identified?

_____
_____
_____
_____

Think Globally!

What is a biome?

Each ecosystem has its own unique biotic and abiotic factors. Some ecosystems have few plants and are cold and dry. Others have forests and are hot and moist. This wide diversity of ecosystems can be organized into categories. Large regions characterized by climate and communities of species are grouped together as **biomes**. A biome can contain many ecosystems. Major land biomes include tropical rain forest, tropical grassland, temperate grassland, desert, temperate deciduous forest, temperate rain forest, taiga, and tundra.

What characteristics define a biome?

All of the ecosystems in a biome share some traits. They share climate conditions, such as temperature and rainfall, and have similar communities.

Climate Conditions

Active Reading 11 **Identify** As you read, underline the climate factors that characterize biomes.

Temperature is an important climate factor that characterizes biomes. For example, some biomes have a constant temperature. The taiga and tundra have cold temperatures all year. Tropical biomes are warm all year. In other biomes, the temperature changes over the course of a year. Temperate biomes have warm summers and colder winters. In some biomes, major temperature changes occur within a single day. For example, some deserts are hot during the day but cold at night.

Biomes also differ in the amount of precipitation they receive. For example, tropical biomes receive a lot of rainfall, while deserts receive little precipitation. The taiga and tundra have moist summers and dry winters.

This temperate rain forest gets a lot of rainfall. The organisms here have adapted to the wet climate.

Think Outside the Book Inquiry

12 **Apply** What biome do you live in? Describe your climate and make a list of the living things that are found in natural undeveloped areas nearby. Research which biome has these features. Then look at a biome map to see if your observations match the biome that is mapped for your location.

Communities of Living Things

Biomes contain communities of living things that have adapted to the climate of the region. Thus, ecosystems within the same biome tend to have similar species across the globe. Monkeys, vines, and colorful birds live in hot and humid tropical rain forests. Grasses, large mammals, and predatory birds inhabit tropical grasslands on several continents.

Only certain types of plants and animals can live in extreme climate conditions. For example, caribou, polar bears, and small plants live in the tundra, but trees cannot grow there. Similarly, the plant and animal species that live in the desert are also unique. Cacti and certain animal species have adaptations that let them tolerate the dry desert climate.

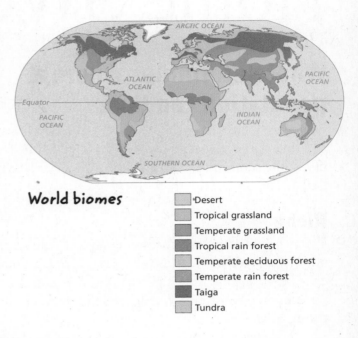

World biomes

- Desert
- Tropical grassland
- Temperate grassland
- Tropical rain forest
- Temperate deciduous forest
- Temperate rain forest
- Taiga
- Tundra

Visualize It!

13 Compare The photos below show two different biomes. Use what you learned about the characteristics of biomes to compare these environments, and then explain why they are categorized as different biomes. Write your answers in the space provided.

Compare: _____

Explain: _____

Home Sweet Home

What determines where a population can live?

Ecologists study the specific needs of different kinds of organisms and the role each species plays in the environment. Organisms that live in the same area have different ways of getting the resources they need.

Niche

Each population in an ecosystem plays a specific role. A population's **niche** (NICH) is the role the population plays in the ecosystem, such as how it gets food and interacts with other populations. For example, one part of a shark population's niche is eating fish.

A **habitat** is the place where an organism usually lives and is part of an organism's niche. The habitat must provide all of the resources that an organism needs to grow and survive. Abiotic factors, such as temperature, often influence whether a species can live in a certain place. Biotic factors, such as the interactions with other organisms that live in the area, also play a role. For example, the habitat of a shark must include populations of fish it can eat.

Two populations cannot occupy exactly the same niche. Even small differences in habitats, roles, and adaptations can allow similar species to live together in the same ecosystem. For example, green and brown anoles sometimes live on the same trees, but they avoid competition by living in different parts of the trees.

14 Relate How is a habitat like a person's address? How is a niche like a person's job?

_____

_____

_____

_____

_____

_____

_____

Visualize It!

15 Infer Describe the prairie dog's niche. How does it find shelter and impact the environment?

_____

_____

_____

_____

_____

Prairie dogs dig burrows in grassy plains. They eat plants and are hunted by predators such as owls and foxes.

Lizard Invasion

Green anole lizards (*Anolis carolinensis*) have been part of the South Florida ecosystem for a long time. Recently, a closely related lizard, the nonnative brown anole (*Anolis sagrei*), invaded the green anoles' habitat. How do they avoid competing with each other for resources?

Home Base
Green anoles live on perches throughout a tree. Brown anoles live mainly on branches that are close to the ground. If they have to share a tree, green anoles will move away from perches close to the ground. In this way, both kinds of anoles can live in the same tree while avoiding competition with each other.

Intrusive Neighbors
Although brown and green anoles can coexist by sharing their habitats, they do not live together peacefully. For example, brown anoles affect green anoles by eating their young.

Extend

Inquiry

16 Describe How do green and brown anoles avoid competition? Draw a picture of a tree showing both green and brown anoles living in it.

17 Research What are other examples of two species dividing up the parts of a habitat?

18 Relate Infer what would happen if the habitats of two species overlapped. Present your findings in a format such as a short story, a music video, or a play.

Visual Summary

To complete this summary, circle the correct word. Then use the key below to check your answers. You can use this page to review the main concepts of the lesson.

Ecology and Ecosystems

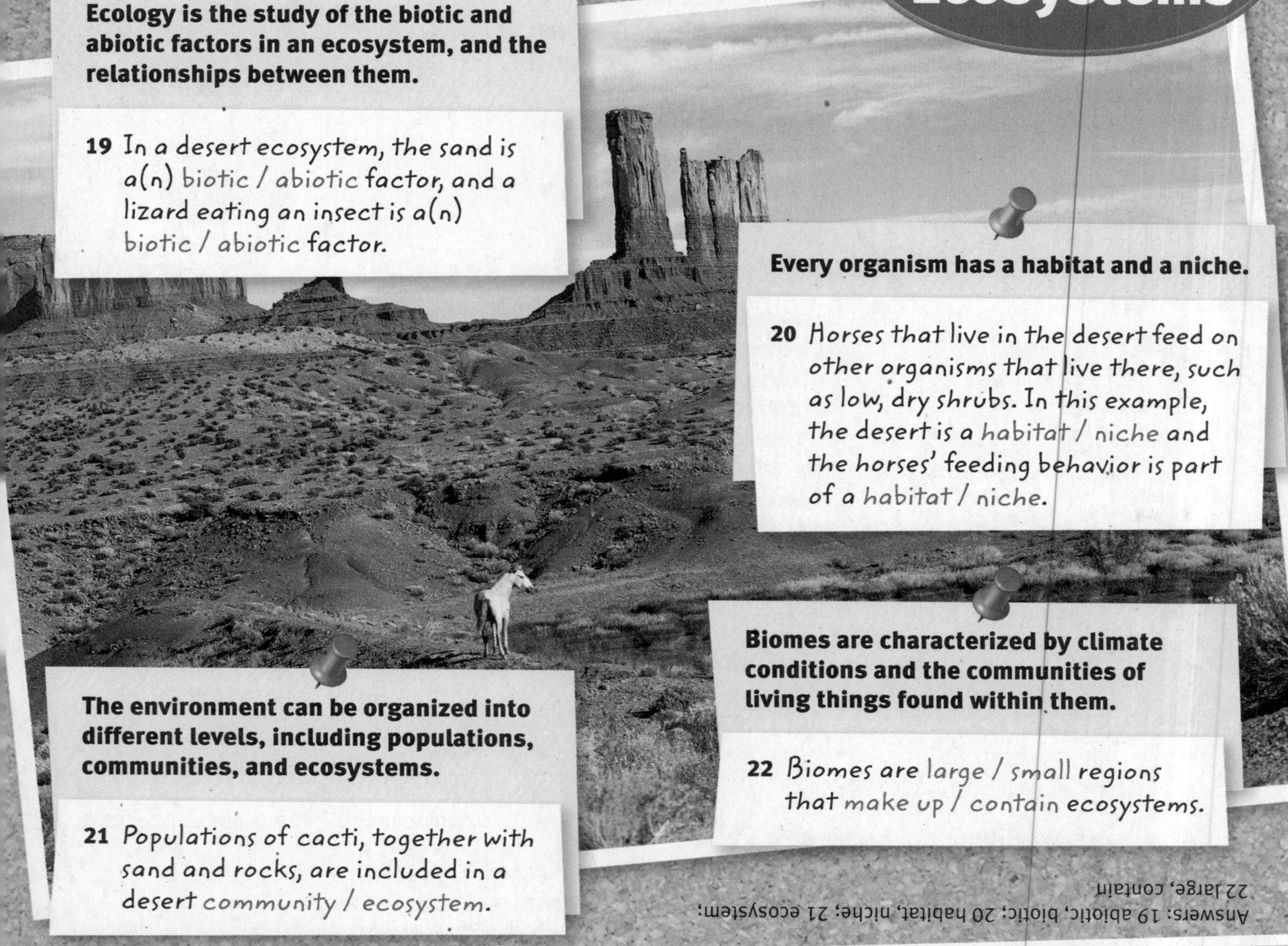

Ecology is the study of the biotic and abiotic factors in an ecosystem, and the relationships between them.

19 In a desert ecosystem, the sand is a(n) biotic / abiotic factor, and a lizard eating an insect is a(n) biotic / abiotic factor.

Every organism has a habitat and a niche.

20 Horses that live in the desert feed on other organisms that live there, such as low, dry shrubs. In this example, the desert is a habitat / niche and the horses' feeding behavior is part of a habitat / niche.

The environment can be organized into different levels, including populations, communities, and ecosystems.

21 Populations of cacti, together with sand and rocks, are included in a desert community / ecosystem.

Biomes are characterized by climate conditions and the communities of living things found within them.

22 Biomes are large / small regions that make up / contain ecosystems.

Answers: 19 abiotic, biotic; 20 habitat, niche; 21 ecosystem; 22 large, contain

23 **Predict** In the desert ecosystem shown above, name a biotic factor, and describe the effect on the horses if it were removed from the ecosystem.

Lesson Review

Vocabulary

1 Explain how the meanings of the terms *biotic factor* and *abiotic factor* differ.

_____

_____

_____

2 In your own words, write a definition for *ecology*.

_____

_____

_____

3 Explain how the meanings of the terms *habitat* and *niche* differ.

_____

_____

_____

Key Concepts

4 Compare What is the relationship between ecosystems and biomes?

_____

_____

_____

5 Explain Within each biome, how can the environment be organized into levels from complex to simple?

_____

_____

_____

_____

6 Infer How do the populations in a community depend on each other?

_____

_____

_____

7 Identify What factors determine where a population can live?

_____

_____

_____

_____

Critical Thinking

8 Predict What might happen in a tropical rain forest biome if the area received very little rain for an extended period of time?

_____

_____

_____

9 Infer Owls and hawks both eat rodents. They are also found in the same habitats. Since no two populations can occupy exactly the same niche, how can owls and hawks coexist?

_____

_____

_____

Use this graph to answer the following question.

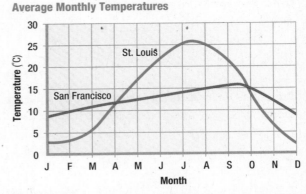

Average Monthly Temperatures

10 Interpret What is the difference in average temperature between the two cities in July?

My Notes

Kenneth Krysko

ECOLOGIST

Snakes have fascinated Dr. Kenneth Krysko since he was four years old. Now he is an ecologist specializing in herpetology—the study of snakes. You can often find him in the Florida Everglades looking for Burmese pythons. He tracks these pythons to help limit the effect they have on Florida ecosystems.

Burmese pythons can grow to be 6 meters long. They are native to southeast Asia and were illegally brought to Florida as pets. Many owners released them into the wild when the snakes grew too large. The snakes breed well in Florida's subtropical climate. And they eat just about any animal they can swallow, including many native species. Dr. Krysko tracks down these invasive pythons. Through wildlife management, molecular genetics, and other areas of study, he works with other scientists to search for ways to reduce the python population.

Dr. Krysko studies many other invasive species, that is, nonnative species that can do harm in Florida ecosystems. He shares what he learns, including ways to identify and deal with invasive species with other ecologists. Along with invasion ecology, he has done research in reproduction and conservation biology. Dr. Krysko also works as a collections manager in the herpetology division at the Florida Museum of Natural History.

Dr. Krysko works to get a handle on what to do about the invasive pythons.

JOB BOARD

Park Naturalist

What You'll Do: Teach visitors at state and national parks about the park's ecology, geology, and landscape. Lead field trips, prepare and deliver lectures with slides, and create educational programs for park visitors. You may participate in research projects and track organisms in the park.

Where You Might Work: State and national parks

Education: An advanced degree in science and teacher certification

Other Job Requirements: You need to be good at communicating and teaching. Having photography and writing skills helps you prepare interesting educational materials.

Conservation Warden

What You'll Do: Patrol an area to enforce rules, and work with communities and groups to help educate the public about conservation and ecology.

Where You Might Work: Indoors and outdoors in state and national parks and ecologically sensitive areas

Education: A two-year associate's degree or at least 60 fully accredited college-level credits

Other Job Requirements: To work in the wild, good wilderness skills, map-reading, hiking, and excellent hearing are useful.

PEOPLE IN SCIENCE NEWS

Phil McCRORY

Saved by a Hair!

Phil McCrory, a hairdresser in Huntsville, Alabama, asked a brilliant question when he saw an otter whose fur was drenched with oil from the Exxon Valdez oil spill. If the otter's fur soaked up oil, why wouldn't human hair do the same? McCrory gathered hair from the floor of his salon and performed his own experiments. He stuffed hair into a pair of pantyhose and tied the ankles together. McCrory floated this bundle in his son's wading pool and poured used motor oil into the center of the ring. When he pulled the ring closed, not a drop of oil remained in the water! McCrory's discovery was tested as an alternative method for cleaning up oil spills. Many people donated their hair to be used for cleanup efforts. Although the method worked well, the engineers conducting the research concluded that hair is not as useful as other oil-absorbing materials for cleaning up large-scale spills.

Roles in Energy Transfer

ESSENTIAL QUESTION

How does energy flow through an ecosystem?

By the end of this lesson, you should be able to relate the roles of organisms to the transfer of energy in food chains and food webs.

Energy is transferred from the sun to producers, such as kelp. It flows through the rest of the ecosystem.

This fish also needs energy to live. How do you think it gets this energy? From the sun like kelp do?

👋 **Lesson Labs**

Quick Labs
• Making Compost
• Energy Role Game
Field Lab
• Food Webs

🧠 Engage Your Brain

1 Describe Most organisms on Earth get energy from the sun. How is energy flowing through the ecosystem pictured on the opposite page?

_____

_____

_____

_____

_____

2 Predict List two of your favorite foods. Then, explain how the sun's energy helped make those foods available to you.

_____

_____

_____

_____

_____

_____

_____

✏️ Active Reading

3 Synthesize You can often define an unknown word if you know the meaning of its word parts. Use the word parts and sentences below to make an educated guess about the meaning of the words *herbivore* and *carnivore*.

Word part	Meaning
-vore	to eat
herbi-	plant
carni-	meat

Example sentence
A koala bear is an <u>herbivore</u> that eats eucalyptus leaves.

herbivore:

_____

_____

_____

Example sentence
A great white shark is a <u>carnivore</u> that eats fish and other marine animals.

carnivore:

_____

_____

_____

Vocabulary Terms

• producer	• carnivore
• decomposer	• omnivore
• consumer	• food chain
• herbivore	• food web

4 Apply As you learn the definition of each vocabulary term in this lesson, create your own definition or sketch to help you remember the meaning of the term.

Get Energized!

How do organisms get energy?

Energy is all around you. Chemical energy is stored in the bonds of molecules and holds molecules together. The energy from food is chemical energy in the bonds of food molecules. All living things need a source of chemical energy to survive.

Active Reading **6 Identify** As you read, underline examples of producers, decomposers, and consumers.

Think Outside the Book

5 Apply Record what you eat at your next meal. Where do you think these items come from, before they reach the market?

Producers Convert Energy Into Food

A **producer**, also called an autotroph, uses energy to make food. Most producers use sunlight to make food in a process called photosynthesis. The sun powers most life on Earth. In photosynthesis, producers use light energy to make food from water, carbon dioxide, and nutrients found in water and soil. The food contains chemical energy and can be used immediately or stored for later use. All green plants, such as grasses and trees, are producers. Algae and some bacteria are also producers. The food that these producers make supplies the energy for other living things in an ecosystem.

Decomposers Break Down Matter

An organism that gets energy and nutrients by breaking down the remains of other organisms is a **decomposer**. Fungi, such as the mushrooms on this log, and some bacteria are decomposers. Decomposers are nature's recyclers. By converting dead organisms and animal and plant waste into materials such as water and nutrients, decomposers help move matter through ecosystems. Decomposers make these simple materials available to other organisms.

This plant is a producer. Producers make food using light energy from the sun.

These mushrooms are decomposers. They break down the remains of plants and animals.

Consumers Eat Other Organisms

A **consumer** is an organism that eats other organisms. Consumers use the energy and nutrients stored in other living organisms because they cannot make their own food. A consumer that eats only plants, such as a grasshopper or bison, is called an **herbivore**. A **carnivore**, such as a badger or this wolf, eats other animals. An **omnivore** eats both plants and animals. A *scavenger* is a specialized consumer that feeds on dead organisms. Scavengers, such as the turkey vulture, eat the leftovers of the meals of other animals or eat dead animals.

This wolf is a consumer. It eats other organisms to get energy.

Consumers

Visualize It!

7 List Beside each image, place a check mark next to the word that matches the type of consumer the animal is.

Name: Hedgehog
What I eat: leaves, earthworms, insects

What am I?
☐ herbivore
☐ omnivore
☐ carnivore

Name: Moose
What I eat: grasses, fruits

What am I?
☐ herbivore
☐ omnivore
☐ carnivore

Name: Komodo dragon
What I eat: insects, birds, mammals

What am I?
☐ herbivore
☐ omnivore
☐ carnivore

8 Infer Explain how carnivores might be affected if the main plant species in a community were to disappear.

_____
_____
_____
_____

Energy Transfer

How is energy transferred among organisms?

Organisms change energy from the environment or from their food into other types of energy. Some of this energy is used for the organism's activities, such as breathing or moving. Some of the energy is saved within the organism to use later. If an organism is eaten or decomposes, the consumer or decomposer takes in the energy stored in the original organism. Only chemical energy that an organism has stored in its tissues is available to consumers. In this way, energy is transferred from organism to organism.

Active Reading **9 Infer** When a grasshopper eats grass, only some of the energy from the grass is stored in the grasshopper's body. How does the grasshopper use the rest of the energy?

_____

_____

This tree gets its energy from the sun.

10 Identify By what process does this tree get its energy?

_____

_____

This ant eats plants like the mesquite tree, and other insects.

11 Apply What type of energy is this ant consuming?

_____

_____

Energy Flows Through a Food Chain

A **food chain** is the path of energy transfer from producers to consumers. Energy moves from one organism to the next in one direction. The arrows in a food chain represent the transfer of energy, as one organism is eaten by another. Arrows represent the flow of energy from the body of the consumed organism to the body of the consumer of that organism.

Producers form the base of food chains. Producers transfer energy to the first, or primary, consumer in the food chain. The next, or secondary, consumer in the food chain consumes the primary consumer. A tertiary consumer eats the secondary consumer. Finally, decomposers recycle matter back to the soil.

Visualize It!

The photographs below show a typical desert food chain. Answer the following four questions from left to right based on your understanding of how energy flows in a food chain.

This hawk eats the lizard. It is at the top of the food chain.

13 Predict If nothing ever eats this hawk, what might eventually happen to the energy that is stored in its body?

_____

This lizard eats mostly insects.

12 Apply What does the arrow between the ant and the lizard represent?

_____

_____

World Wide Webs

How do food webs show energy connections?

Active Reading

14 Identify Underline the type of organism that typically forms the base of the food web.

Few organisms eat just one kind of food. So, the energy and nutrient connections in nature are more complicated than a simple food chain. A **food web** is the feeding relationships among organisms in an ecosystem. Food webs are made up of many food chains.

The next page shows a coastal food web. Most of the organisms in this food web live in the water. The web also includes some birds that live on land and eat fish. Tiny algae called phytoplankton form the base of this food web. Like plants on land, phytoplankton are producers. Tiny consumers called zooplankton eat phytoplankton. Larger animals, such as fish and squid, eat zooplankton. At the top of each chain are top predators, animals that eat other animals but are rarely eaten. In this food web, the killer whale is a top predator. Notice how many different energy paths lead from phytoplankton to the killer whale.

Visualize It!

15 Apply Complete the statements to the right with the correct organism names from the food web.

ENERGY

Energy flows up the food web when
_____ eat puffins.

Puffins are connected to many organisms in the food web.

ENERGY

Puffins get energy by eating

_____ ,

_____ ,

and _____ .

Food Web

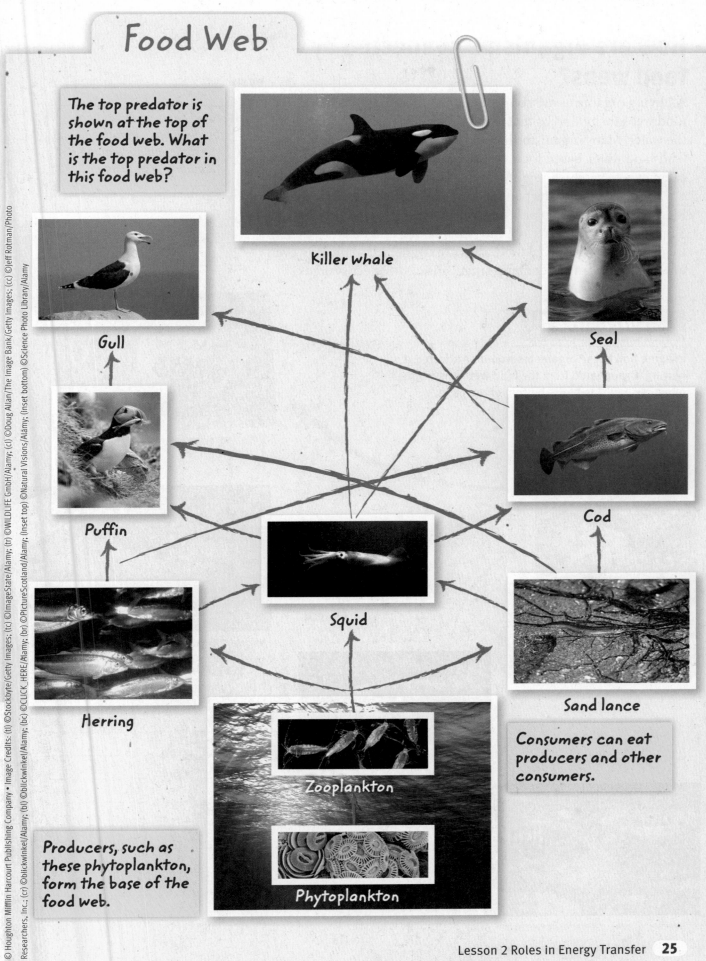

The top predator is shown at the top of the food web. What is the top predator in this food web?

Killer whale

Seal

Gull

Puffin

Cod

Squid

Herring

Sand lance

Zooplankton

Phytoplankton

Consumers can eat producers and other consumers.

Producers, such as these phytoplankton, form the base of the food web.

How are organisms connected by food webs?

All living organisms are connected by global food webs. Global food webs include webs that begin on land and webs that begin in the water. Many organisms have feeding relationships that connect land- and water-based food webs. For example, algae might be eaten by a fish, which might then be eaten by a bird.

Food webs that start on land may also move into the water. Many insects that eat plants on land lay their eggs in the water. Some fish eat these eggs and the insect larvae that hatch from them. Because the global food webs are connected, removing even one organism can affect many organisms in other ecosystems.

👁 Visualize It!

Imagine how these organisms would be affected if herring disappeared from the food web. Answer the questions starting at the bottom of the page.

■ Puffin

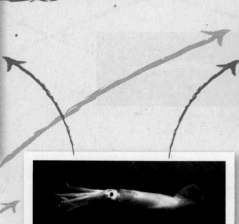
■ Squid

Herring

16 Identify Put a check mark next to the organisms that eat herring.

18 Infer Gulls don't eat herring but they are still connected by the food web. How might gull populations be affected?

_____
_____
_____
_____

■ Gull

■ Cod

17 Predict With no herring to eat, how might the eating habits of cod change?

_____
_____
_____
_____
_____
_____
_____
_____
_____

Dangerous Competition

Sometimes species are introduced into a new area. These invasive species often compete with native species for energy resources, such as sunlight and food.

Full Coverage
The kudzu plant was introduced to stop soil erosion, but in the process it outgrew all the native plants, preventing them from getting sunlight. Sometimes it completely covers houses or cars!

Destructive Zebras
The zebra mussel is one of the most destructive invasive species in the United States. They eat by filtering tiny organisms out of the water, often leaving nothing for the native mussel species.

Across the Grass
The walking catfish can actually move across land to get from one pond to another! As a result, sometimes the catfish competes with native species for food.

Extend

Inquiry

19 Relate Describe how the competition between invasive and native species might affect a food web.

20 Describe Give an example of competition for a food resource that may occur in an ecosystem near you.

21 Illustrate Provide an illustration of your example of competition in a sketch or a short story. Be sure to include the important aspects of food webs that you learned in the lesson.

Visual Summary

To complete this summary, circle the correct word. Then use the key below to check your answers. You can use this page to review the main concepts of the lesson.

Energy Transfer
in Ecosystems

Organisms get energy in different ways.

- Producers make their own food.
- Consumers eat other living organisms.
- Decomposers break down dead organisms.

22 Herbivores, carnivores, and omnivores are three types of producers / consumers / decomposers.

Food chains and food webs describe the flow of energy in an ecosystem.

23 All food chains start with producers / consumers / decomposers.

Answers: 22 consumers; 23 producers

24 Predict Describe the effects on global food webs if the sun's energy could no longer reach Earth.

Food Web

Lesson Review

Vocabulary

Fill in the blanks with the term that best completes the following sentences.

1 _____ is the primary source of energy for most ecosystems.

2 A _____ eats mostly dead matter.

3 A _____ contains many food chains.

4 _____ is the process by which light energy from the sun is converted to food.

Key Concepts

5 Describe What are the roles of producers, consumers, and decomposers in an ecosystem?

_____

_____

_____

_____

6 Apply What types of organisms typically make up the base, middle, and top of a food web?

_____

_____

_____

_____

_____

7 Describe Identify the two types of global food webs and describe how they are connected.

_____

_____

_____

_____

_____

Use the figure to answer the following questions.

8 Apply Describe the flow of energy in this food chain. Be sure to use the names of the organisms and what role they serve in the food chain (producer, consumer, or decomposer). If an organism is a consumer, identify whether it is an herbivore, carnivore, or omnivore.

_____

_____

_____

_____

9 Apply What do the arrows represent in the figure above?

_____

_____

_____

Critical Thinking

10 Predict Give an example of a decomposer, and explain what would happen if decomposers were absent from a forest ecosystem.

_____

_____

_____

_____

11 Predict How would a food web be affected if a species disappeared from an ecosystem?

_____

_____

_____

_____

_____

My Notes

Population Dynamics

ESSENTIAL QUESTION

What determines a population's size?

By the end of this lesson, you should be able to explain how population size changes in response to environmental factors and interactions between organisms.

By looking like a snake, this caterpillar may scare off predators. However, the effectiveness of this defense depends on population size. If there are few real snakes, predators won't be fooled for long.

🖐 Lesson Labs

Quick Labs
• What Factors Influence a Population Change?
• Investigate an Abiotic Limiting Factor

Exploration Lab
• How Do Populations Interact?

🌍 Engage Your Brain

1 Predict Check T or F to show whether you think each statement is true or false.

T F

☐ ☐ Plants compete for resources.

☐ ☐ Populations of organisms never stop growing.

☐ ☐ Animals never help other animals survive.

☐ ☐ Living things need the nonliving parts of an environment to survive.

2 Explain When a chameleon eats a butterfly, what happens to the number of butterflies in the population? How could a sudden decrease in butterflies affect chameleons?

_____

_____

_____

📖 Active Reading

3 Synthesize You can often define an unknown word if you know the meaning of its word parts. Use the word parts and sentences below to make an educated guess about the meaning of the words *immigrate* and *emigrate*.

Word part	Meaning
im-	into
e-	out
-migrate	move

Example sentence
Many deer will <u>immigrate</u> to the new park.

immigrate:

_____

_____

Example sentence
Birds will <u>emigrate</u> from the crowded island.

emigrate:

_____

Vocabulary Terms

• carrying capacity   • competition
• limiting factor   • cooperation

4 Identify This list contains the vocabulary terms you'll learn in this lesson. As you read, circle the definition of each term.

Movin' Out

How can a population grow or get smaller?

Active Reading **5 Identify** As you read, underline the processes that can cause a population to grow or to get smaller.

A population is a group of organisms of one species that lives in the same area at the same time. If new individuals are added to the population, it grows. The population gets smaller if individuals are removed from it. The population stays at about the same size if the number of individuals that are added is close to the number of individuals that are removed.

By Immigration and Emigration

Populations change in size when individuals move to new locations. *Immigration* occurs when individuals join a population. For example, fruit flies may travel on fruit to a new island. The population of fruit flies on the new island grows as fruit flies immigrate. *Emigration* occurs when individuals leave a population. The population of fruit flies on the original island decreases when fruit flies emigrate.

Fruit fly population sizes change as individuals move between islands.

Maui

A

B

If fruit flies move to a new island, that island's population increases.

Visualize It!

6 Apply Label the arrow that shows *emigration* from Maui and the arrow that shows *immigration* to Maui.

© Houghton Mifflin Harcourt Publishing Company • Image Credits: (t) ©Robert Postma/First Light/Corbis; (b) ©StockTrek Images/Getty Images

By Birth and Death

Populations increase as individuals are born. For example, consider a population of 100 deer in a forest. The population will increase if 20 fawns are born that year. But what if 12 deer are killed by predators or disease that year? Populations decrease as individuals die. If 20 deer are added and 12 are lost, the population will have an overall increase. At the end of the year, there will be 108 deer. The number of births compared to the number of deaths helps to determine if a population is increasing or decreasing.

Visualize It!

7 Apply Use the terms *birth*, *death*, and *immigration* to label each way that this population is changing.

An individual being carried off by a predator

A

A wandering male joins the population

B

A mother with nursing babies

C

Know Your Limits

What environmental factors influence population size?

A tropical rain forest can support large populations of trees. A desert, however, will probably support few or no trees. Each environment has different amounts of the resources that living things need, such as food, water, and space.

Resource Availability

The amount of resources in an area influences the size of a population. If important resources are lost from the environment, a population may shrink. The population may grow if the amount of resources in the environment is increased. But if the population continues to grow, the individuals would eventually run out of resources. The **carrying capacity** is the maximum number of individuals of one species that the environment can support. For example, the carrying capacity, or the number of owls that a forest can support, depends on how many mice are available to eat and how many trees are available for the owls to live in.

Deforestation causes a sudden change in resource availability.

Visualize It!

8 Identify Make a list of each population in the image that would be affected by drought.

_____

_____

_____

_____

Animals use plants as food and shelter. Plants depend on sunlight and water as resources.

Changes in the Environment

The carrying capacity can change when the environment changes. For example, after a rainy season, plants may produce a large crop of leaves and seeds. This large amount of food may allow an herbivore population to grow. But what if important resources are destroyed? A population crash occurs when the carrying capacity of the environment suddenly drops. Natural disasters, such as forest fires, and harsh weather, such as droughts, can cause population crashes. The carrying capacity can also be reduced when new competitors enter an area and outcompete existing populations for resources. This would cause existing populations to become smaller or crash.

Active Reading **9 Describe** What are two ways in which the environment can influence population size?

_____

_____

_____

_____

Drought slowly reduces the amount of water available as a resource to different populations.

Think Outside the Book

10 Apply With a classmate, discuss how the immigration of new herbivores might affect the carrying capacity of the local zebra population.

Maximum Capacity

What factors can limit population size?

A part of the environment that keeps a population's size at a level below its full potential is called a **limiting factor**. Limiting factors can be living or nonliving things in an environment.

Abiotic Factors

The nonliving parts of an environment are called *abiotic factors*. Abiotic factors include water, nutrients, soil, sunlight, temperature, and living space. Organisms need these resources to survive. For example, plants use sunlight, water, and carbon dioxide to make food. If there are few rocks in a desert, lizard populations that use rocks for shelter will not become very large.

Biotic Factors

Relationships among organisms affect each one's growth and survival. A *biotic factor* is an interaction between living things. For example, zebras interact with many organisms. Zebras eat grass, and they compete with antelope for this food. Lions prey on zebras. Each of these interactions is a biotic factor that affects the population of zebras.

Houghton Mifflin Harcourt Publishing Company • Image Credits: (t) ©Nigel Cattlin/Photo Researchers, Inc.; (c) ©Stock Connection Distribution/Alamy Images; (b) ©CW Images/Alamy Images

Inquiry

11 Apply Think about how people limit the populations of pests such as insects and mice. List one abiotic factor and one biotic factor that humans use to limit these pest populations.

Abiotic _____

Biotic _____

Visualize It!

12 Identify Label each of the following factors that limits plant population growth as abiotic or biotic.

This plant has a disease.

A

This plant grows between the rocks.

B

Herbivores are eating this leaf.

C

A Fungus Among Us!

In many parts of the world, frog populations are shrinking. We now know that many of these frogs have died because of a fungal infection.

Meet the fungus

Chytrid fungi [KY•trid FUHN•jy] live in water. They are important decomposers. One of them, called Bd, infects frogs.

Stop the Spread

Bd is found in wet mud. If you go hiking in muddy places, washing and drying your boots can help stop Bd from spreading.

Deadly Disease

Frogs take in oxygen and water through their skin. Bd interferes with this process. The fungus also affects an infected frog's nervous system.

Extend

Inquiry

13 Describe How does Bd fungus harm frogs?

14 Recommend Imagine that an endangered frog lives near an area where Bd was just found. How could you help protect that frog species?

15 Apply Design an experiment to test whether using soap or using bleach is the better way to clean boots to prevent Bd contamination. What are the independent and dependent variables? Remember to include a control in designing your experiment.

Teamwork

Animals compete for access to water.

What interactions between organisms can influence population size?

As living things try to gather the resources they need, they often interact with each other. Sometimes interactions help one individual and harm another. At other times, all of the organisms benefit by working together.

Competition

When two or more individuals or populations try to use the same limited resource, such as food, water, shelter, space, or sunlight, it is called **competition**. Competition can happen among individuals within a population. The elk in a forest compete with each other for the same food plants. This competition increases in winter when many plants die. Competition also happens among populations. For example, different species of trees in a forest compete with each other for sunlight and space.

Visualize It!

16 Predict The image above shows individuals from two populations competing for access to water.

What would happen to the size of the lion population if elephants usually won this competition?

_____

_____

What would happen to each population if lions usually won this competition?

_____

_____

_____

Active Reading 17 **Identify** As you read, underline how cooperation can influence population dynamics.

Cooperation

Cooperation occurs when individuals work together. Some animals, such as killer whales, hunt in groups. Emperor penguins in Antarctica stay close together to stay warm. Some populations have a structured social order that determines how the individuals work with each other. For example, ants live in colonies in which the members have different jobs. Some ants find food, others defend the colony, and others take care of the young. Cooperation helps individuals get resources, which can make populations grow.

18 **Compare** Make an analogy between an ant colony and a sports team. How does each group work together to achieve a goal?

_____

_____

_____

_____

_____

These ants cooperate to protect aphids that produce a substance that ants eat.

Visual Summary

To complete this summary, fill in the blanks with the correct word or phrase. Then use the key below to check your answers. You can use this page to review the main concepts of the lesson.

Population Dynamics

Populations grow due to birth and immigration and get smaller due to death and emigration.

19 If more individuals are born in a population than die or emigrate, the population will _____

Both populations and individuals can compete or cooperate.

21 Some birds warn other birds when predators are close. This type of interaction is called

_____

The carrying capacity is the maximum number of individuals of one species an environment can support.

20 If the amount of resources in an environment decreases, the carrying capacity for a population will probably

_____

Answers: 19 grow; 20 decrease; 21 cooperation

22 Synthesize Describe how a change in the environment could lead to increased immigration or emigration.

Lesson Review

Vocabulary

Circle the term that best completes the following sentences.

1 Individuals joining a population is an example of *emigration / immigration*.

2 A part of the environment that prevents a population from growing too large is a(n) *abiotic / limiting / biotic* factor.

3 Individuals *cooperate / compete* when they work together to obtain resources.

Key Concepts

4 Identify What is a limiting factor?

_____
_____
_____

5 Describe How do limiting factors affect the carrying capacity of an environment?

_____
_____
_____
_____
_____
_____

6 Explain Give one example of how cooperation can help organisms survive.

_____
_____
_____

7 Provide Name two factors that increase population size and two factors that decrease population size.

_____
_____
_____
_____

Critical Thinking

Use the illustration to answer the following questions.

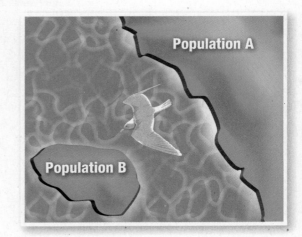

8 Infer What might cause birds in Population A to immigrate to the island?

_____
_____
_____

9 Predict How will the level of competition among birds in Population B change if many birds from Population A join Population B?

_____
_____
_____

10 Conclude Explain how a change in the environment could cause a population crash.

_____
_____
_____
_____

11 Relate How does population size relate to resource availability in an environment?

_____
_____
_____
_____

My Notes

Interactions in Communities

ESSENTIAL QUESTION

How do organisms interact?

By the end of this lesson, you should be able to predict the effects of different interactions in communities.

These birds, called tickbirds, eat ticks and flies on a rhinoceros. This behavior helps the rhino. The ticks are also parasites that sometimes drink the rhino's blood!

Lesson Labs

Quick Labs
- Prey Coloration
- Identifying Predators and Prey

Exploration Lab
- Modeling the Predator-Prey Cycle

Engage Your Brain

1 Predict Check T or F to show whether you think each statement is true or false.

T	F	
☐	☐	Different animals can compete for the same food.
☐	☐	Parasites help the organisms that they feed on.
☐	☐	Some organisms rely on each other for necessities such as food or shelter.
☐	☐	Organisms can defend themselves against predators that try to eat them.

2 Explain Draw an interaction between two living things that you might observe while on a picnic. Write a caption to go with your sketch.

Active Reading

3 Synthesize You can often define an unknown word if you know the meaning of its word parts. Use the word parts and sentence below to make an educated guess about the meaning of the word *symbiosis*.

Word part	Meaning
bio-	life
sym-	together

Example sentence

The relationship between a sunflower and the insect that pollinates it is an example of symbiosis.

symbiosis:

_____

_____

_____

Vocabulary Terms

- predator
- prey
- symbiosis
- mutualism
- commensalism
- parasitism
- competition

4 Apply As you learn the meaning of each vocabulary term in this lesson, create your own definition or sketch to help you remember the meaning of the term.

Feeding Frenzy!

How do predator and prey interact?

Every organism lives with and affects other organisms. Many organisms must feed on other organisms in order to get the energy and nutrients they need to survive. These feeding relationships establish structure in a community.

Predators Eat Prey

In a predator–prey relationship, an animal eats another animal for energy and nutrients. The **predator** eats another animal. The **prey** is an animal that is eaten by a predator. An animal can be both predator and prey. For example, if a warthog eats a lizard, and is, in turn, eaten by a lion, the warthog is both predator and prey.

Predators and prey have adaptations that help them survive. Some predators have talons, claws, or sharp teeth, which provide them with deadly weapons. Spiders, which are small predators, use their webs to trap unsuspecting prey. Camouflage (CAM•ah•flaj) can also help a predator or prey to blend in with its environment. A tiger's stripes help it to blend in with tall grasses so that it can ambush its prey, and the wings of some moths look just like tree bark, which makes them difficult for predators to see. Some animals defend themselves with chemicals. For example, skunks and bombardier beetles spray predators with irritating chemicals.

Active Reading

5 Identify As you read, underline examples of predator–prey adaptations.

This lion is a predator. The warthog is its prey.

Adaptations of Predators and Prey

Most organisms wouldn't last a day without their adaptations. This bald eagle's vision and sharp talons allow it to find and catch prey.

sharp talons

Predators and Prey Populations Are Connected

Predators rely on prey for food, so the sizes of predator and prey populations are linked together very closely. If one population grows or shrinks, the other population is affected. For example, when there are a lot of warthogs to eat, the lion population may grow because the food supply is plentiful. As the lion population grows, it requires more and more food, so more and more warthogs are hunted by the lions. The increased predation may cause the warthog population to shrink. If the warthog population shrinks enough, the lion population may shrink due to a shortage in food supply. If the lion population shrinks, the warthog population may grow due to a lack of predators.

This lion is hunting down the antelope. If most of the antelope are killed, the lions will have less food to eat.

6 Compare Fill in the Venn diagram to compare and contrast predators and prey.

Predators   Both   Prey

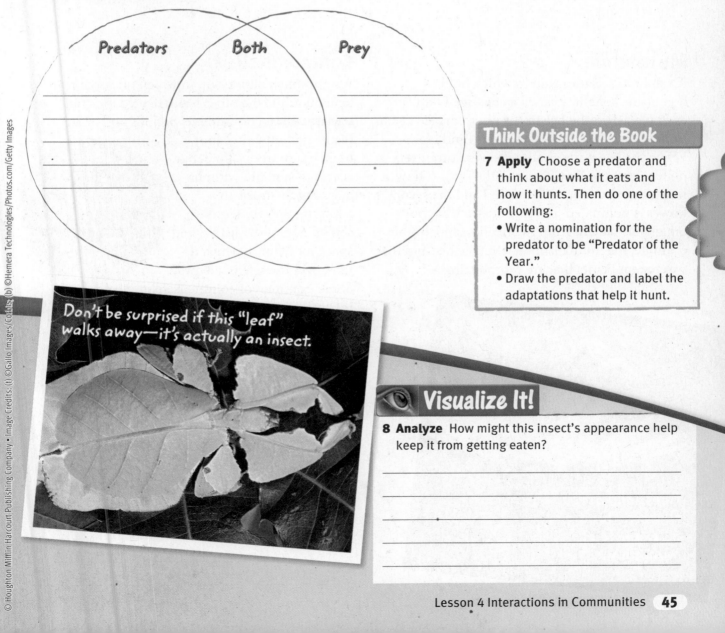

Don't be surprised if this "leaf" walks away—it's actually an insect.

Think Outside the Book

7 Apply Choose a predator and think about what it eats and how it hunts. Then do one of the following:
- Write a nomination for the predator to be "Predator of the Year."
- Draw the predator and label the adaptations that help it hunt.

Visualize It!

8 Analyze How might this insect's appearance help keep it from getting eaten?

_____
_____
_____
_____
_____

Living Together

What are the types of symbiotic relationships?

A close long-term relationship between different species in a community is called **symbiosis** (sim•bee•OH•sis). In symbiosis, the organisms in the relationship can benefit from, be unaffected by, or be harmed by the relationship. Often, one organism lives in or on the other organism. Symbiotic relationships are classified as mutualism, commensalism, or parasitism.

Active Reading **9 Identify** As you read, underline examples of symbiotic relationships.

Mutualism

A symbiotic relationship in which both organisms benefit is called **mutualism**. For example, when the bee in the photo drinks nectar from a flower, it gets pollen on its hind legs. When the bee visits another flower, it transfers pollen from the first flower to the second flower. In this interaction, the bee is fed and the second flower is pollinated for reproduction. So, both organisms benefit from the relationship. In this example, the mutualism benefits the bee and the two parent plants that are reproducing.

Bees pollinate flowers. This is an example of mutualism.

Commensalism

A symbiotic relationship in which one organism benefits while the other is unaffected is called **commensalism.** For example, orchids and other plants that often live in the branches of trees gain better access to sunlight without affecting the trees. In addition, the tree trunk shown here provides a living space for lichens, which do not affect the tree in any way. Some examples of commensalism involve protection. For example, certain shrimp live among the spines of the fire urchin. The fire urchin's spines are poisonous but not to the shrimp. By living among the urchin's spines, the shrimp are protected from predators. In this relationship, the shrimp benefits and the fire urchin is unaffected.

Lichens can live on tree bark.

10 Compare How does commensalism differ from mutualism?

_____

_____

_____

_____

© Houghton Mifflin Harcourt Publishing Company • Image Credits: (l) ©Jason Hosking/Getty Images; (r) ©Kathy Wright/Alamy

Think Outside the Book Inquiry

12 **Predict** Observe and take notes about how the organisms in your area interact with one another. Imagine what would happen if one of these organisms disappeared. Write down three effects that you can think of.

parasite

host

Parasitism

A symbiotic relationship in which one organism benefits and another is harmed is called **parasitism** (PAR•uh•sih•tiz•uhm). The organism that benefits is the *parasite*. The organism that is harmed is the *host*. The parasite gets food from its host, which weakens the host. Some parasites, such as ticks, live on the host's surface and feed on its blood. These parasites can cause diseases such as Lyme disease. Other parasites, such as tapeworms, live within the host's body. They can weaken their host so much that the host dies.

11 **Summarize** Using the key, complete the table to show how organisms are affected by symbiotic relationships.

Symbiosis	Species 1	Species 2
Mutualism	+	
	+	0
Parasitism		

Key + organism benefits
0 organism not affected
− organism harmed

Let the Games Begin!

Why does competition occur in communities?

In a team game, two groups compete against each other with the same goal in mind—to win the game. In a biological community, organisms compete for resources. **Competition** occurs when organisms fight for the same limited resource. Organisms compete for resources such as food, water, sunlight, shelter, and mates. If an organism doesn't get all the resources it needs, it could die.

Sometimes competition happens among individuals of the same species. For example, different groups of lions compete with each other for living space. Males within these groups also compete with each other for mates.

Competition can also happen among individuals of different species. Lions mainly eat large animals, such as zebras. They compete for zebras with leopards and cheetahs. When zebras are scarce, competition increases among animals that eat zebras. As a result, lions may steal food or compete with other predators for smaller animals.

Active Reading

13 Identify Underline each example of competition.

14 Predict In the table below, fill in the missing cause and effect of two examples of competition in a community.

Cause	Effect
A population of lions grows too large to share their current territory.	
	Several male hyenas compete to mate with the females present in their area.

Many organisms rely on the same water source.

Think Outside the Book

15 Apply With a classmate, discuss how competition might affect the organisms in this photo.

Strange Relationships

Glow worms? Blind salamanders? Even creepy crawlers in this extreme cave community interact in ways that help them meet their needs. How do these interactions differ from ones in your own community?

A Blind Hunter

Caves are very dark and, over generations, these salamanders have lost the use of their eyes for seeing. Instead of looking for food, they track prey by following water movements.

Guano Buffet

Cave swiftlets venture out of the cave daily to feed. The food they eat is recycled as bird dung, or guano, which piles up beneath the nests. The guano feeds many cave dwellers, such as insects. As a result, these insects never have to leave the cave!

Sticky Traps

Bioluminescent glow worms make lines of sticky beads to attract prey. Once a prey is stuck, the worm pulls in the line to feast.

Extend

Inquiry

16 Identify Name the type of relationship illustrated in two of the examples shown above.

17 Research Name some organisms in your community and the interactions they have.

18 Create Illustrate two of the interactions you just described by doing one of the following:
- make a poster
- write a song
- write a play
- draw a graphic novel

Visual Summary

To complete this summary, fill in the blanks with the correct word or phrase. Then, use the key below to check your answers. You can use this page to review the main concepts of the lesson.

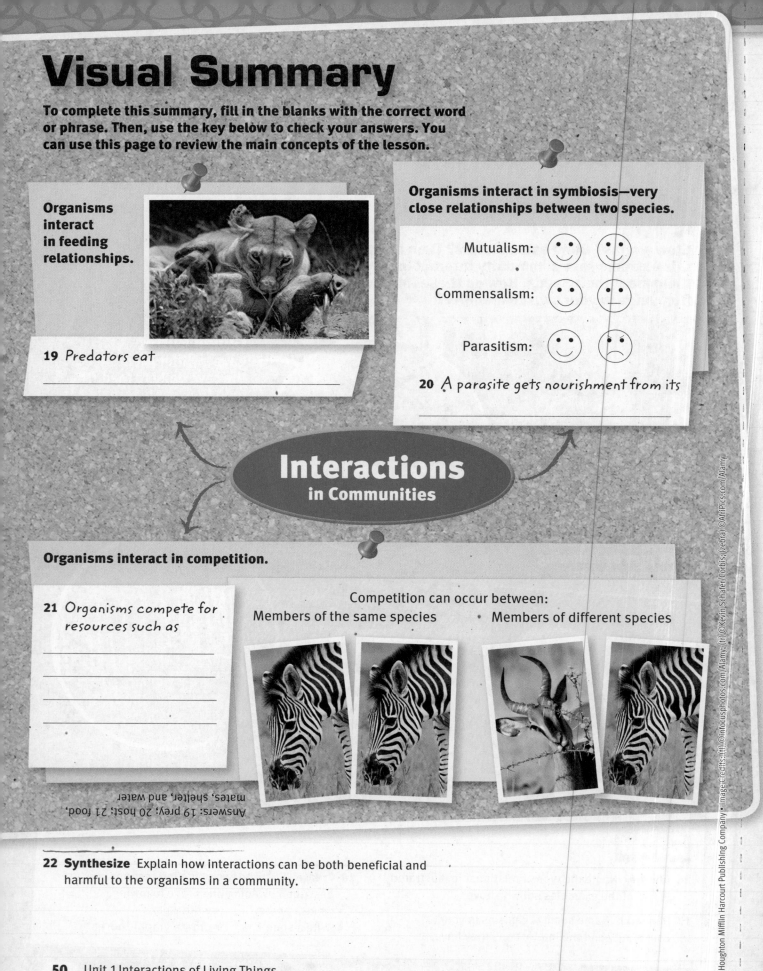

Organisms interact in feeding relationships.

19 Predators eat

_____

Organisms interact in symbiosis—very close relationships between two species.

Mutualism: ☺ ☺

Commensalism: ☺ 😐

Parasitism: ☺ ☹

20 A parasite gets nourishment from its

_____

Interactions
in Communities

Organisms interact in competition.

21 Organisms compete for resources such as

_____

_____

_____

_____

Competition can occur between:

Members of the same species   ·   Members of different species

Answers: 19 prey, 20 host, 21 food, mates, shelter, and water.

22 Synthesize Explain how interactions can be both beneficial and harmful to the organisms in a community.

_____

Lesson Review

Vocabulary

Fill in the blank with the term that best completes the following sentences.

1 A _____ is an animal that kills and eats another animal, known as prey.

2 A long-term relationship between two different species within a community is called

_____

3 _____ occurs when organisms fight for limited resources.

Key Concepts

Fill in the table below.

Example	Type of symbiosis
4 Identify Tiny organisms called mites live in human eyelashes and feed on dead skin, without harming humans.	
5 Identify Certain bacteria live in human intestines, where they get food and also help humans break down their food.	

6 Describe Think of an animal, and list two resources that it might compete for in its community. Then describe what adaptations the animal has to compete for these resources.

_____
_____
_____
_____
_____
_____

7 Explain What is the relationship between the size of a predator population and the size of a prey population?

_____
_____
_____

Critical Thinking

Use this graph to answer the following question.

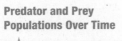

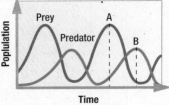

Predator and Prey Populations Over Time

8 Analyze At which point (A or B) on this graph would you expect competition within the predator population to be the highest?

_____

9 Infer Think of a resource, and predict what happens to the resource when competition for it increases.

_____
_____
_____

10 Apply Identify a community near where you live, such as a forest, a pond, or your own backyard. Think about the interactions of the organisms in this community. Describe an interaction and identify it as predation, mutualism, commensalism, parasitism, or competition.

_____
_____
_____
_____
_____

My Notes

Lesson 1

ESSENTIAL QUESTION
How are different parts of the environment connected?

Analyze the parts of an environment.

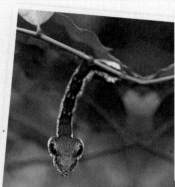

Lesson 3

ESSENTIAL QUESTION
What determines a population's size?

Explain how population size changes in response to environmental factors and interactions between organisms.

Lesson 2

ESSENTIAL QUESTION
How does energy flow through an ecosystem?

Relate the roles of organisms to the transfer of energy in food chains and food webs.

Lesson 4

ESSENTIAL QUESTION
How do organisms interact?

Predict the effects of different interactions in communities.

Connect ESSENTIAL QUESTIONS
Lessons 1 and 3

1 Explain Do organisms compete for abiotic resources? Explain your answer.

_____

_____

_____

_____

Think Outside the Book

2 Synthesize Choose one of these activities to help synthesize what you have learned in this unit.

☐ Using what you learned in lessons 2 and 3, write a short story that describes what might happen in a food web when a new species is introduced to an ecosystem.

☐ Using what you learned in lessons 1 through 4, choose an ecosystem and explain three interactions that might occur within it. In your poster presentation, use the terms *cooperation, competition, predator,* and *prey.*

Name _____

Vocabulary

Check the box to show whether each statement is true or false.

T	F	
☐	☐	**1** Competition occurs when organisms try to use the same limited resource.
☐	☐	**2** Biomes are characterized by temperature, precipitation, and the plant and animal communities that live there.
☐	☐	**3** A habitat is the role of a population in its community, including its environment and its relationship with other species.
☐	☐	**4** A food chain is the feeding relationships among all of the organisms in an ecosystem.
☐	☐	**5** A limiting factor is an environmental factor that increases the growth of a population.

Key Concepts

Read each question below, and circle the best answer.

6 A small fish called a cleaner wrasse darts in and out of a larger fish's mouth, removing and eating parasites and dead tissue. Which term best describes the relationship between the cleaner wrasse and the large fish?

A mutualism

B commensalism

C parasitism

D competition

7 Bees have a society in which different members have different responsibilities. The interaction among bees is an example of what type of behavior?

A cooperation

B competition

C consumerism

D commensalism

8 After a mild winter with plenty of food, a deer population grew rapidly. What most likely happened to the wolf population in that same ecosystem?

A It was unaffected.

B It grew.

C It shrank.

D It became extinct.

9 The diagram below shows an aquatic ecosystem.

What is one abiotic factor shown in this diagram?

A the snails

B the water

C the crab

D the tree roots

10. Which of the following is an example of a biotic limiting factor for a population?

A water availability

B climate

C disease

D natural disasters

11 Which of the following is the most likely reason that a population might crash?

A The competition for the same resource suddenly drops.

B The number of prey suddenly increases.

C The number of predators suddenly decreases.

D The carrying capacity of the environment suddenly drops.

12 Grizzly bears are classified in the order Carnivora. Their diet consists of roots, tubers, berries, nuts, fungi, insects, rodents, and fish. What ecological role best describes grizzly bears?

A carnivores

B omnivores

C herbivores

D producers

Name _____

13 The graph below shows the size of a squirrel population over 20 years.

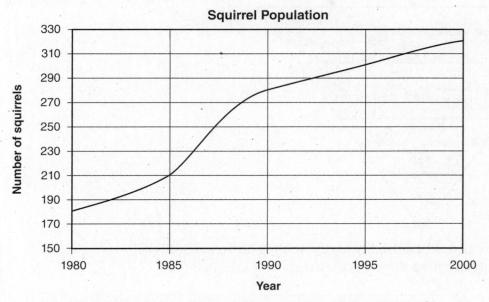

Squirrel Population

The trend displayed on the graph could be a result of what factor?

A emigration   **C** increased death rate

B immigration   **D** scarce resources

Critical Thinking

Answer the following questions in the space provided.

14 The diagram below shows how a manatee gets its energy.

Energy source   Sea grass   Manatee

What provides the energy for the sea grass, the manatee, and most life on Earth? _____.

What role does the sea grass play in this food chain? _____

According to this diagram, what type of consumer is the manatee? _____

15 Use the diagram to help you answer the following question.

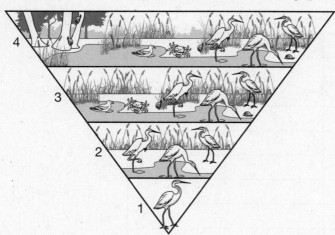

If there is a decrease in food availability for the wading birds, how will the different levels of organization shown in the diagram be affected?

_____

_____

_____

_____

Connect ESSENTIAL QUESTIONS
Lessons 2 and 4

Answer the following question in the space provided.

16 The diagram below shows an example of a food web.

What traits do the prey animals shown here have in common that help them survive?

_____

What important ecological group is missing from this food web? _____

What might happen if the rabbit population suddenly shrank due to disease?

_____

_____

Earth's Biomes and Ecosystems

Big Idea
Matter and energy together support life within an environment.

Mangroves

What do you think?

Mangroves and Roseate Spoonbills are both found in Florida. How do organisms like these get and use matter and energy?

Roseate Spoonbill

Unit 2
Earth's Biomes and Ecosystems

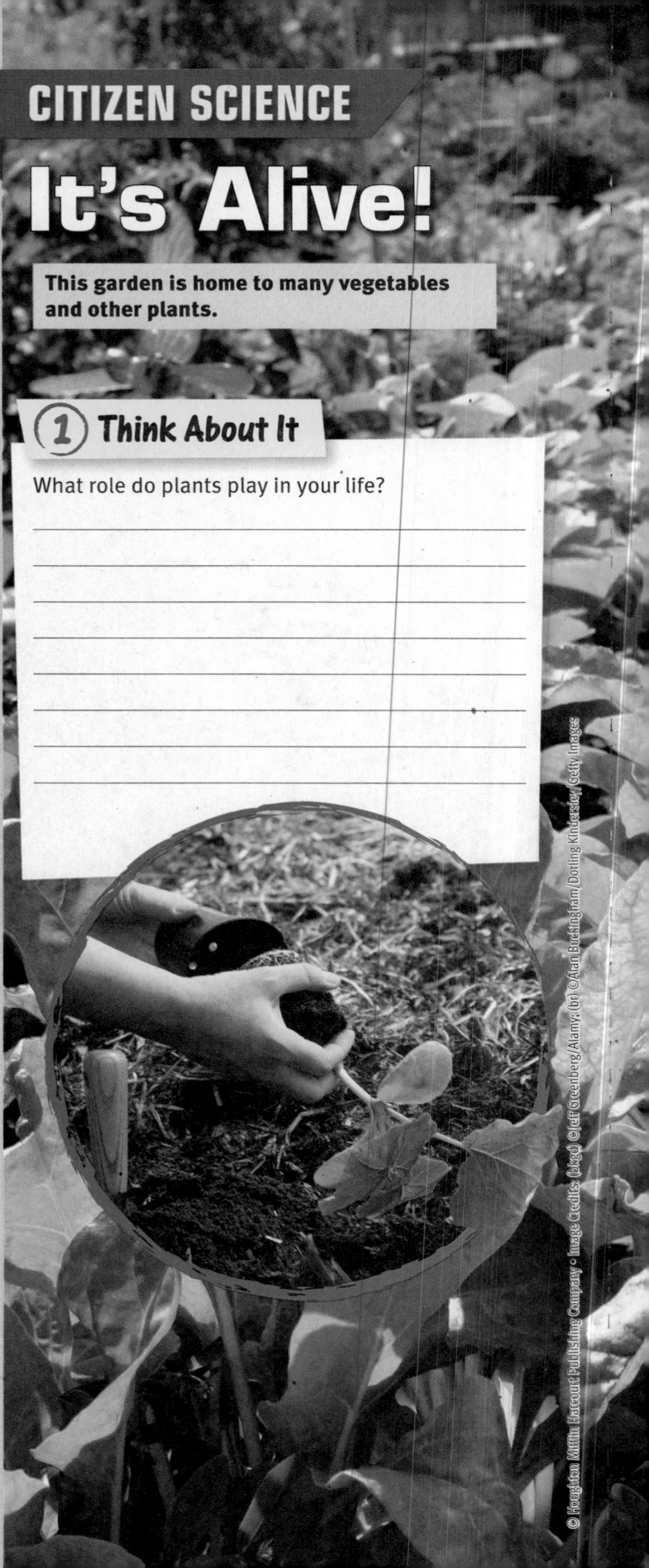

CITIZEN SCIENCE
It's Alive!

This garden is home to many vegetables and other plants.

① Think About It

What role do plants play in your life?

_____

_____

_____

_____

_____

_____

_____

② Ask A Question

How do plants use matter and energy?

As a class, design a plan for a garden plot or window box garden in which the class can grow a variety of plants. Remember that plants have different growing periods and requirements.

Sketch It!

Draw your plan to show where each plant will be placed.

③ Apply Your Knowledge

A What do your plants need in order to grow?

_____

_____

_____

B Which of the things you listed above are examples of matter? Which are examples of energy?

_____

_____

_____

_____

C Create and care for your classroom garden and observe the plant growth.

Take It Home

Describe an area in your community that is used for growing food. If there is no such area, initiate a plan to plant in an area that you think could be used.

Land Biomes

ESSENTIAL QUESTION

What are land biomes?

By the end of this lesson, you should be able to describe the characteristics of different biomes that exist on land.

The North American prairie is an example of a grassland biome. It is home to grazing animals such as the bison.

Herds of thousands of bison used to roam the prairies. Bison became rare as people hunted them and developed the prairie into farmland.

Lesson Labs

Quick Labs
• Climate Determines Plant Life
• Identify Your Land Biome

Field Lab
• Survey of a Biome's Biotic and Abiotic Factors

Engage Your Brain

1 Compare How are the two biomes in the pictures at right different from each other?

_____

_____

_____

_____

_____

_____

2 Infer Which of these biomes gets more rain? Explain your answer.

_____

_____

_____

_____

_____

_____

Active Reading

3 Word Parts Parts of words that you know can help you find the meanings of words you don't know. The suffix *-ous* means "possessing" or "full of." Use the meanings of the root word and suffix to write the meaning of the term *coniferous tree.*

Root Word	Meaning
conifer	tree or shrub that produces cones

coniferous tree:

_____

_____

_____

Vocabulary Terms

• biome
• tundra
• taiga
• coniferous tree

• desert
• grassland
• deciduous tree

4 Apply As you learn the definition of each vocabulary term in this lesson, create your own definition or sketch to help you remember the meaning of the term.

Home Sweet Biome

What is a biome?

If you could travel Earth from pole to pole, you would pass through many different biomes. A **biome** is a region of Earth where the climate determines the types of plants that live there. The types of plants in a biome determine the types of animals that live there. Deserts, grasslands, tundra, taiga, temperate forests, and tropical forests are all types of biomes.

What makes one biome different from another?

Each biome has a unique community of plants and animals. The types of organisms that can live in a biome depend on the biome's climate and other abiotic, or nonliving, factors.

Climate

Climate is the main abiotic factor that characterizes a biome. Climate describes the long-term patterns of temperature and precipitation in a region. The position of a biome on Earth affects its climate. Biomes that are closer to the poles receive less annual solar energy and have colder climates. Biomes that are near the equator receive more annual solar energy and have warmer climates. Biomes that are close to oceans often have wet climates.

The taiga is a northern latitude biome that has low average temperatures, nutrient-poor soil, and coniferous trees.

Earth's Major Land Biomes

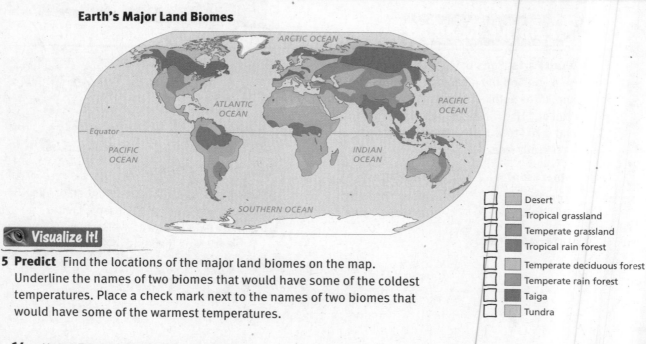

Legend:
- Desert
- Tropical grassland
- Temperate grassland
- Tropical rain forest
- Temperate deciduous forest
- Temperate rain forest
- Taiga
- Tundra

Visualize It!

5 Predict Find the locations of the major land biomes on the map. Underline the names of two biomes that would have some of the coldest temperatures. Place a check mark next to the names of two biomes that would have some of the warmest temperatures.

Other Abiotic Factors

Other abiotic factors that characterize a biome include soil type, amount of sunlight, and amount of water that is available. Abiotic factors affect which organisms can live in a biome.

Plant and Animal Communities

Adaptations are features that allow organisms to survive and reproduce. Plants and animals that live in a biome have adaptations to its unique conditions. For example, animals that live in biomes that are cold all year often grow thick fur coats. Plants that live in biomes with seasonal temperature changes lose their leaves and become inactive in winter. Plants that live in warm, rainy biomes stay green and grow all year long.

© Houghton Mifflin Harcourt Publishing Company • Image Credits: (tr) ©Jan Carroll/Alamy; (bl) ©Mike Grandmaison/First Light/Alamy; (br) ©Grambo/First Light/Corbis

Active Reading

6 Identify As you read, underline the abiotic factors besides climate that characterize a biome.

Visualize It!

7 Infer Place a check mark in each box to predict the average temperature range for each of the biomes shown.

- ☐ Warm All Year
- ☐ Cool All Year
- ☐ Seasonal Temperatures

- ☐ Warm All Year
- ☐ Cool All Year
- ☐ Seasonal Temperatures

- ☐ Warm All Year
- ☐ Cool All Year
- ☐ Seasonal Temperatures

Life in a Biome

How are ecosystems related to biomes?

Most biomes stretch across huge areas of land. Within each biome are smaller areas called ecosystems. Each *ecosystem* includes a specific community of organisms and their physical environment. A temperate forest biome can contain pond or river ecosystems. Each of these ecosystems has floating plants, fish, and other organisms that are adapted to living in or near water. A grassland biome can contain areas of small shrubs and trees. These ecosystems have woody plants, insects, and nesting birds.

Visualize It!

Three different ecosystems are shown in this temperate rain forest biome. Different organisms live in each of these ecosystems.

8 Identify List three organisms that you see in the picture that are part of each ecosystem within the biome.

Tree Canopy Ecosystem

_____

_____

_____

Stream Ecosystem

_____

_____

Forest Floor Ecosystem

_____

_____

_____

What are the major land biomes?

There are six major land biomes. These include tundra, taiga, desert, grassland, temperate forest, and tropical forest.

Active Reading **9 Identify** Underline the abiotic features that characterize tundra and taiga biomes.

Tundra

Tundra has low average temperatures and very little precipitation. The ground contains permafrost, a thick layer of permanently frozen soil beneath the surface. Tundra is found in the Arctic and in high mountain regions. Tundra plants include mosses and woody shrubs. These plants have shallow roots, since they cannot grow into the permafrost. Tundra winters are dark, cold, and windy. Animals such as musk oxen have thick fur and fat deposits that protect them from the cold. Some animals, such as caribou, migrate to warmer areas before winter. Ground squirrels hibernate, or become dormant, underground.

Taiga

Taiga is also called the boreal forest. **Taiga** has low average temperatures like those in the tundra biome, but more precipitation. The soil layer in taiga is thin, acidic, and nutrient-poor. Taiga biomes are found in Canada and northern Europe and Asia. Taiga plants include **coniferous trees**, which are trees that have evergreen, needlelike leaves. These thin leaves let trees conserve water and produce food all year long. Migratory birds live in taiga in summer. Wolves, owls, and elk live in taiga year-round. Some animals, such as snowshoe hares, experience a change in fur color as the seasons change. Hares that match their surroundings are not seen by predators as easily.

Visualize It!

10 Describe Below each picture, describe how organisms that you see are adapted to the biome in which they live.

Tundra

Taiga

_____ _____

_____ _____

_____ _____

Desert

Desert biomes are very dry. Some deserts receive less than 8 centimeters (3 inches) of precipitation each year. Desert soil is rocky or sandy. Many deserts are hot during the day and cold at night, although some have milder temperatures. Plants and animals in this biome have adaptations that let them conserve water and survive extreme temperatures. Members of the cactus family have needlelike leaves that conserve water. They also contain structures that store water. Many desert animals are active only at night. Some animals burrow underground or move into shade to stay cool during the day.

11 Identify As you read, underline the characteristics of deserts.

Visualize It!

12 Describe List the ways that each plant or animal in the picture is adapted to the desert biome.

Saguaro Cactus
_____
_____
_____
_____

Desert Tortoise

A tortoise can crawl into shade or retreat into its shell to avoid the heat. A tortoise has thick skin that prevents water loss.

Kangaroo Rat
_____
_____
_____
_____
_____

Tropical Grassland

Temperate Grassland

Tropical Grassland

A **grassland** is a biome that has grasses and few trees. Tropical grasslands, such as the African savanna, have high average temperatures throughout the year. They also have wet and dry seasons. Thin soils support grasses and some trees in this biome. Grazing animals, such as antelope and zebras, feed on grasses. Predators such as lions hunt grazing animals. Animals in tropical grasslands migrate to find water during dry seasons. Plants in tropical grasslands are adapted to survive periodic fires.

Temperate Grassland

Temperate grasslands, such as the North American prairie, have moderate precipitation, hot summers, and cold winters. These grasslands have deep soils that are rich in nutrients. Grasses are the dominant plants in this biome. Bison, antelope, prairie dogs, and coyotes are common animals. Periodic fires sweep through temperate grasslands. These fires burn dead plant material and kill trees and shrubs. Grasses and other nonwoody plants are adapted to fire. Some of these plants regrow from their roots after a fire. Others grow from seeds that survived the fire.

Visualize It!

13 Describe Write captions to explain how fire shapes a temperate grassland biome.

Between fires, small trees begin to grow in a temperate grassland.

C

B

A

© Houghton Mifflin Harcourt Publishing Company • Image Credits: (tl) ©Charles V. Angelo/Photo Researchers, Inc.; (tr) ©Andrew Woodley/Alamy

Temperate Deciduous Forest

Temperate deciduous forests have moderate precipitation, hot summers, and cold winters. These forests are located in the northeastern United States, East Asia, and much of Europe. This biome has **deciduous trees**, which are broadleaf trees that drop their leaves as winter approaches. Fallen leaves decay and add organic matter to the soil, making it nutrient-rich. Songbirds nest in these forests during summer, but many migrate to warmer areas before winter. Animals such as chipmunks and black bears hibernate during winter. Deer and bobcats are active year-round.

Temperate Rain Forest

Temperate rain forests have a long, cool wet season and a relatively dry summer. Temperate rain forests exist in the Pacific Northwest and on the western coast of South America. This biome is home to many coniferous trees, including Douglas fir and cedar. The forest floor is covered with mosses and ferns and contains nutrient-rich soil. Plants grow throughout the year in the temperate rain forest. Animals in this biome include spotted owls, shrews, elk, and cougars.

Temperate Rain Forest

A. Climate: _____

_____

B. Soil: _____

_____

C. Plants: _____

_____

D. Animals: _____

_____

👁 Visualize It!

14 Summarize Fill in the missing information on the cards to describe each of these temperate forest biomes.

Temperate Deciduous Forest

A. Climate: _____

_____

B. Soil: _____

_____

C. Plants: _____

_____

D. Animals: _____

_____

Think Outside the Book Inquiry

15 Apply With a classmate, compare the adaptations of animals that migrate, hibernate, or stay active year-round in a temperate deciduous forest.

Tropical Rain Forest

Tropical rain forests are located near Earth's equator. This biome is warm throughout the year. It also receives more rain than any other biome on Earth. The soil in tropical rain forests is acidic and low in nutrients. Even with poor soil, tropical rain forests have some of the highest biological diversity on Earth. Dense layers of plants develop in a tropical rain forest. These layers block sunlight from reaching the forest floor. Some plants such as orchids grow on tree branches instead of on the dark forest floor. Birds, monkeys, and sloths live in the upper layers of the rain forest. Leaf-cutter ants, jaguars, snakes, and anteaters live in the lower layers.

Visualize It!

16 Display Color in the band labeled *Light Level* next to the picture of the tropical rain forest. Make the band darkest at the level where the forest would receive the least light. Make the band lightest at the level where the forest would receive the most light.

Light Level

Emergent Layer

Canopy

Understory

Forest Floor

Visual Summary

To complete this summary, fill in the answers to the questions. Then, use the key below to check your answers. You can use this page to review the main concepts of the lesson.

Land Biomes

A biome is a region of Earth characterized by a specific climate and specific plants and animals.

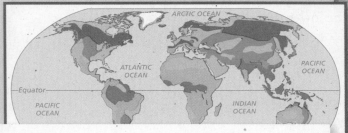

ARCTIC OCEAN
ATLANTIC OCEAN
PACIFIC OCEAN
Equator
PACIFIC OCEAN
INDIAN OCEAN

17 What are the major land biomes?

_____

_____

_____

Plants and animals are adapted to the conditions in their biome.

19 The plant below is adapted to what conditions?

_____

_____

Each biome can contain many ecosystems.

18 How are ecosystems different from biomes?

_____

_____

_____

20 Predict Describe what might happen to the organisms in a desert if the climate changed and rainfall increased.

Lesson Review

Vocabulary

Define Draw a line to connect the following terms to their definitions.

1 a region that has a specific climate and a specific community of plants and animals

A taiga

2 a region with low average temperatures and little precipitation

B climate

3 long-term temperature and precipitation patterns in a region

C biome

Key Concepts

4 Identify What are the abiotic factors that help to characterize a biome?

_____
_____
_____
_____

5 Describe Describe a tropical grassland biome.

_____
_____
_____
_____

6 Explain How does climate determine the organisms that live in a biome?

_____
_____
_____
_____

7 Summarize Why can many ecosystems exist in one biome?

_____
_____
_____

Critical Thinking

Use the Venn diagram to answer the following questions.

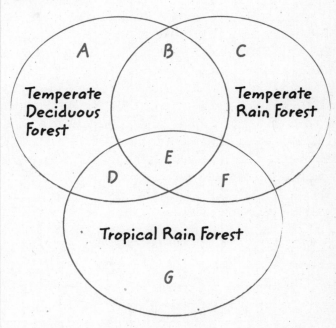

8 Infer In which space on the Venn diagram would you write *coniferous trees*?

_____

9 Analyze What is common among all three types of forests in the diagram?

_____
_____
_____
_____

10 Relate What biome do you think you live in? Explain your answer.

_____
_____
_____
_____
_____
_____

My Notes

Aquatic Ecosystems

ESSENTIAL QUESTION

What are aquatic ecosystems?

By the end of this lesson, you should be able to describe the characteristics of marine, freshwater, and other aquatic ecosystems.

Coral reefs are coastal ocean ecosystems that are located in many tropical areas. Coral reefs have some of the highest biological diversity on Earth.

🐟 Engage Your Brain

1 Predict Check T or F to show whether you think each statement is true or false.

T	F	
☐	☐	Wetlands can protect areas close to shorelines from flooding.
☐	☐	Most ponds contain both salt water and fresh water.
☐	☐	Plants and animals cannot live in fast-moving waters.
☐	☐	The deep ocean is colder and darker than other marine ecosystems.

2 Predict How do you think organisms like this squid are adapted to life in the deep ocean?

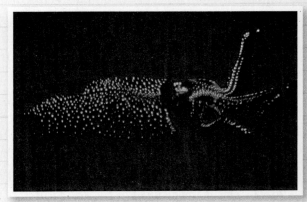

_____

_____

_____

✏️ Active Reading

3 Synthesize You can often define an unknown word if you know the meaning of its word parts. Use the word parts and sentence below to make an educated guess about the meaning of the word *wetland*.

Word part	Meaning
wet-	having water or liquid on the surface
-land	solid part of Earth's surface

Example sentence:
Many species of birds and mammals rely on <u>wetlands</u> for food, water, and shelter.

wetland:

_____

_____

Vocabulary Terms

• wetland   • estuary

4 Identify As you read, place a question mark next to any words that you don't understand. When you finish reading the lesson, go back and review the text you marked. Work with a classmate to define the words that are still unclear.

Splish Splash

What are the major types of aquatic ecosystems?

Have you ever gone swimming in the ocean, or fishing on a lake? Oceans and lakes support many of the aquatic ecosystems on Earth. An *aquatic ecosystem* includes any water environment and the community of organisms that live there.

The three main types of aquatic ecosystems are freshwater ecosystems, estuaries, and marine ecosystems. Freshwater ecosystems can be found in rivers, lakes, and wetlands. Marine ecosystems are found in oceans. Rivers and oceans form estuaries where they meet at a coastline.

What abiotic factors affect aquatic ecosystems?

Abiotic factors are the nonliving things in an environment. The major abiotic factors that affect aquatic ecosystems include water temperature, water depth, amount of light, oxygen level, water pH, salinity (salt level), and the rate of water flow. An aquatic ecosystem may be influenced by some of these factors but not others. For example, a river would be influenced by rate of water flow but not typically by salinity.

Visualize It!

5 Identify Fill in the major types of aquatic ecosystems in the picture.

Freshwater and marine ecosystems meet at a coastline. These ecosystems form estuaries, which have a mixture of fresh water and salt water.

Ⓐ _____

estuary

Ⓑ _____

6 Compare What is the main difference in the water that is in freshwater ecosystems, estuaries, and marine ecosystems?

_____
_____
_____

Where are examples of freshwater ecosystems found?

Freshwater ecosystems contain water that has very little salt in it. Freshwater ecosystems are found in lakes, ponds, wetlands, rivers, and streams. Although freshwater ecosystems seem common, they actually contain less than one percent of all the water on Earth.

In Lakes and Ponds

Lakes and ponds are bodies of water surrounded by land. Lakes are larger than ponds. Some plants grow at the edges of these water bodies. Others live underwater or grow leaves that float on the surface. Protists such as algae and amoebas float in the water. Frogs and some insects lay eggs in the water, and their young develop there. Clams, bacteria, and worms live on the bottom of lakes and ponds and break down dead materials for food. Frogs, turtles, fish, and ducks have adaptations that let them swim in water.

Active Reading

7 Identify As you read, underline the names of organisms that live in or near lakes and ponds.

Visualize It!

8 Describe Pick a plant and animal in the picture. Describe how each is adapted to a pond.

Plant

_____

_____

_____

Animal

_____

_____

_____

In Wetlands

A **wetland** is an area of land that is saturated, or soaked, with water for at least part of the year. Bogs, marshes, and swamps are types of wetlands. Bogs contain living and decomposing mosses. Many grasslike plants grow in marshes. Swamps have trees and vines. Plants that live in wetlands are adapted to living in wet soil.

Wetlands have high species diversity. Common wetland plants include cattails, duckweed, sphagnum moss, sedges, orchids, willows, tamarack, and black ash trees. Animals found in wetlands include ducks, frogs, shrews, herons, and alligators. Water collects and slowly filters through a wetland. In this way, some pollutants are removed from the water. Since wetlands can hold water, they also protect nearby land and shore from floods and erosion.

Think Outside the Book Inquiry

9 Apply Use library and Internet resources to put together an identification guide to common wetland plants.

Visualize It!

Wetland

Development That Replaced Wetland

10 Describe What can happen when a wetland is replaced by a development in an area?

_____

_____

_____

_____

_____

In Rivers and Streams

Water moves in one direction in a stream. As water moves, it interacts with air and oxygen is added to the water. A large stream is called a river. Rivers and streams are home to many organisms, including fish, aquatic insects, and mosses. Freshwater ecosystems in streams can have areas of fast-moving and slow-moving water. Some organisms that live in fast-moving water have adaptations that let them resist being washed away. Immature black flies can attach themselves to rocks in a fast-moving stream. Rootlike rhizoids let mosses stick to rocks. In slow-moving waters of a stream, water striders are adapted to live on the water's surface.

The slope of a river's channel and the river's depth determine how quickly water moves.

Visualize It!

11 Match Match the correct captions to the pictures showing areas of fast-moving and slow-moving water.

A Water striders move across the surface of a pool of water in a river.

B Rocks form small waterfalls in areas of some streams.

C Aquatic plants can live below the surface of a river.

D Mosses can grow on the surface of rocks even in fast-moving water.

Inquiry

12 Infer Why might stream water have more oxygen in it than pond water does?

_____

_____

_____

_____

Where River Meets Sea

What is an estuary?

An **estuary** is a partially enclosed body of water formed where a river flows into an ocean. Because estuaries have a mixture of fresh water and salt water, they support ecosystems that have a unique and diverse community of organisms. Seagrasses, mangrove trees, fish, oysters, mussels, and water birds all live in estuaries. Fish and shrimp lay eggs in the calm waters of an estuary. Their young mature here before moving out into the ocean. Many birds feed on the young shrimp and fish in an estuary.

Organisms in estuaries must be able to survive in constantly changing salt levels due to the rise and fall of tides. Some estuary grasses, such as smooth cordgrass, have special structures in their roots and leaves that let them get rid of excess salt.

Visualize It!

13 Describe Fill in the rest of the name tags for each estuary organism. List at least one way the organism uses an estuary to survive.

Hello, I'm a:
great blue heron. I hunt for the young fish that live in this estuary.

Hello, I'm a:
shrimp.

Hello, I'm a:
catfish.

Hello, I'm a:
seagrass.

Houghton Mifflin Harcourt Publishing Company

Protecting Estuaries

Why are estuaries important? The mixture of salt water and nutrient-rich fresh water in an estuary supports breeding grounds for birds, commercial fish, and shellfish such as crabs and shrimp. The grasses in estuaries also protect coastal areas from erosion and flooding.

Oil Spill!

In 2010, a major oil spill occurred in the Gulf of Mexico. Oil flowed into the ocean for almost three months.

Coastal Damage

Estuaries along the northern Gulf Coast were affected. Oil killed birds and other animals. It soaked seagrasses and damaged fish and shellfish nurseries.

Cleaning Up

A large cleanup effort began after the spill. Continuing work will be important to restore ecosystems and protect fishing and tourism jobs in the area.

Extend

Inquiry

14 Explain What are the economic benefits from estuaries?

15 Research Find out about another damaged estuary ecosystem. How has the estuary been restored?

16 Hypothesize Form a hypothesis about how the loss of estuaries can increase erosion along shorelines.

By the Beautiful Sea

The open ocean is vast and contains a variety of life forms. The ocean's largest, fastest, and deepest-diving organisms are found here.

Where are examples of marine ecosystems found?

Marine ecosystems are saltwater ecosystems. They cover more than 70 percent of Earth's surface. Marine ecosystems are found in the coastal ocean, the open ocean, and the deep ocean. Different abiotic, or nonliving, factors affect each marine ecosystem.

In and Along Coastal Oceans

Marine ecosystems in and along coastal oceans include the intertidal zone and the neritic zone. The intertidal zone is the land between high and low tides that includes beaches and rocky shores. Organisms that live in this zone are often adapted to changing water depth, wave action, exposure to air, and changing salinity. Crabs and seagrasses live on beaches. Barnacles and anemones live in tidal pools on rocky shores.

The neritic zone is the underwater zone from the shore to the edge of the continental shelf. Light reaches the bottom of the neritic zone, allowing algae and many plants to live there. Coral reefs and kelp forests are found in the neritic zone. Coral reefs are located mainly in warm tropical areas. They support many species of colorful fish, anemones, and coral. Kelp forests are found in cold, nutrient-rich waters. Kelp forests support brown and red algae, shrimp, fish, brittle stars, and sea otters.

Visualize It!

17 List Below each photo, list abiotic factors that affect the coastal ocean ecosystem that is shown.

Sandy Beach	Rocky Shore	Coral Reef	Kelp Forest

A	B	C	D

In Open Oceans

The open ocean includes all surface waters down to a depth of about 2,000 meters (6,562 feet). Ecosystems at the surface are often dominated by tiny floating organisms called plankton. Organisms that are adapted to dark and cold conditions live at greater depths. Because the open ocean is so large, the majority of sea life is found there. Animals found in open ocean ecosystems include sharks, whales, dolphins, fish, and sea turtles. Ecosystems in the bathyal zone, which extends from the edge of the continental shelf to its base, are also considered open ocean ecosystems.

In Deep Oceans

The deep ocean has the coldest and darkest conditions. Deep ocean ecosystems include those in the abyssal zone, which is the part of the ocean below 2,000 meters (6,562 feet). Some species that live in the deep ocean have bioluminescence, which lets them produce a glowing light to attract mates or prey. Female anglerfish attract prey using bioluminescent structures that act as bait.

No light can reach the deep ocean, so no photosynthesis can happen there. Organisms in the deep ocean must get energy in other ways. Some feed on the organic material that is constantly falling from shallower ocean depths. Microorganisms living near hydrothermal vents use chemicals in the water as an energy source.

Active Reading

18 Infer How do organisms in the deep ocean get energy to live?

_____

_____

Hydrothermal vents release super-hot, acidic water in the deep ocean. Microorganisms called archaea convert chemicals from the vents into food using chemosynthesis. Archaea, tube worms, crabs, clams, and shrimp are part of hydrothermal vent communities.

Visual Summary

To complete this summary, fill in the answer to each question. Then, use the key below to check your answers. You can use this page to review the main concepts of the lesson.

Aquatic Ecosystems

Freshwater ecosystems contain still or moving fresh water.

19 Where are freshwater ecosystems found?

_____

_____

An estuary is an ecosystem that forms where a river empties into an ocean.

Marine ecosystems are located in or near oceans.

20 Where are ecosystems found in the ocean?

_____

_____

21 Which abiotic factor would likely have the greatest effect on an estuary?

_____

_____

Sample answers: 19 in lakes, ponds, wetlands, rivers, and streams; 20 in the coastal ocean, open ocean, and deep ocean; 21 changing salinity

22 Compare How are estuaries and coral reefs similar?

_____

Lesson Review

Vocabulary

Fill in the blank with the term that best completes the following sentences.

1 A(n) _____ is a partially enclosed body of water formed where a river flows into an ocean.

2 A(n) _____ is an area of land that is covered or saturated with water for at least part of the year.

Key Concepts

3 Identify What kinds of organisms live in estuaries?

_____

_____

_____

_____

_____

4 Describe What types of adaptations would be needed by organisms that live in a river?

_____

_____

_____

_____

_____

5 Describe Describe the characteristics of the four zones found in the ocean.

_____

_____

_____

_____

_____

_____

_____

_____

_____

Critical Thinking

Use the photo to answer the following question.

6 Predict Organisms in the aquatic ecosystem in the picture must be adapted to which abiotic factors?

_____

_____

_____

_____

7 Draw Draw an organism that is adapted to the abyssal zone of the ocean, and label its adaptations.

8 Analyze Salt water is denser than fresh water. What ecosystem would be most affected by this fact? Explain your answer.

_____

_____

_____

_____

_____

My Notes

Interpreting Circle Graphs

Scientists display data in tables and graphs in order to organize it and show relationships. A *circle graph*, also called a *pie graph*, is used to show and compare the pieces of a whole.

Tutorial

In a circle graph, the entire circle represents the whole, and each piece is called a *sector*. Follow the instructions below to learn how to interpret a circle graph.

1 Evaluating Data Data on circle graphs may be given in one of two ways: as values (such as dollars, days, or numbers of items) or as percentages of the whole.

2 Changing Percentage to Value The word *percent* means "per hundred," so 25% means 25 per 100, or 25/100. To find the total volume represented by a sector, such as the volume of fresh water in surface water, multiply the whole value by the percent of the sector, and then divide by 100.

$$35{,}030{,}000 \text{ km}^3 \times \frac{0.3}{100} = 105{,}090 \text{ km}^3 \text{ of Earth's fresh water is in surface water.}$$

3 Changing Value to Ratio The sum of the sectors, 35,030,000 km³, is the whole, or total value. Divide the value of a sector, such as the icecaps and glaciers sector, by the value of the whole. Simplify this fraction to express it as a ratio.

$$\frac{24{,}065{,}610 \text{ km}^3}{35{,}030{,}000 \text{ km}^3} \approx \frac{25}{35} = \frac{5}{7}$$

About $\frac{5}{7}$ of Earth's fresh water is in icecaps and glaciers.

This ratio can be expressed as $\frac{5}{7}$, 5:7, or 5 to 7.

4 Changing Value to Percentage The whole circle graph is 100%. To find the percentage of a sector, such as the world's fresh water that is found as groundwater, divide the value of the sector by the value of the whole, and then multiply by 100%.

$$\frac{10{,}544{,}030 \text{ km}^3}{35{,}030{,}000 \text{ km}^3} \times 100\% = 30.1\% \text{ of Earth's fresh water is groundwater.}$$

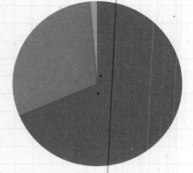

Distribution of Fresh Water (in values)

- ■ Icecaps and Glaciers 24,065,610 km³
- ■ Ground Water 10,544,030 km³
- ■ Surface Water 105,090 km³
- ■ Other 315,270 km³

Source: Gleick, P. H., 1996: Water resources. In Encyclopedia of Climate and Weather, ed. by S. H. Schneider, Oxford University Press, New York, vol. 2, pp.817-823

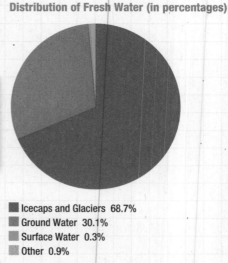

Distribution of Fresh Water (in percentages)

- ■ Icecaps and Glaciers 68.7%
- ■ Ground Water 30.1%
- ■ Surface Water 0.3%
- ■ Other 0.9%

Source: Gleick, P. H., 1996: Water resources. In Encyclopedia of Climate and Weather, ed. by S. H. Schneider, Oxford University Press, New York, vol. 2, pp.817-823

You Try It!

Use the circle graphs below to answer the following questions.

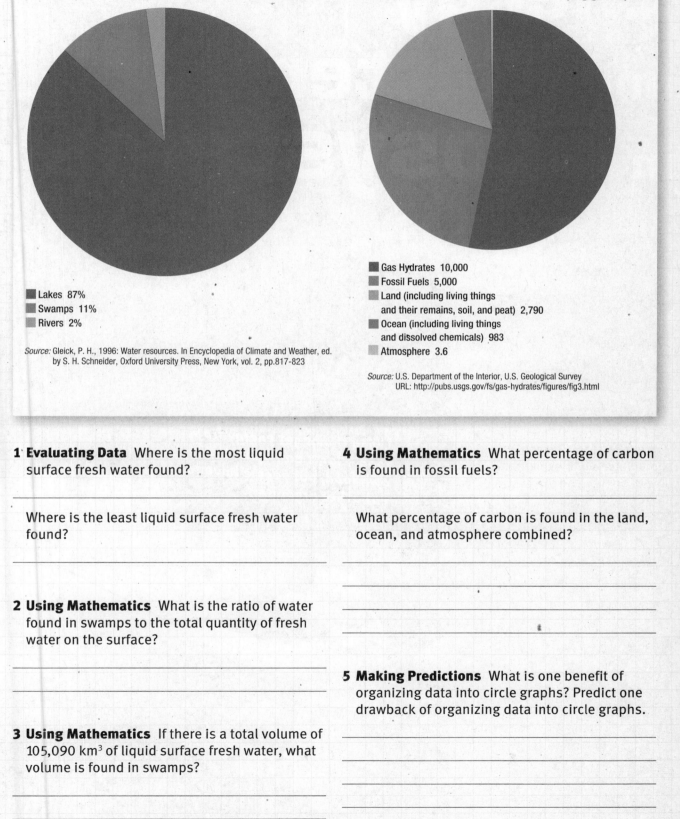

Distribution of Liquid Surface Fresh Water (in percentages)

- Lakes 87%
- Swamps 11%
- Rivers 2%

Source: Gleick, P. H., 1996: Water resources. In Encyclopedia of Climate and Weather, ed. by S. H. Schneider, Oxford University Press, New York, vol. 2, pp.817-823

Distribution of Organic Carbon in Earth (in gigatons)

- Gas Hydrates 10,000
- Fossil Fuels 5,000
- Land (including living things and their remains, soil, and peat) 2,790
- Ocean (including living things and dissolved chemicals) 983
- Atmosphere 3.6

Source: U.S. Department of the Interior, U.S. Geological Survey URL: http://pubs.usgs.gov/fs/gas-hydrates/figures/fig3.html

1 Evaluating Data Where is the most liquid surface fresh water found?

Where is the least liquid surface fresh water found?

2 Using Mathematics What is the ratio of water found in swamps to the total quantity of fresh water on the surface?

3 Using Mathematics If there is a total volume of 105,090 km³ of liquid surface fresh water, what volume is found in swamps?

4 Using Mathematics What percentage of carbon is found in fossil fuels?

What percentage of carbon is found in the land, ocean, and atmosphere combined?

5 Making Predictions What is one benefit of organizing data into circle graphs? Predict one drawback of organizing data into circle graphs.

Energy and Matter in Ecosystems

ESSENTIAL QUESTION

How do energy and matter move through ecosystems?

By the end of this lesson, you should be able to explain the flow of energy and the cycles of matter in ecosystems.

Living things get energy from food. Plants can make their own food, but people have to eat other organisms.

Lesson Labs

Quick Labs
- Pyramid of Energy
- Model the Carbon Cycle
- Condensation and Evaporation

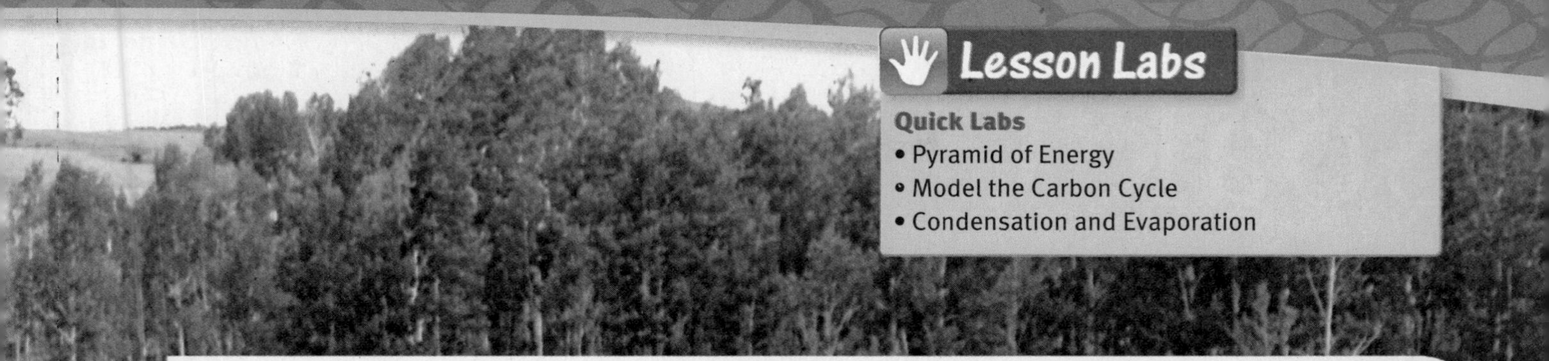

Engage Your Brain

1 Predict Organisms get energy from food. Underline the organisms in the list below that get food by eating other organisms.

Lizard	Butterfly
Pine tree	Cactus
Grass	Mountain lion
Salamander	Bluebird
Turtle	Moss

2 Diagram Choose a nearby ecosystem, and draw a diagram below of the flow of energy from the sun to the organisms in the ecosystem.

Active Reading

3 Apply Many scientific words, such as *energy*, also have everyday meanings. Use context clues to write your own definition for each meaning of the word *energy*.

You could feel the energy in the crowd during the homecoming game.

___

___

When she had the flu, Eliza slept all day because she felt completely drained of energy.

___

___

The brightly colored painting was full of energy.

___

___

Vocabulary Terms

- **energy**
- **matter**
- **law of conservation of energy**
- **law of conservation of mass**
- **energy pyramid**
- **water cycle**
- **nitrogen cycle**
- **carbon cycle**

4 Apply As you learn the definition of each vocabulary term in this lesson, create your own definition or sketch to help remember the meaning of the term.

Soak Up the Sun

How do organisms get energy and matter?

To live, grow, and reproduce, all organisms need matter and energy. **Matter** is anything that has mass and takes up space. Organisms use matter in chemical processes, such as digestion and breathing. For these processes to occur, organisms need energy. **Energy** is the ability to do work and enables organisms to use matter in life processes. Organisms have different ways of getting matter and energy from their environment.

Active Reading

5 Identify As you read, underline the characteristics of producers and consumers.

From the Sun

Organisms called *producers* use energy from their surroundings to make their own food. In most ecosystems, the sun is the original source of energy. Producers, like most plants and algae, use sunlight to convert water and carbon dioxide into sugars. In a few ecosystems, producers use chemical energy instead of light energy to make food. Producers take in matter, such as carbon dioxide, nitrogen, and water from air and soil.

From Other Organisms

Consumers are organisms that get energy by eating producers or other consumers. They get materials such as carbon, nitrogen, and phosphorus from the organisms they eat. So, consumers take in both energy and matter when they eat other organisms.

Roots help trees get matter, such as water and nutrients, from the soil.

6 Infer Use this table to identify where producers and consumers get energy and matter.

Type of organism	How it gets energy	How it gets matter
Producer		
Consumer		

What happens to energy and matter in ecosystems?

Energy and matter are constantly moving through ecosystems. Organisms need energy and matter for many functions, such as moving, growing, and reproducing. Some producers use carbon dioxide and water to make sugars, from which they get energy. They also collect materials from their environment for their life processes. Consumers get energy and matter for their life processes by eating other organisms. During every process, some energy is lost as heat. And, matter is returned to the physical environment as wastes or when organisms die.

Energy and Matter Are Conserved

The **law of conservation of energy** states that energy cannot be created or destroyed. Energy changes forms. Some producers change light energy from the sun to chemical energy in sugars. When sugars are used, some energy is given off as heat. Much of the energy in sugars is changed to another form of chemical energy that cells can use for life functions. The **law of conservation of mass** states that mass cannot be created or destroyed. Instead, matter moves through the environment in different forms.

Energy and Matter Leave Ecosystems

Ecosystems do not have clear boundaries, so energy and matter can leave them. Matter and energy can leave an ecosystem when organisms move. For example, some birds feed on fish in the ocean. When birds fly back to land, they take the matter and energy from the fish out of the ocean. Matter and energy can leave ecosystems in moving water and air. Even though the matter and energy enter and leave an ecosystem, they are never destroyed.

Visualize It!

7 Analyze How might energy and matter leave the ecosystem shown in the picture above?

_____

_____

_____

_____

_____

8 Compare Use the Venn diagram below to relate how energy and matter move through ecosystems.

Energy

Matter

Both

Energy and matter are conserved.

Cycle *and* Flow

How does energy move through an ecosystem?

Energy enters most ecosystems as sunlight, which some producers use to make food. Primary consumers, such as herbivores, get energy by consuming producers. Secondary consumers, such as carnivores, get energy by eating primary consumers, and so on up the food chain. An organism uses most of the energy it takes in for life processes. However, some energy is lost to the environment as heat. A small amount of energy is stored within an organism. Only this stored energy can be used by a consumer that eats the organism.

An **energy pyramid** is a tool that can be used to trace the flow of energy through an ecosystem. The pyramid's shape shows that there is less energy and fewer organisms at each level. At each step in the food chain, energy is lost to the environment. Because less energy is available, fewer organisms can be supported at higher levels. The bottom level—the producers—has the largest population and the most energy. The other levels are consumers. At the highest level, consumers will have the smallest population because of the limited amount of energy available to them.

The amount of energy available and population size decrease as you go up the energy pyramid.

Tertiary consumers

Secondary consumers

Primary consumers

Producers

Visualize It!

9 Analyze Describe how energy flows through each level in this energy pyramid. Is all the matter and energy from one level transferred to the next level?

_____

_____

_____

_____

_____

_____

_____

_____

_____

How does matter move through an ecosystem?

Matter cycles through an ecosystem. For example, water evaporates from Earth's surface into the atmosphere and condenses to form clouds. After forming clouds, water falls back to Earth's surface, completing a cycle.

Carbon and nitrogen also cycle through an ecosystem. Producers take in compounds made of carbon and nitrogen from the physical environment. They use these compounds for life processes. Primary consumers get matter by consuming producers.

Secondary consumers eat primary consumers. The matter in primary consumers is used in chemical processes by secondary consumers. In this way, carbon and nitrogen flow from producers through all levels of consumers.

Consumers do not use all of the matter that they take in. Some of the matter is turned into waste products. Decomposers, such as bacteria and fungi, break down solid waste products and dead organisms, returning matter to the physical environment. Producers can then reuse this matter for life processes, starting the cycles of matter again.

All of these cycles can take place over large areas. Matter leaves some ecosystems and enters other ecosystems. For example, water that evaporates from a lake in the middle of a continent can later fall into an ocean. Because matter can enter and leave an ecosystem, it is called an *open system*.

Active Reading **10 Identify** What is the role of decomposers in cycling matter?

_____

_____

_____

Visualize It!

11 Analyze Describe how water is moving through the ecosystem on this page.

_____

_____

_____

_____

_____

_____

What is the water cycle?

The movement of water between the oceans, atmosphere, land, and living things is known as the **water cycle**. Three ways water can enter the atmosphere are evaporation, transpiration, and respiration. During *evaporation*, the sun's heat causes water to change from liquid to vapor. Plants release water vapor from their leaves in *transpiration*. Organisms release water as waste during *respiration*.

In *condensation*, the water vapor cools and returns to liquid. The water that falls from the atmosphere to the land and oceans is *precipitation*. Rain, snow, sleet, and hail are forms of precipitation. Most precipitation falls into the ocean. The precipitation that falls on land and flows into streams and rivers is called *runoff*. Some precipitation seeps into the ground and is stored underground in spaces between or within rocks. This water, called *groundwater*, will slowly flow back into the soil, streams, rivers, and oceans.

Active Reading

12 Explain How does water from the atmosphere return to Earth's surface?

_____

_____

_____

_____

_____

_____

Visualize It!

13 Label Use the terms *evaporation*, *transpiration*, and *respiration* to correctly complete the diagram. Be sure the arrow for each term leads from the proper source.

Condensation

Precipitation

Water vapor in air

Runoff

A

B

Groundwater

C

The water cycle describes how water travels from Earth's surface to the atmosphere and back.

What is the nitrogen cycle?

Organisms need nitrogen to build proteins and DNA for new cells. The movement of nitrogen between the environment and living things is called the **nitrogen cycle**. Most of Earth's atmosphere is nitrogen gas. But most organisms cannot use nitrogen gas directly. However, bacteria in the soil are able to change nitrogen gas into forms that plants can use. This process is called *nitrogen fixation*. Lightning can also fix nitrogen into usable compounds. Plants take in and use fixed nitrogen. Consumers can then get the nitrogen they need by eating plants or other organisms.

When organisms die, decomposers break down their remains. Decomposition releases a form of nitrogen into the soil that plants can use. Finally, certain types of bacteria in the soil can convert nitrogen into a gas, which is returned to the atmosphere.

Nitrogen gas in air

Nitrogen fixed by lightning

Plants eaten by animals

Decay and waste

Nitrogen fixed by bacteria

Nitrogen taken in by plants

Bacteria convert nitrogen back into gas

Usable nitrogen in soil

In the nitrogen cycle, nitrogen gas is converted into usable nitrogen by bacteria and lightning. Plants take in the usable nitrogen. Consumers get the nitrogen they need from the organisms they eat.

Visualize It! (Inquiry)

14 Hypothesize What would happen to the ecosystem if there were no nitrogen-fixing bacteria?

_____

_____

_____

_____

What is the carbon cycle?

Carbon is an important building block of organisms. It is found in sugars, which store the chemical energy that organisms need to live. It also is found in the atmosphere (as carbon dioxide gas), in bodies of water, in rocks and soils, in organisms, and in fossil fuels. Carbon moves through organisms and between organisms and the physical environment in the **carbon cycle**.

Active Reading **15 List** Identify five places where carbon may be found.

_____

_____

_____

Respiration

Photosynthesis

Photosynthesis

During photosynthesis, producers in the water and on land take in light energy from the sun and use carbon dioxide and water to make sugars. These sugars contain carbon and store chemical energy. Oxygen gas is also a product of photosynthesis.

Respiration

Cellular respiration occurs in producers and consumers on land and in water. During respiration, sugars are broken down to release energy. The process uses oxygen gas. Energy, carbon dioxide, and water are released.

carbon in organisms

carbon dioxide dissolved in water

Visualize It!

16 Relate Briefly describe how carbon enters and exits a consumer, such as the sheep shown in this diagram.

_____

_____

_____

_____

_____

Combustion

Combustion is the burning of materials, including wood and fossil fuels. Burning once-living things releases carbon dioxide, water, heat, and other materials into the environment. It may also produce pollution.

carbon dioxide in air

Combustion

Photosynthesis

Respiration

carbon in organisms

Decomposition

Decomposition is the breakdown of dead organisms and wastes. Decomposers get energy from this material by respiration. Decomposition returns carbon dioxide, water, and other nutrients to the environment.

Decomposition

carbon in fossil fuels

Fossil Fuels

Fossil fuels formed from decomposing organisms that were buried deeply millions of years ago. Fossil fuels are burned during combustion, releasing carbon dioxide into the air.

Think Outside the Book Inquiry

17 **Apply** With a partner, choose an ecosystem with which you are familiar. Make a diagram of how carbon cycles in the ecosystem and how energy flows through it. Be sure to label your diagram.

Visual Summary

To complete this summary, fill in the blanks with the correct word or phrase. Then use the key below to check your answers. You can use this page to review the main concepts of the lesson.

Energy and Matter in Ecosystems

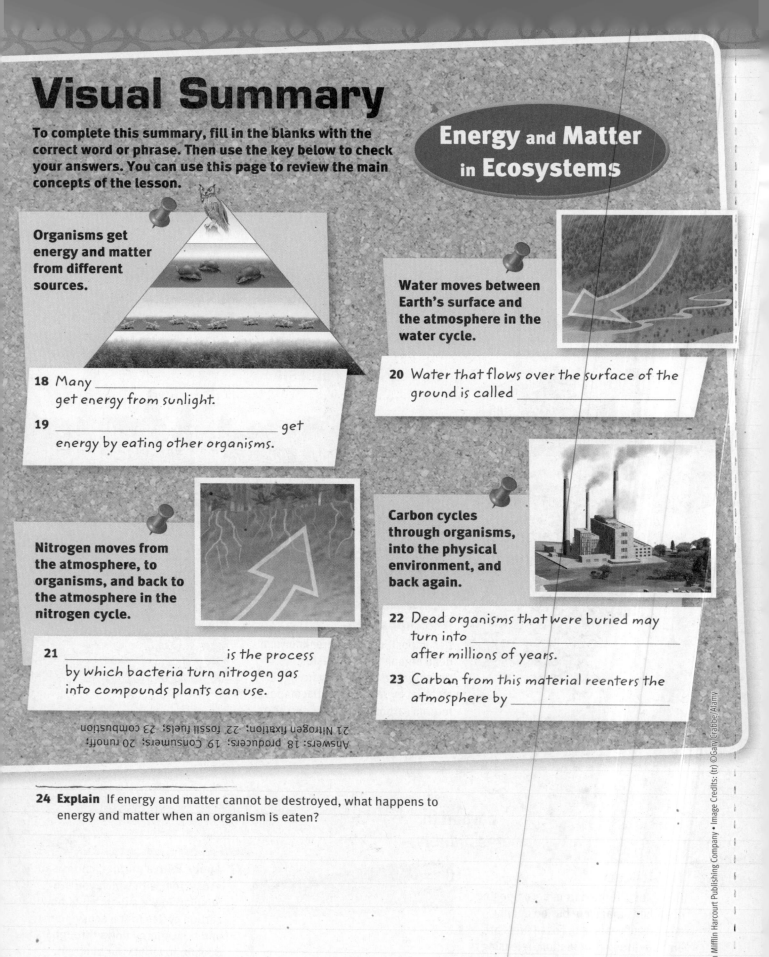

Organisms get energy and matter from different sources.

18 Many _____ get energy from sunlight.

19 _____ get energy by eating other organisms.

Water moves between Earth's surface and the atmosphere in the water cycle.

20 Water that flows over the surface of the ground is called _____

Nitrogen moves from the atmosphere, to organisms, and back to the atmosphere in the nitrogen cycle.

21 _____ is the process by which bacteria turn nitrogen gas into compounds plants can use.

Carbon cycles through organisms, into the physical environment, and back again.

22 Dead organisms that were buried may turn into _____ after millions of years.

23 Carbon from this material reenters the atmosphere by _____

Answers: 18 producers; 19 Consumers; 20 runoff; 21 Nitrogen fixation; 22 fossil fuels; 23 combustion

24 **Explain** If energy and matter cannot be destroyed, what happens to energy and matter when an organism is eaten?

Lesson Review

Vocabulary

Fill in the blanks with the term that best completes the following sentences.

1 The ability to do work is called _____

2 _____ is anything that has mass and takes up space.

3 A(n) _____ can be used to trace the flow of energy through an ecosystem.

Key Concepts

4 Describe Explain the difference between a producer, a consumer, and a decomposer.

_____

_____

_____

5 Compare How are the law of conservation of energy and the law of conservation of mass similar?

_____

_____

_____

_____

_____

6 Explain Why do organisms need nitrogen?

_____

_____

_____

_____

Critical Thinking

7 Analyze In an ecosystem, which would have a larger population: producers or primary consumers? Explain.

_____

_____

_____

_____

Use the graph to answer the following questions.

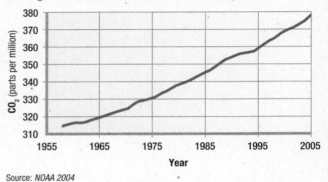

Average Carbon Dioxide Levels at Mauna Loa, Hawaii

Source: *NOAA 2004*

8 Analyze What process of the carbon cycle is likely causing the increase in carbon dioxide levels shown in the graph above?

9 Identify What is the most likely source of the increase in carbon dioxide in the atmosphere shown in the graph above?

10 Evaluate If people planted huge numbers of trees and other plants, how might the carbon dioxide levels in the graph above change? Explain your answer.

_____

_____

_____

_____

11 Apply Water is traveling up a tree carrying nutrients. Use the water cycle to explain how that water later becomes groundwater.

_____

_____

_____

_____

My Notes

Changes in Ecosystems

ESSENTIAL QUESTION

How do ecosystems change?

By the end of this lesson, you should be able to describe how natural processes change ecosystems and help them develop after a natural disturbance.

Ecosystems are always changing. Many changes in ecosystems are due to natural disturbances. This forest fire in Yellowstone National Park was caused by lightning.

✋ Lesson Labs

Quick Labs
- Measuring Species Diversity
- Investigate Evidence of Succession

Field Lab
- Predicting How Succession Follows a Human Disturbance

Engage Your Brain

1 Predict Check T or F to show whether you think each statement is true or false.

T	F	
☐	☐	Some damaged ecosystems can recover after a disturbance.
☐	☐	Ecosystems only change slowly after natural disturbances.
☐	☐	Changes in ecosystems proceed in a fairly predictable way after a disturbance occurs.
☐	☐	Ecosystems eventually stop changing.

2 Describe Use the picture below to describe how beavers change their environment.

_____

_____

_____

Active Reading

3 Synthesize A compound term is a term made from two or more words. The term *pioneer species* is a compound term. Use the definitions and sentence below to make an educated guess about the meaning of the compound term *pioneer species*.

Word	Meaning
pioneer	the first ones to do something
species	a group of very similar organisms

Example sentence
Lichens and other <u>pioneer species</u> break down rock and leave organic matter that mix together to make soil.

pioneer species:

_____

_____

Vocabulary Terms

- eutrophication
- succession
- pioneer species
- biodiversity

4 Identify As you read, create a reference card for each vocabulary term. On one side of the card, write the term and its meaning. On the other side, draw a picture that illustrates or makes a connection to the term. These cards can be used as bookmarks in the text. You can also refer to the cards while studying.

Nothing Stays the Same

How quickly do ecosystems change?

Ecosystems and organisms are constantly changing and responding to daily, seasonal, and long-term changes in the environment. Most ecosystem changes are gradual. Some are sudden and irregular.

Active Reading **5 Describe** As you read, underline one example of a slow change and one example of a sudden change in an ecosystem.

Ecosystems May Change Slowly

Some changes happen slowly. Over time, a pond can develop into a meadow. **Eutrophication** (yoo•trohf•ih•KAY• shuhn) is the process in which organic matter and nutrients slowly build up in a body of water. The nutrients increase the growth of plants and microorganisms. When these organisms die, decaying matter sinks to the bottom of the pond. This organic matter can eventually fill the pond and become soil that grasses and other meadow plants can grow in.

Ecosystem changes can also be caused by seasonal or long-term changes in climate.

Ecosystems May Change Suddenly

Ecosystems can suddenly change due to catastrophic natural disturbances. A hurricane's strong winds can blow down trees and destroy vegetation in a few hours. Lightning can start a forest fire that rapidly clears away plants and alters animal habitats. A volcano, such as Washington's Mount St. Helens, can erupt and cause massive destruction to an ecosystem. But destruction is not the end of the story. Recovery brings new changes to an ecosystem and the populations that live in it.

Visualize It! Inquiry

6 Hypothesize What natural ecological change might happen to the meadow that forms where the pond was?

_____

_____

The organic matter growing in a pond dies and falls to the bottom. The pond gets shallower as the matter piles up.

Eventually, the pond fills in, and land plants grow there. The pond becomes a level meadow.

A CHANGING WORLD

Ruin and Recovery

Ecosystems can change very fast. The volcanic eruption of Mount St. Helens in southern Washington devastated the mountain on May 18, 1980, killing 57 people. The hot gas and debris also killed native plant and animal species and damaged 596 square kilometers (230 square miles) of forest.

1979

Today

A Changed Landscape

The eruption changed the ecosystem dramatically. Trees fell and forests burned. Much of the ice and snow melted. The water mixed with ash and dirt that covered the ground. Thick mud formed and slid down the mountain. Flowing mud removed more trees and changed the shape of the landscape.

Road to Recovery

How did the ecosystem recover? Snow patches and ice protected some species. Some small mammals were sheltered in burrows. With the trees gone, more sunlight reached the ground. Seeds sprouted, and the recovery began.

Extend

Inquiry

7 Explain How do sudden catastrophes such as the eruption of Mount St. Helens change the landscape of ecosystems?

8 Research Find out about how natural catastrophic events, such as volcanic eruptions, can affect the climate on Earth.

9 Hypothesize Form a hypothesis based on your research in question 8 about how changes in climate can lead to changes in ecosystems.

Houghton Mifflin Harcourt Publishing Company • Image Credits: (bg) ©Science Source/Photo Researchers, Inc.; (t) ©Science Source/Photo Researchers, Inc.; (b) ©EdBookPhoto/Alamy

What are the two types of ecological succession?

Ecosystems can develop from bare rock or cleared land. This development is the result of slow and constructive gradual changes. The slow development or replacement of an ecological community by another ecological community over time is called **succession**.

Primary Succession

A community may start to grow in an area that has no soil. This process is called primary succession. The first organisms to live in an uninhabited area are called **pioneer species**. Pioneer species, such as lichens, grow on rock and help to form soil in which plants can grow.

Visualize It!

10 Label Write a title for each step of primary succession.

A _____

A slowly retreating glacier exposes bare rock where nothing lives, and primary succession begins.

B _____

Acids from lichens break down the rock into particles. These particles mix with the remains of dead lichens to make soil.

C _____

After many years, there is enough soil for mosses to grow. The mosses replace the lichens. Insects and other small organisms begin to live there, enriching the soil.

D _____

As the soil deepens, mosses are replaced by ferns. The ferns may slowly be replaced by grasses and wildflowers. If there is enough soil, shrubs and small trees may grow.

E _____

After hundreds or even thousands of years, the soil may be deep and fertile enough to support a forest.

Secondary Succession

Succession also happens to areas that have been disturbed but that still have soil. Sometimes an existing ecosystem is damaged by a natural disaster, such as a fire or a flood. Sometimes farmland is cleared but is left unmanaged. In either case, if soil is left intact, the original community may regrow through a series of stages called secondary succession.

11 Identify Underline one or two distinctive features of each stage of secondary succession.

Think Outside the Book

12 Describe Find an example of secondary succession in your community, and make a poster that describes each stage.

A

The first year after a farmer stops growing crops or the first year after some other major disturbance, wild plants start to grow. In farmland, crabgrass often grows first.

B

By the second year, new wild plants appear. Their seeds may have been blown into the field by the wind, or they may have been carried by insects or birds. Horseweed is common during the second year.

C

In 5 to 15 years, small conifer trees may start growing among the weeds. The trees continue to grow, and after about 100 years, a forest may form.

D

As older conifers die, they may be replaced by hardwoods, such as oak or maple trees, if the climate can support them.

It's a Balancing Act

What are two signs of a mature ecosystem?

In the early stages of succession, only a few species live and grow in an area. As the ecosystem matures, more species become established.

Climax Species

Succession can happen over decades or over hundreds of years. A community of producers forms first. These organisms are followed by decomposers and consumers. Over time, a stable, balanced ecosystem develops.

As a community matures, it may become dominated by well-adapted *climax species*. The redwoods in a temperate rain forest are a climax species. An ecosystem dominated by climax species is stable until the ecosystem is disturbed.

Biodiversity

As succession moves along, richer soil, nutrients, and other resources become available. This increase in resource availability lets more species become established. By the time climax species are established, the resources in the area support many different kinds of organisms. The number and variety of species that are present in an area is referred to as **biodiversity**.

A diverse forest is more stable and less likely to be destroyed by sudden changes, such as an insect invasion. Most plant-damaging insects attack only one kind of plant. The presence of a variety of plants can reduce the impact of the insects. Even if an entire plant species dies off, other similar plant species may survive.

Active Reading **13 Summarize** How is biodiversity beneficial to an ecosystem?

_____

_____

_____

Rain forests are not just found at the equator. Temperate rain forests along the Pacific Northwest host a diversity of life. Temperate rain forests are often dominated by conifers. Rain forests can receive 350 cm or more of rain annually.

Ferns and other small plants live on the wet, shady forest floor.

Shorter trees and shrubs form an understory. The plants of the forest provide food and shelter for animals such as birds and mammals.

A desert is very different from a rain forest, but it can also be an example of a mature ecosystem. Deserts receive as little as 8 cm of rain per year. But a desert has climax species well-adapted to its dry climate. These species form a balanced ecosystem.

Large cactuses are climax species in deserts.

Desert plants are adapted to live in hot, dry conditions and provide food and shelter for animals.

14 Compare Use the Venn diagram to compare and contrast deserts and rain forests.

Rain Forest Ecosystem

Both

Desert Ecosystem

Visual Summary

To complete this summary, fill in the blanks with the correct word or phrase. Then use the key below to check your answers. You can use this page to review the main concepts of the lesson.

Changes in Ecosystems

Ecosystems are always changing.

Ecosystems can change rapidly or slowly.

15 A pond fills in with organic matter during _____

Secondary succession occurs in damaged ecosystems that still have soil.

17 Soil in damaged ecosystems enables _____ to grow right away.

Primary succession begins with bare rock.

16 In primary succession, _____ grow on bare rock.

Mature ecosystems include many kinds of diverse organisms living in balance.

18 Many mature ecosystems are dominated by a community of _____

Answers: 15 eutrophication; 16 lichens; 17 plants; 18 climax species

19 Relate How is diversity related to changes in ecosystems?

Lesson Review

Vocabulary

Fill in the blank with the term that best completes the following sentences.

1 _____ are the first organisms to live in an uninhabited area.

2 _____ is the number and variety of species that are present in an area.

3 The gradual development or replacement of one ecological community by another is called

_____

Key Concepts

4 Describe Explain how eutrophication can change an aquatic ecosystem into a land ecosystem.

_____
_____
_____
_____
_____
_____

5 Compare What is the major difference between primary and secondary succession?

_____
_____
_____
_____
_____

6 Summarize Explain the important role a pioneer species plays in succession.

_____
_____
_____
_____
_____

Critical Thinking

Use the diagram to answer the following questions.

| Visit 1 | Visit 2 | Visit 3 | Visit 4 | Visit 5 | Visit 6 | Visit 7 |

7 Analyze Between visits 1 and 7, what kind of ecological succession is shown? Explain your answer.

_____
_____
_____

8 Predict If a fire occurs at visit 5, what kind of ecological succession is more likely to occur thereafter?

_____
_____
_____

9 Synthesize How might biodiversity help an ecosystem recover from a volcanic eruption?

_____
_____
_____
_____
_____
_____

My Notes

Houghton Mifflin Harcourt Publishing Company

Engineering Design Process

Skills

Skills
Identify a need
✔ Conduct research
Brainstorm solutions
✔ Select a solution
✔ Build a prototype
✔ Test and evaluate
✔ Redesign to improve
✔ Communicate results

Objectives

- Explain the flow of energy in an ecosystem.
- Build and analyze a closed ecosystem.

Design an Ecosystem

An ecosystem is a community of organisms that interact with each other and with the nonliving environment in a specific area. Factors, such as temperature, the amount of sunlight, water, and minerals, determine which species can live in an ecosystem. Populations of organisms in an ecosystem can be classified by their function. Some producers, such as algae and green plants, make their own food by using sunlight through a process called photosynthesis. Consumers can be carnivores, herbivores, or omnivores. Decomposers, such as fungi and some bacteria, are consumers that break down dead plants and animals and recycle them as nutrients that other organisms can use.

1 Identify On the illustration of the ecosystem, label A through D as a producer, a consumer, or a decomposer.

A

B

Energy in Ecosystems

A food web is the feeding relationship among organisms within an ecosystem. Energy and nutrients are transferred within a food web as organisms feed. Producers form the base of the food web. When producers, such as plants, are consumed, only one tenth of the energy they get from the sun is passed up the food web to primary consumers. The primary consumers, for example herbivores, use the energy they get from plants to grow, reproduce, and live. In turn, when herbivores are eaten, only about one tenth of the energy is passed to secondary consumers, which are carnivores. The decreasing amounts of energy transferred to higher levels is shown by the energy pyramid here.

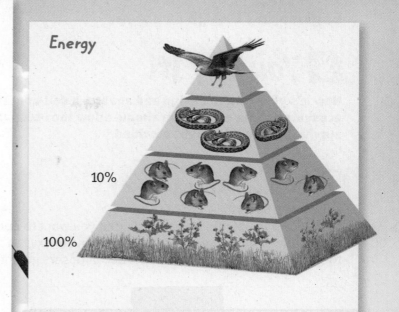

Energy

10%

100%

2 Infer In this example, what percentage of the energy that was available in the grass would reach the snakes? What percentage would reach the eagle? Explain your reasoning.

_____

_____

_____

C

D

✋ You Try It! ⟶

Now it's your turn to design a self-contained aquatic ecosystem.

✋ You Try It!

Now it's your turn to design and analyze a self-contained aquatic ecosystem. Your ecosystem should allow the occupants to survive just from the light provided.

1 Conduct Research

Write down the plants and animals that you want to put into your ecosystem. Use fast-growing plants to provide oxygen and food for the animals. Also, write down how decomposers get into the system.

_____

_____

_____

_____

You Will Need

✓ one-gallon glass jar with tight-fitting lid or sealable clear plastic container

✓ fresh water; can use tap water, but water from natural source is preferable

✓ gravel

✓ aquatic plants and animals to be selected by students

✓ light source if needed

✓ decorative aquarium items (optional)

2 Select a Solution

Based on the flow of energy and biomass in an ecosystem, determine the rough proportion of producers and consumers needed in the ecosystem you are designing. Write down how many plants to animals you think that you will need. Explain your reasoning.

_____

_____

_____

3 Build a Prototype

Follow these steps to build a prototype of your system.

- Clean your container, and record its mass.
- Put enough gravel in to cover the bottom.
- Fill the container with water, and add decorative items.
- Let the water and decorative items settle for at least 24 hours to allow the chemicals in the water to evaporate and the water to come to room temperature.
- Add your plants, and wait 24 hours.

- Before releasing the animals into the tank, float the containers holding the animals in the water in the tank for a few hours. This allows the animals to adjust to the temperature of the water in the tank.
- Close the lid tightly to prevent evaporation, and then record the mass of your ecosystem.
- Store your ecosystem where it will receive indirect sunlight.

④ Test and Evaluate

List five things that you think would be important to record before you close your system completely. Keep a journal in which you record daily observations of your ecosystem for several weeks.

_____

_____

_____

_____

_____

⑤ Redesign to Improve

After observing your system and keeping a journal for several weeks, what would you change about your system?

_____

_____

_____

_____

_____

_____

_____

⑥ Communicate Results

Summarize the observations you made in your journal. Consider these questions: What things do you think made your ecosystem successful or unsuccessful? What things, if any, would you change to improve your ecosystem even more? Finally, make a report of your ecosystem to present to the class.

_____

_____

_____

_____

_____

_____

_____

Human Activity and Ecosystems

ESSENTIAL QUESTION

How do human activities affect ecosystems?

By the end of this lesson, you should be able to describe the effects of human activities on ecosystems, and explain the role of conservation in protecting natural resources.

Human activities can disturb habitats and wildlife. Coastal developments may prevent species such as leatherback sea turtles from reproducing.

Engage Your Brain

1 Explain Think about what you see as you go to and from school. What is one example of human activity that you would change if you could?

_____

Why and how would you make this change?

_____

_____

_____

_____

2 Describe Write your own caption to this photo.

_____

_____

_____

Active Reading

3 Synthesize Many English words have their roots in other languages. Use the Latin words below to make an educated guess about the meaning of the words *urbanization* and *biodiversity*.

Latin word	Meaning
urbanus	city
divertus	diverse
bio	life

Example sentence
The population of Los Angeles increased during the 20th century because of <u>urbanization</u>.

urbanization:

_____

_____

Example sentence
The <u>biodiversity</u> of our food crops has decreased over the last several decades.

biodiversity:

_____

_____

Vocabulary Terms

• urbanization
• biodiversity
• eutrophication
• stewardship
• conservation

4 Identify As you read, place a question mark next to any words that you don't understand. After you finish reading the lesson, go back and review the text that you marked. If the information is still confusing, consult a classmate or your teacher.

Growing Pains

How do humans negatively affect ecosystems?

Human activities can change and even harm ecosystems. An *ecosystem* is all of the living and nonliving things within a given area. Changing one thing in an ecosystem can affect many other things, because everything in an ecosystem is connected.

Humans can affect ecosystems through pollution. *Pollution* is caused by any material or condition that harms the environment. For example, factories and automobiles burn fossil fuels. This releases harmful chemicals into the environment. Farms that produce our food may also burn fossil fuels and release chemicals, such as pesticides or fertilizers, into the environment.

Even simple actions can harm ecosystems. For example, the trash we throw out may end up in a landfill. Landfills take up space and may contain harmful materials like batteries. Toxic metals in batteries can leak into soil or groundwater, with drastic consequences for organisms and ecosystems.

5 Relate Identify a form of pollution that you observe in your community.

_____

_____

Tons of garbage are put into landfills every day.

As cities and suburbs expand closer to natural areas, wildlife may wander into our backyards and onto our streets.

© Houghton Mifflin Harcourt Publishing Company • Image Credits: (bg) ©Arno Massee/Photo Researchers, Inc.; (c) ©Rex Ziak/Stone/Getty Images

By Depleting Resources

The number of people on Earth has increased from 1 billion to more than 6 billion people in the last 200 years. The growing human population has created a greater need for natural resources. This need has created problems for ecosystems. When we cut down trees, we remove a resource that many organisms need for food and shelter. The loss of many trees in an area can affect shade and local temperatures. These changes can disturb ecosystems.

The overuse of resources causes them to be depleted, or used up. *Resource depletion* occurs when a large fraction of a resource has been used up. Fresh water was once a renewable resource. But in some areas, humans use fresh water faster than it can be replenished by the water cycle.

By Destroying Habitats

Human population growth in and around cities is called **urbanization** (er•buh•nih•ZAY•shuhn). Urban growth within ecosystems often destroys natural habitats. Roads can divide habitats and prevent animals from safely roaming their territory. If animals cannot interact with each other and their surroundings, the ecosystem will not thrive.

An ecosystem may be converted into housing and shopping areas that further shrink habitats. This can bring humans and wildlife into contact. Deer, raccoons, and even coyotes have become common sights in some suburban areas.

Every habitat has its own number and variety of organisms, or **biodiversity**. If a habitat is damaged or destroyed, biodiversity is lost. Because living things are connected with each other and with their environment, loss of biodiversity affects the entire ecosystem.

Active Reading 6 **Provide** Give one example of how urbanization affects natural ecosystems.

_____

_____

_____

An open-pit mine like this one is one way that humans remove minerals from the ground. Minerals are nonrenewable resources.

Cutting down forests destroys habitats and affects the physical features of the ecosystem.

Think Outside the Book Inquiry

7 **Apply** Do research to find out what the environment around your school looked like 100 years ago.

Water, Water Everywhere?

How do humans impact oceans?

Active Reading

8 Identify As you read, underline the sources of ocean pollution.

Oceans support a variety of ecosystems that together contain nearly half of Earth's species. Pollution from human activities damages ocean ecosystems and threatens marine biodiversity.

Point-source pollution comes from one source. Oil spills, such as the one shown above, are an example of this. Spilled oil pollutes open waters and coastal habitats. *Nonpoint-source pollution* comes from many sources. For example, chemicals such as fertilizers and pesticides may be washed into oceans, where they harm many marine organisms.

Raw sewage and trash are frequently dumped into marine habitats. Plastic bags and packaging are dangerous to marine animals. Some animals mistake bags for food or become tangled in packaging. Dumping trash in the ocean is illegal. Many people and agencies work hard to enforce laws that protect the oceans.

Visualize It!

9 Predict Compare these pictures. What is one problem that could arise if a sea turtle sees the plastic bag underwater?

_____

_____

Jellyfish have translucent, sac-like bodies. Sea turtles and dolphins eat jellyfish.

Underwater, plastic bags look like jellyfish.

Through Fishing and Overfishing

A greater demand for seafood from the growing human population has led to *overfishing* of some ocean species. Many fish species cannot reproduce fast enough to replace individuals that are harvested for food. When large numbers of a single fish population are caught, the remaining population may be too small to successfully reproduce. If the population cannot replace itself, it can become locally extinct. The local loss of a species can disturb ocean food webs and threaten ecosystem stability.

Through Coastal Development

The growing human population also has led to increased coastal development. That means building homes and businesses on and near beaches and wetlands. Sadly, this can destroy the very coastlines we want to be near. Roads and shopping centers divide habitats. Increased human activity increases pollution both on shore and in coastal waters.

In some places, development has almost completely replaced natural coastlines. For example, construction of new homes and businesses is rapidly destroying mangrove forests. Mangroves are unique trees found only in certain coastal regions. Mangrove forests play a key role in maintaining coastlines. The thick roots stabilize the sandy soil and prevent erosion. The trees are home to a wide range of species.

Human activity has also damaged coral reefs, but people and scientists are working to correct this damage. Coral reefs are vital ecosystems because so many species live in or around them. To replace this lost habitat, scientists have created artificial reefs. First, different fish species will find safety in the structures. Next, algae and soft corals begin to grow. Over time, hard corals grow and other sea life can be seen. Artificial reefs preserve the reef food web and stabilize the ecosystem.

Overfishing means that the rate at which fish are caught exceeds the rate at which the species can reproduce.

10 List What are three ways that human activities impact ocean ecosystems?

_____

_____

_____

Artificial reefs, such as sunken ships or other human-made objects, are being used to make up for the loss of natural coral reefs.

How do humans affect freshwater ecosystems?

Active Reading

11 Identify As you read, number the steps involved in the formation of acid rain.

Human activities have decreased the amount of water, or *water quantity*, in many river ecosystems. Dams and river channelization are two examples of this. Dams block the flow of river water. That means there is less water downstream of the dam. Channelization is used to straighten rivers to improve travel and other activities. However, changing the natural course of a river also changes the amount of water in it. Differences in water levels can change water temperature and chemistry. These changes can affect the reproduction and survival of many river species.

Human activities can also decrease *water quality*, or change how clean or polluted the water is, in ecosystems. Pollution disturbs water quality. Animal waste and fertilizer from farms contain nutrients that can enter ponds and lakes as runoff. An increase in the amount of nutrients, such as nitrates, in an aquatic ecosystem is called **eutrophication** (yoo•trohf•ih•KAY•shuhn). The extra nutrients cause overgrowth of algae. The excess algae die and decompose, using up the pond's dissolved oxygen. As dissolved oxygen levels decrease, fish begin to die. If eutrophication continues, the pond ecosystem will not recover.

Water quality is also affected by air pollution. For example, some freshwater ecosystems are affected by acid rain. Burning fossil fuels releases chemicals into the air. Some of these combine with rain to form acids. Small amounts of acid in rain cause its pH to fall below its normal value of 5.6. Acid rain can damage both aquatic and land ecosystems.

Eutrophication causes overgrowth of algae and can disrupt pond ecosystems.

© Houghton Mifflin Harcourt Publishing Company • Image Credits: ©James Leighton/Corbis

Why It Matters

Exotic Species

An organism that makes a home for itself in a new place outside its native home is an *exotic species*. Exotic species often thrive in new places because they are free from the predators found in their native homes. Exotic species that outcompete native species for resources, such as food or space, are known as *invasive* exotic species.

European rabbits were introduced into Australia in 1859 for sport hunting. With plenty of space and food—and no predators—Australia's rabbit population exploded.

The rabbits threatened the survival of many native Australian animals and plants. Many efforts were made to control the rabbit population. Their dens were poisoned. Rabbit-proof fences were built. Rabbits were even "herded" by cowboys.

So far, all efforts to remove rabbits have failed. There are still more than 200 million rabbits in Australia.

Extend

Inquiry

12 Explain How do exotic species contribute to habitat destruction?

13 Hypothesize Form a hypothesis about a method that might be effective in controlling an invasive exotic species.

14 Research Identify a non-native plant species that has been introduced into the United States. Explain where the species came from, how or why it was brought to the United States, and how it has affected the ecosystem.

Save It!

Active Reading

15 Identify As you read, underline the definition of stewardship.

How do humans protect ecosystems?

There are many ways that humans can protect ecosystems. One way is by using Earth's resources in a careful manner. The careful and responsible management of a resource is called **stewardship**. The resources of an ecosystem include all of its living and nonliving parts.

By Maintaining Biodiversity

The organisms in an ecosystem depend on each other and interact with each other in a vast interconnected food web. Each species has a place in this web and a role to play. The loss of a species or introduction of an exotic species creates gaps in the web. This can disrupt species interactions. Protecting habitats and helping species survive protects the biodiversity in an ecosystem. The greater the biodiversity, the healthier the ecosystem.

16 State What are two ways that humans can help maintain biodiversity in ecosystems?

_____

_____

_____

You can reduce pollution by participating in a local cleanup project.

You can protect habitats by staying on marked trails when visiting national parks and forests.

By Conserving Natural Resources

Humans can protect ecosystems through conservation. **Conservation** is the protection and wise use of natural resources. Practicing conservation means using fewer natural resources and reducing waste. It also helps prevent habitat destruction.

The "three Rs" are three ways to conserve resources.

- *Reduce* what you buy and use—this is the first goal of conservation.
- *Reuse* what you already have. For example, carry water in a reusable bottle and lunch in a reusable lunch bag.
- *Recycle* by recovering materials from waste and by always choosing to use recycling bins.

You can practice conservation every day by making wise choices. Even small changes make a difference!

17 Synthesize Suppose you wanted to stop eating fast food to cut down on excess fat and sodium. How might this benefit the environment as well?

_____

_____

_____

_____

You can help prevent water shortages by turning off the water as you brush your teeth.

You can reduce pesticide use by supporting responsible agriculture.

You can reduce the use of fossil fuels by turning off lights and supporting alternative energy sources.

Visual Summary

To complete this summary, fill in the blanks with the correct word. Then use the key below to check your answers. You can use this page to review the main concepts of the lesson.

Human demand for resources and land can destroy habitats and disturb ecosystems.

18 Habitat destruction can lead to a loss of _____

Human Activity and Ecosystems

Dumping trash and chemicals into waterways can damage aquatic ecosystems.

19 Materials that cause unwanted changes in the environment cause _____

Conservation and stewardship help protect ecosystems.

20 The protection and wise use of natural resources is called _____

Answers: 18 biodiversity; 19 pollution; 20 conservation

21 Predict Imagine that everyone in the United States chose to ride bicycles rather than drive cars. What effect would this have on your local ecosystem?

_____

_____

_____

Lesson Review

Vocabulary

In your own words, define the following terms.

1 eutrophication

_____

_____

2 stewardship

_____

_____

3 urbanization

_____

_____

Key Concepts

4 Illustrate Name two ways that humans affect land ecosystems.

_____

_____

5 Describe Explain the difference between an *exotic species* and an *invasive exotic species*.

_____

_____

_____

_____

6 Summarize What is pollution?

_____

_____

_____

_____

_____

7 Identify What are two ways to practice conservation?

_____

_____

_____

Critical Thinking

Use this table to answer the following questions.

Human Population Growth

Human population		Year
1 billion		1804
2 billion		1927
3 billion		1960
4 billion		1975
5 billion		1987
6 billion		1999
Projected		
7 billion		2012
8 billion		2026

8 Calculate How many years did it take for the population to double from 1 billion to 2 billion?

_____

_____

9 Calculate How many years did it take for the population to double from 3 billion to 6 billion?

_____

_____

10 Hypothesize If Earth's population continues to increase without limit, how might this affect natural ecosystems? Be specific in your answer.

_____

_____

_____

_____

_____

11 Synthesize Some detergents contain phosphates, chemicals that act like fertilizers. If wastewater from washing machines enters a local lake, will the fish population increase or decrease? Explain your answer.

_____

_____

_____

My Notes

Houghton Mifflin Harcourt Publishing Company

Unit 2 [Big Idea] Matter and energy together support life within an environment.

Lesson 1
ESSENTIAL QUESTION
What are land biomes?

Describe the characteristics of different biomes that exist on land.

Lesson 4
ESSENTIAL QUESTION
How do ecosystems change?

Describe how natural processes change ecosystems and help them develop after a natural disturbance.

Lesson 2
ESSENTIAL QUESTION
What are aquatic ecosystems?

Describe the characteristics of marine, freshwater, and other aquatic ecosystems.

Lesson 5
ESSENTIAL QUESTION
How do human activities affect ecosystems?

Describe the effect of human activities on ecosystems, and explain the role of conservation in protecting natural resources.

Lesson 3
ESSENTIAL QUESTION
How do energy and matter move through ecosystems?

Explain the flow of energy and the cycles of matter in ecosystems.

Connect ESSENTIAL QUESTIONS
Lessons 4 and 5

1 Explain How might human activity cause secondary succession? In your answer, identify each stage of secondary succession.

_____

_____

_____

_____

Think Outside the Book

2 Synthesize Choose one of these activities to help synthesize what you have learned in this unit.

☐ Using what you learned in lessons 1 and 2, create a brochure that describes the characteristics of the biome in which you live. In your brochure list what aquatic systems, if any, can also be found where you live.

☐ Using what you learned in lessons 1, 2, and 3, choose a biome or aquatic ecosystem and draw or make a collage of an energy pyramid that might be found in it. Label each tier of the energy pyramid and identify the species shown.

Unit 2 Review

Vocabulary

Fill in each blank with the term that best completes the following sentences.

1 The _____ states that energy cannot be created or destroyed.

2 A _____ is a community of organisms at a major regional or global level.

3 A _____ tree has leaves that drop in the winter as an adaptation to cold temperatures.

4 _____ is an increase in the ratio or density of people living in urban areas rather than rural areas.

5 A _____ is one of the first species of organisms to live in an area.

Key Concepts

Read each question below, and circle the best answer.

6 Where do producers, such as trees, get the energy that they need to survive?

   A from the sun   **C** from the organisms they eat

   B from the air   **D** from the remains of organisms

7 What are the ocean zones of a marine ecosystem, from most shallow to deepest?

   A intertidal, neritic, bathyal, abyssal

   B abyssal, neritic, intertidal, bathyal

   C neritic, intertidal, bathyal, abyssal

   D bathyal, abyssal, intertidal, neritic

8 Resource depletion, pollution, and habitat loss are all environmental problems caused by what factor?

   A acid rain   **C** introduced species

   B eutrophication   **D** human activities

9 Below is an energy pyramid diagram.

Energy Pyramid

Why is the level at 4 so much smaller than the level at 1?

A Organisms gain energy as the food chain moves down the pyramid.

B Fewer organisms are supported as you move down the pyramid.

C Only the energy that is used is available to organisms at a higher level.

D Only the energy that is stored is available to organisms at a higher level.

10 What element can be changed by lightning into a form that plants can use?

A oxygen   **C** phosphorous

B carbon   **D** nitrogen

11 Below is a diagram of the carbon cycle.

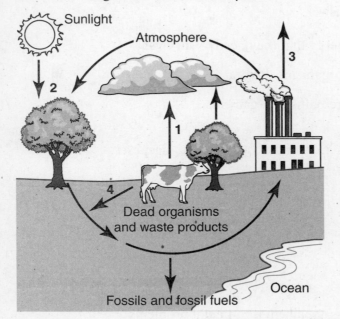

Which number corresponds to combustion and the release of CO_2, water, and the loss of energy as heat into the environment?

A 1   **C** 3

B 2   **D** 4

12 What is an adaptation that allows some animals to survive in the tundra?

    A living underground   **C** being active at night only

    B having thick layers of fur   **D** living within the upper branches of trees

13 Some grass species need fire in order for their seeds to germinate. Why might this adaptation be useful for grasses?

    A Fire allows trees to grow and provide shade for the grasses.

    B The hot temperature of the fire helps the grasses grow faster.

    C Seeds can germinate in an area that has been cleared by a fire.

    D Fire discourages grazing by large animals so grass can grow higher.

Critical Thinking

Answer the following questions in the space provided.

14 Draw a diagram of the water cycle and label it with the terms given below.

In the space provided, identify what each term means.

Precipitation: _____

Evaporation: _____

Transpiration: _____

Condensation: _____

15 The picture below shows a land ecosystem that experiences annual flooding.

Is this ecosystem more likely a result of primary succession or secondary succession? _____

Predict what would happen if a fast growing non-native species of plant was introduced to this ecosystem.

_____

_____

Connect **ESSENTIAL QUESTIONS**
Lessons 2 and 5

Answer the following question in the space provided.

16 Below is an example of an aquatic food web common in mangrove forests.

Mangrove Food Web

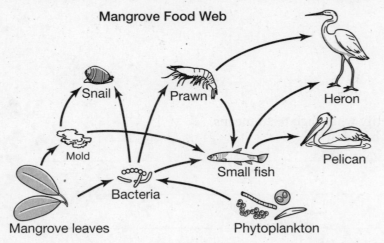

Mangroves commonly grow in estuaries. What are the characteristics of an estuary? _____

What might happen if the prawns and fish shown in the diagram were fished to near extinction? _____

_____

Earth's Resources

Common building materials such as lumber, bricks, and glass are all made from natural resources.

Big Idea

Humans depend on natural resources for materials and for energy.

Wood for buildings comes from forests that have to be managed wisely.

What do you think?

The resources that humans need to live are found on Earth or come from the sun. What would happen if one or more of these resources were used up?

CITIZEN SCIENCE

Energy Sources

The world is filled with valuable resources. How we use, reuse, or use up those resources is important to this and future generations.

① Think About It

Every time you walk into school on a normal school day, the lights are on, the rooms are comfortable, and there are material resources available for teacher and student use. Where does your school get its energy? Is it from a renewable or nonrenewable resource? Could the energy be used more efficiently?

_____

_____

_____

_____

The type of lighting as well as the quality of doors and windows can make a difference in a building's energy costs and efficiency.

② Ask a Question

What is the energy source for your school's heating and cooling system?

With a partner or as a class, learn more about the source of energy for your school's heating and cooling system and the energy efficiency of your school building. As you talk about it, consider the items below.

Things to Consider

☐ Does your school have more than one energy source?

☐ Is your school building energy efficient?

Many older schools have been modified with new windows, doors, and insulation. These changes were made to save on heating and cooling costs and to provide a more comfortable learning environment.

③ Make a Plan

Once you have learned about your school building's energy efficiency, develop a proposal for your principal. Propose an alternative energy source for the heating and cooling system and ways to improve the building's energy efficiency.

A Describe the current energy source for your school's heating and cooling system.

_____

_____

B Describe one alternative energy source your school could use.

_____

_____

C List any noted energy inefficiencies and suggestions for improvements.

_____

_____

_____

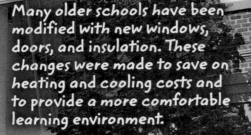

Ideas for saving resources can help schools save money.

Take It Home

What energy sources supply your home? With an adult, talk about possible ways to improve energy efficiency where you live.

135

Earth's Support of Life

ESSENTIAL QUESTION

How can Earth support life?

By the end of this lesson, you should be able to explain how the unique properties of Earth make it possible for life to exist.

Earth's land, water, and atmosphere help to support life on the planet's surface and in its oceans.

✋ **Lesson Labs**

Quick Labs
• How Water Forms on Earth's Surface
• Temperature Variations on Earth

Exploration Lab
• Modeling the Greenhouse Effect

🧠 Engage Your Brain

1 Describe What kind of life is found on Earth?

_____

_____

2 Compare Look at the differences between the pictures of Earth and Mars. Why do you think that Mars does not support the kind of life found on Earth?

_____

_____

_____

_____

_____

Mars

✏️ Active Reading

3 Synthesize You can often define an unknown word if you know the meaning of its word parts. Use the word parts and sentence below to make an educated guess about the meaning of the word *atmosphere*.

Word part	Meaning
atmo-	vapor, steam
-sphere	globe, ball

Example sentence
Earth's <u>atmosphere</u> is made of different layers of gases.

atmosphere:

_____

_____

_____

Vocabulary Terms

• **photosynthesis**
• **atmosphere**
• **ultraviolet radiation**
• **ozone**

4 Identify As you read, place a question mark next to any words that you don't understand. When you finish reading the lesson, go back and review the text that you marked. If the information is still confusing, consult a classmate or teacher.

Living it Up

What do living things need to survive?

Earth is covered in living things. Plants, animals, and other organisms live in oceans, rivers, forests, and any other place that you can think of. What do these organisms need to survive? Animals like the poison dart frog in the picture need to breathe air, drink water, and eat food. They need a place to live where they have protection from things that can harm them and where they can dispose of wastes. What do plants need to stay alive? Plants like the bromeliad in the picture need many of the same basic things that animals do. The basic necessities of life are air, water, a source of energy, and a habitat to live in.

How do Earth and the sun interact to support life on Earth?

The sun is a star, so it radiates energy out into space. Some of this energy reaches Earth's surface. Plants on Earth use the sun's energy to make food through the process of photosynthesis. During **photosynthesis**, plants convert carbon dioxide and water to oxygen and glucose. Glucose is a sugar that can be stored in cells. When plants need energy, they break down and use the glucose they have stored. Plant life on Earth forms the foundation of many food chains. Some animals eat plants to gain energy. Other animals eat these animals. In this way, energy from the sun is passed from plants to other organisms.

---

6 Identify Underline the food that is produced during photosynthesis.

$$\text{carbon dioxide} + \text{water} \xrightarrow{\text{solar energy}} \text{oxygen} + \text{glucose}$$

Visualize It!

5 List What necessities of life does the frog get from the bromeliad?

_____

_____

_____

_____

Plants use energy from sunlight to perform photosynthesis.

Earth's Rotation Distributes Solar Energy

Earth rotates continuously on its axis, spinning around completely every 24 hours. Earth's rotation allows most regions of Earth to receive sunlight regularly. Regular sunlight allows plants to grow in almost all places on Earth. Earth's rotation also protects areas on Earth from temperature extremes. Imagine how hot it would be if your town always faced the sun. And imagine how cold it would be if your town never faced the sun!

Earth Has a Unique Temperature Range

Earth's distance from the sun also protects it from temperature extremes. If Earth were closer to the sun, it might be like Venus. Venus has extremely high temperatures because it is closer to the sun, and because it has a very thick atmosphere. These factors make it is too hot to support life. If Earth were farther away from the sun, it might be like Mars. Mars has extremely low temperatures, so it is too cold to support life as we know it. Earth has an average temperature of 15° C (59° F). Regions of Earth range from freezing temperatures below 0° C (32° F) to hot temperatures above 38° C (100° F). This temperature range allows life to survive in even the coldest and hottest places on Earth.

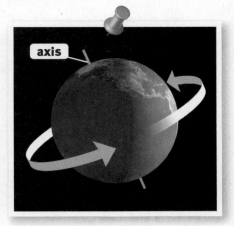

Earth's rotation allows all parts of Earth to receive energy from the sun.

Think Outside the Book Inquiry

7 Apply Write a news story about what would happen to life on Earth if Earth stopped rotating.

Visualize It!

8 Identify Write whether each planet in the drawing is too hot, too cold, or just right to support life.

Water, Water Everywhere

What is unique about Earth's water?

When you look at a picture of Earth, you see lots and lots of water. How did Earth get so much water? Early Earth formed from molten materials, such as iron, nickel, and silica. These materials separated into layers and began to cool. As Earth cooled, it released steam and other gases into the air around its surface. The steam formed clouds, and water fell to Earth as rain. This was the beginning of Earth's oceans. Some of Earth's water also came from space. Icy comets and meteors impacted Earth and added water to Earth's oceans.

Only Earth Has Liquid Water to Support Life

Earth is unique in the solar system because it contains water in three states: solid, liquid, and gas. Most of Earth's water is in liquid form. In fact, Earth is the only known planet with a large supply of liquid water on its surface. About 71% of Earth's surface is now covered with water. Liquid water is essential to life because cells need liquid water in order to perform life processes. Water remains a liquid on Earth because surface temperatures generally stay above the freezing point of water. Temperatures also stay far below water's boiling point.

Active Reading

9 Infer As you read, underline the reason that liquid water is essential to life.

Visualize It!

10 Summarize The pictures below show how Earth's oceans formed. Write a caption for the last two pictures in your own words.

Earth's Formation

As Earth cooled, it released steam. The steam cooled to form clouds. Rain fell and began to form oceans.

Objects from Space

_____
_____
_____
_____

Modern Earth

_____
_____
_____
_____

Extremophiles

Extremophiles are organisms that live in extreme environments. Most extremophiles are unicellular, but some are multicellular. Extremophiles live in some of the coldest, hottest, driest, and saltiest places on Earth.

Living in the Cold
The Antarctic is home to ice-covered lakes and cold, dry valleys. Surprisingly, life can still be found in these harsh conditions.

Extreme Adaptations
A type of worm called a nematode survives in the cold by producing antifreeze in its cells. The nematode can also dry itself out when groundwater is not available. The nematode can then become active when water flows again underground.

Life on Other Planets?
The cold, dry Antarctic has some similarities to the cold, dry surface of Mars. The presence of organisms in extreme environments on Earth makes it seem more possible that some kind of life could exist in the extreme conditions on other planets.

Extend

11 Explain What is an extremophile?

12 Describe What are some adaptations that an extremophile might have in order to survive in a very salty environment?

13 Extend How could a greater knowledge of extremophiles help scientists to search for life on other planets?

Inquiry

Security Blanket

How does Earth's atmosphere support life?

Take a deep breath. The air you are breathing is part of Earth's atmosphere. An **atmosphere** is a mixture of gases that surround a planet, moon, or other space object.

Some space objects have atmospheres, and some do not. It often depends on the object's gravity. Earth and Venus have atmospheres because their gravity is strong enough to hold gases in place. Mercury and the Moon each have weaker gravity, so they do not have atmospheres.

Gases Fuel Life Processes

Earth's atmosphere is composed mainly of nitrogen and oxygen. It also has traces of other gases like carbon dioxide. Carbon dioxide and oxygen support most forms of life. Plants and some single-celled organisms use carbon dioxide for photosynthesis. Plants, animals, and most other organisms use oxygen to perform cell processes. Anaerobic bacteria are some forms of life that do not need oxygen to survive.

Earth's atmosphere has not always contained nitrogen, oxygen, and carbon dioxide. It was originally just hydrogen and helium. These gases were too light for Earth's gravity to hold, so they escaped into space. Volcanoes released water vapor, carbon dioxide, and ammonia into Earth's early atmosphere. Solar energy broke ammonia apart to add nitrogen and hydrogen to the atmosphere. Hydrogen escaped into space, but the nitrogen stayed in the atmosphere. Bacteria used carbon dioxide to perform photosynthesis, which released oxygen into the atmosphere.

Planet	% Gravity Compared to Earth
Mercury	38%
Venus	91%
Earth	100%

14 Infer Why doesn't Mercury have an atmosphere?

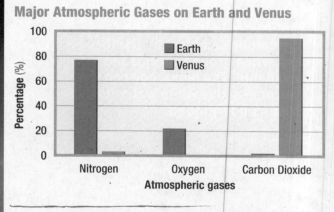

Major Atmospheric Gases on Earth and Venus

15 Infer If Venus has an atmosphere, why doesn't it support the kind of life that is now found on Earth?

Gases Insulate Earth

The gases in Earth's atmosphere support life in other ways. As radiation from the sun reaches Earth's atmosphere, some of it is reflected back into space. Some is absorbed by water vapor, carbon dioxide, and other gases in the atmosphere. Some solar radiation passes through the atmosphere and is absorbed by Earth's surface. Radiation from Earth's surface then moves into the atmosphere. This energy is absorbed and re-radiated by atmospheric gases, through a process called the greenhouse effect. The greenhouse effect keeps Earth warmer than it would be if Earth had no atmosphere.

The Ozone Layer Protects Earth

One type of solar radiation that can harm life is **ultraviolet radiation**. Ultraviolet radiation is harmful because it can damage the genetic material in organisms. Earth has a protective ozone layer that blocks most ultraviolet radiation before it reaches Earth's surface. The ozone layer contains ozone gas in addition to the other atmospheric gases. **Ozone** is a molecule that is made up of three oxygen atoms. Some human-made chemicals have damaged the ozone layer by breaking apart ozone molecules. International laws have banned the use of these ozone-destroying chemicals.

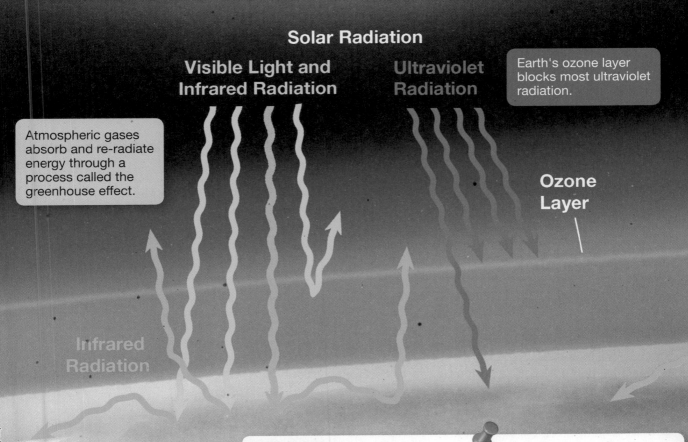

Solar Radiation

Visible Light and Infrared Radiation

Ultraviolet Radiation

Earth's ozone layer blocks most ultraviolet radiation.

Atmospheric gases absorb and re-radiate energy through a process called the greenhouse effect.

Ozone Layer

Infrared Radiation

Visualize It!

16 Explain How does the ozone layer protect life on Earth?

_____

_____

_____

Visual Summary

To complete this summary, answer each question in the space provided. Then use the key below to check your answers. You can use this page to review the main concepts of the lesson.

Earth's Support of Life

Organisms need certain things to survive.

17 What do animals need to survive?

_____

Earth's rotation and distance from the sun allow it to support life.

19 How does the sun support life on Earth?

_____
_____

Liquid water supports life on Earth.

18 Why is liquid water important to life?

_____
_____

Earth's atmosphere protects life on Earth.

20 What is an atmosphere?

_____
_____

Sample answers: **17** air, water, food, and a place to live; **18** Cells need liquid water to perform life processes; **19** It provides energy that warms Earth and allows plants to make food; **20** a blanket of gases around a space object

21 Describe How does Earth's position in space affect water on Earth?

Lesson Review

Vocabulary

Fill in the blank with the term that best completes the following sentences.

1 Plants produce glucose and oxygen during the process of _____

2 Earth's _____ absorbs solar radiation and re-radiates it to Earth's surface.

Key Concepts

3 Describe How does Earth's rotation affect life on Earth?

_____

_____

_____

4 List What are three ways that Earth is different from other planets?

_____

_____

_____

5 Describe How did Earth's oceans form?

_____

_____

_____

_____

_____

6 Explain How does the carbon dioxide in Earth's atmosphere allow Earth to support life?

_____

_____

_____

Critical Thinking

Use the image to answer the following questions.

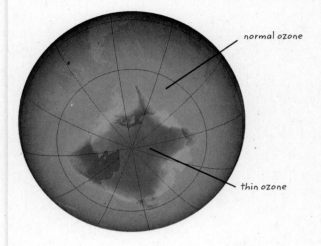

normal ozone

thin ozone

7 Describe The image shows the ozone layer. Why do you think it looks this way?

_____

_____

_____

8 Explain Why is it important to protect the ozone layer?

_____

_____

_____

_____

9 Apply What conditions would you look for if you were looking for life on moons or other planets besides Earth?

_____

_____

_____

_____

My Notes

Natural Resources

ESSENTIAL QUESTION

What are Earth's natural resources?

By the end of this lesson, you should be able to understand the types and uses of Earth's natural resources.

Light produced from electrical energy helps people see at night. Natural resources are needed to produce electrical energy.

Lesson Labs

Quick Labs
Renewable or Not?
Production Impacts

Field Labs
Natural Resources Used at Lunch

Engage Your Brain

1 Predict Check T or F to show whether you think each statement is true or false.

T   F

☐   ☐   Energy from the sun can be used to make electrical energy.

☐   ☐   All of Earth's resources will last forever.

☐   ☐   Food, cloth, rope, lumber, paper, and rubber come from plants.

☐   ☐   Human activity can negatively affect Earth's resources.

2 Describe Name one item that you use every day. Describe how you think that item is made.

_____

_____

_____

_____

_____

_____

_____

Active Reading

3 Apply Many scientific words, such as *natural* and *resource*, also have everyday meanings. Use context clues to write your own definition for each underlined word.

Oranges are a <u>natural</u> source of vitamin C.

natural:

_____

_____

His curly hair is <u>natural</u>.

natural:

_____

_____

A dictionary is a useful <u>resource</u> for learning words.

resource:

_____

_____

In the desert, water is a limited <u>resource</u>.

resource:

_____

_____

Vocabulary Terms

- natural resource
- renewable resource
- nonrenewable resource
- fossil fuel
- material resource
- energy resource

4 Identify This list contains the key terms you'll learn in this lesson. As you read, circle the definition of each term.

It's Only Natural

What are natural resources?

What do the water you drink, the paper you write on, the gasoline used in cars, and the air you breathe all have in common? They all come from Earth's natural resources. A **natural resource** is any natural material that is used by humans. Natural resources include air, soil, minerals, water, oil, plants, and animals.

Earth's natural resources provide everything needed for life. The atmosphere contains the air we breathe and produces rain as part of the water cycle. Rainfall from the atmosphere renews the water in oceans, rivers, lakes, streams, and underground. In turn, these water sources provide water for drinking, cleaning, and other uses. Earth's soil provides nutrients and a place for plants to grow. Plants provide food for some animals and humans. Animals provide food as well. Many of Earth's resources, such as oil and wind, provide energy for human use. The energy in these resources comes from the sun's energy. Earth's resources are also used to make products that make people's lives more convenient.

Active Reading

5 Identify List four examples of natural resources.

_____

_____

_____

_____

Bauxite is a rock that is used to make aluminum.

6 Illustrate Draw or label the missing natural resources.

A

© Houghton Mifflin Harcourt Publishing Company • Image Credits: (inset) ©George Whitely/Photo Researchers, Inc.

How can we categorize natural resources?

There are many different types of natural resources. Some can be replaced more quickly than others. A natural resource may be categorized as a renewable resource or a nonrenewable resource.

Think Outside the Book Inquiry

7 Debate Research why water or soil can be a renewable or nonrenewable resource. Discuss your points with a classmate.

Renewable Resources

Some natural resources can be replaced in a relatively short time. A natural resource that can be replaced at the same rate at which it is consumed is a **renewable resource**. Solar energy, water, and air are all renewable resources. Some renewable resources are considered to be *inexhaustible resources* [in•ig•ZAW•stuh•buhl REE•sohrs•iz] because the resources can never be used up. Solar energy and wind energy, which is powered by the sun, are examples of inexhaustible resources. Other renewable resources are not inexhaustible. Trees and crops that are used for food must be replanted and regrown. Water must be managed so that it does not become scarce.

Nonrenewable Resources

A resource that forms much more slowly than it is consumed is a **nonrenewable resource**. Some natural resources, such as minerals, form very slowly. Iron ore and copper are important minerals. A **fossil fuel** is a nonrenewable resource formed from the buried remains of plants and animals that lived long ago. Coal, oil, and natural gas are examples of fossil fuels. Coal and oil take millions of years to form. Once these resources are used up, humans will have to find other resources to use instead. Some renewable resources, such as water and wood, may become nonrenewable if they are not used wisely.

8 Compare List some examples of renewable and nonrenewable resources.

Renewable resources	Nonrenewable resources

Natural fibers from cotton plants are processed to make fabric.

B

© Houghton Mifflin Harcourt Publishing Company • Image Credits: (inset) ©Inga Spence/Visuals Unlimited/Getty Images

A Material World

How do we use material resources?

Look around your classroom. The walls, windows, desks, pencils, books, and even the clothing you see are made of material resources. Natural resources that are used to make objects, food, or drink are called **material resources**. Material resources can be either renewable or nonrenewable. The cotton used in T-shirts is an example of a renewable resource. The metal used in your desk is an example of a nonrenewable resource.

To Make Food or Drink

Material resources come from Earth's atmosphere, crust, and waters. They also come from organisms that live on Earth. Think about what you eat and drink every day. All foods and beverages are made from material resources. Some foods come from plants, such as the wheat in bread or the corn in tortillas. These resources are renewable, since farmers can grow more. Other foods, such as milk, cheese, eggs, and meat, come from animals. Juices, sodas, and sport drinks contain water, which is a renewable resource.

Active Reading

9 Identify As you read, underline examples of material resources.

Visualize It!

10 List List two types of food or drink that are made from the material resources in each picture.

A

B

C

To Make Objects

Any object you see is made from material resources. For example, cars are made of steel, plastic, rubber, glass, and leather. Steel comes from iron, which is mined from rock. Plastic is made from oil, which must be drilled from areas underground. Natural rubber comes from tropical trees. Glass is made from minerals found in sand. Leather comes from the hides of animals.

Iron, oil, and sand are nonrenewable. If these materials are used too quickly, they can run out. Rubber, leather, and wood are renewable resources. The plants and animals that produce these resources can be managed so that these resources do not run out.

Visualize It!

11 Label Write the name of each material resource that is used to make objects in this house.

A house is made from many material resources.

A

B

C

D

limestone

Change It Up!

Active Reading

12 Identify As you read, underline the different forms of energy.

How do we use energy resources?

Many objects need energy in order to be useful. For example, a bus needs energy so that it can move people around. Natural resources used to generate energy are called **energy resources**.

Energy is often stored in objects or substances. Stored energy is called *potential energy*. Food and products made from oil have potential energy that is stored in their chemical bonds. For this energy to be useful, it must be converted to *kinetic energy,* which is the energy of movement. Body cells perform chemical reactions that convert the potential energy in food to the kinetic energy that moves your body. Gasoline engines break the bonds in gasoline to convert potential energy to the kinetic energy that moves a car.

An object can have potential energy because of its position. An object that is high above the ground has more potential energy than an object that is close to the ground. Potential energy is converted to kinetic energy when the object falls, such as when water falls over a dam to produce electricity in a power plant.

13 List Look at the examples in the table. Write down three more situations in which potential energy changes to kinetic energy.

The gasoline being pumped into this car has potential energy in its chemical bonds.

This car's engine burns gasoline, converting the potential energy in the fuel into the kinetic energy of the moving car.

When Does Potential Energy Change to Kinetic Energy?
when coal burns to produce electrical energy in a power plant
when your body digests food to give you energy to move

How do everyday objects convert energy?

Energy cannot be created or destroyed, and energy must be converted to be useful. Energy conversions happen around us every day. Think about the appliances in your home. An electric oven warms food by converting electrical energy to energy as heat. A television converts electrical energy to light energy and sound energy, which is a type of kinetic energy. A fan moves by converting electrical energy to kinetic energy. Your body converts the chemical energy in food to kinetic energy as well as thermal energy. When you talk on the phone, the sound energy from your voice is converted to electrical energy. The phone on the other end of the conversation changes the electrical energy back to sound.

 **Visualize It!**

14 Identify Which energy conversion allows you to feel warm?

_____

_____

15 Identify Which energy conversion allows this lamp to light up a room?

_____

_____

16 Identify Which energy conversion lets you hear the music?

_____

_____

Power Trip

How is electrical energy produced?

Computers and appliances need electrical energy to work. Electrical energy is available from outlets, but how does this energy get to the outlets?

In most electrical power plants, an energy source converts potential energy to kinetic energy, causing wheels in a turbine to spin. The spinning wheels cause coils of wire to spin inside a magnet in a generator. The generator converts kinetic energy to electrical energy, which travels through wires to your school. Different energy resources can provide the energy for a power plant. Moving wind or water can turn wheels in a turbine. Burning coal or biofuels made from crop plants can warm water, producing steam that moves the turbine.

Fuel cells and batteries are other sources of electrical energy. A battery has chemicals inside that convert chemical energy to electrical energy. Fuel cells convert chemical energy from hydrogen to produce electrical energy.

Visualize It!

18 Describe After looking at the diagram, describe how energy is converted in a power plant to produce electrical energy.

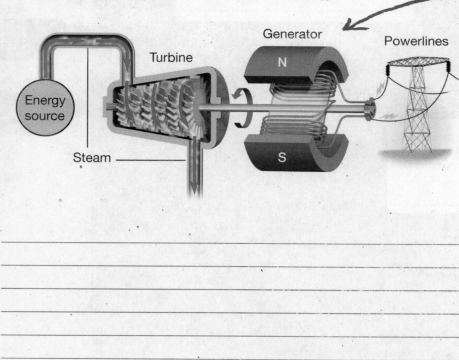

Energy source

Steam

Turbine

Generator

N

S

Powerlines

Electrical energy is generated when coils of wire are turned inside a large magnet. This magnet might look different from bar magnets you have seen, but it still has north and south poles.

_____

_____

_____

_____

_____

Clean Machines

Many car companies are introducing vehicles with hydrogen fuel cells. Hydrogen fuel cells use chemical reactions to produce electrical energy. These reactions produce no pollutants. If hydrogen fuel is made using renewable energy sources, these cars could truly be clean machines.

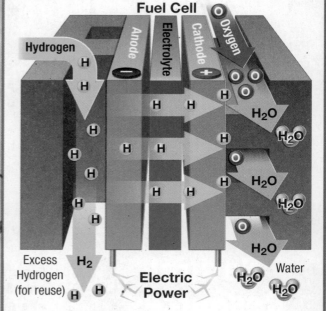

Fuel Cell

Hydrogen · Anode · Electrolyte · Cathode · Oxygen

H₂O

Excess Hydrogen (for reuse) H₂   Electric Power   Water H₂O

Small Packages
The hydrogen fuel cell in a car is about the size of a microwave oven.

HYDROGEN-FUEL CELL ELECTRIC

Cell Technology
The fuel cell removes electrons from hydrogen atoms. Electron movement generates electrical energy. Hydrogen then combines with oxygen to form water. Water and excess hydrogen are the products of this reaction. No carbon dioxide or other pollutants are produced.

driving the future

Extend
Inquiry

19 Explain What kind of energy conversion happens in a hydrogen fuel cell?

20 Compare How is the process of energy conversion different between a fuel-cell vehicle and a gasoline vehicle?

21 Infer Hydrogen fuel must be produced by splitting water into hydrogen and oxygen. This process requires energy. Does it matter if nonrenewable energy is used to produce hydrogen fuel? Support your answer.

Visual Summary

To complete this summary, answer the questions using the lines provided. Then, use the key below to check your answers. You can use this page to review the main concepts of the lesson.

Natural resources can be renewable or nonrenewable.

22 What makes a resource renewable?

_____

_____

Material resources are used to make objects, food, and drink.

23 What are two material resources in this picture?

_____

_____

Natural Resources

Energy can be converted from one form to another. Potential energy in energy resources can be converted to kinetic energy.

24 What are all the energy conversions that happen when wood burns?

_____

_____

_____

Answers: 22 Renewable resources are used more slowly than they are replaced; 23 cattle for food, trees for wood; 24 Chemical energy in the wood is converted to light energy, energy as heat, and sound energy

25 Illustrate Think of a natural resource that can be used as both a material resource and as an energy resource. Draw two pictures to illustrate each use of the resource.

Lesson Review

Vocabulary

Draw a line to connect the following terms to their definitions.

1 fossil fuel

2 material resource

3 natural resource

A resource used to make objects, food, or drink

B any natural material used by people

C a nonrenewable resource formed by buried remains of plants and animals

Key Concepts

4 List Name two material resources and give an example of how each is used.

_____

_____

_____

_____

5 Describe What makes a resource nonrenewable?

_____

_____

_____

6 Explain How can the conversion from potential energy to kinetic energy provide energy that is useful to people.

_____

_____

_____

_____

_____

_____

Critical Thinking

7 Apply What could people do in order to make nonrenewable resources last longer?

_____

_____

_____

_____

Use the drawing to answer the following questions.

8 Analyze What energy conversions are occurring in the illustration?

_____

_____

_____

9 Infer What form of energy that is not useful is being released from the flashlight when it is on?

_____

_____

10 Relate Assume that the batteries in the flashlight are rechargeable. What energy conversion would have to take place in order to recharge the batteries?

_____

_____

_____

My Notes

Nonrenewable Energy Resources

ESSENTIAL QUESTION

How do we use nonrenewable energy resources?

By the end of this lesson, you should be able to describe how humans use energy resources and the role of nonrenewable energy resources in society.

The energy that lights up this city and powers the vehicles comes from energy resources. Most of our energy resources are being used up faster than natural processes can replace them.

Engage Your Brain

1 Identify Unscramble the letters below to find substances that are nonrenewable resources.

ALCO _____

AUNTRLA SGA _____

NUUIMAR _____

MLPEOUTRE _____

2 Describe Write your own caption for this photo.

_____

_____

_____

Active Reading

3 Synthesize Many English words have their roots in other languages. Use the Latin word below to make an educated guess about the meaning of the word *fission*.

Latin word	Meaning
fissus	to split

Example sentence
An atomic nucleus can undergo <u>fission</u>.

fission:

_____

_____

Vocabulary Terms

- energy resource
- nuclear energy
- fossil fuel
- fission

4 Identify This list contains the vocabulary terms you'll learn in this lesson. As you read, circle the definition of each term.

Be Resourceful!

What are the two main types of nonrenewable energy resources?

An **energy resource** is a natural resource that humans use to generate energy and can be renewable or nonrenewable. *Renewable resources* are replaced by natural processes at least as quickly as they are used. *Nonrenewable resources* are used up faster than they can be replaced. Most of the energy used in the United States comes from nonrenewable resources.

Fossil Fuels

A **fossil fuel** is a nonrenewable energy resource that forms from the remains of organisms that lived long ago. Fossil fuels release energy when they are burned. This energy can be converted to electricity or used to power engines. Fossil fuels are the most commonly used energy resource because they are relatively inexpensive to locate and process.

Nuclear Fuel

The energy released when the nuclei of atoms are split or combined is called **nuclear energy**. This energy can be obtained by two kinds of nuclear reactions—fusion and fission. Today's nuclear power plants use fission, because the technology for fusion power plants does not currently exist. The most common nuclear fuel is uranium. Uranium is obtained by mining and processing uranium ore, which is a nonrenewable resource.

You Try It

Nonrenewable Energy Resources Consumed in the U.S. in 2009

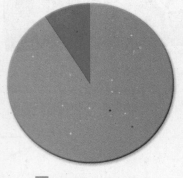

■ Fossil Fuels 90.37%
■ Nuclear Fuel 9.63%

5 Calculate In 2009, 86.8 quadrillion BTUs of the energy used in the United States was produced from nonrenewable energy resources. Using the graph above, calculate how much of this energy was produced from nuclear fuel.

6 Compare Fill in the Venn diagram to compare and contrast fossil fuels and nuclear fuel.

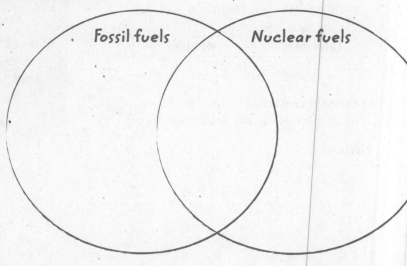

Fossil fuels   Nuclear fuels

What are the three main types of fossil fuels?

All living things contain the element carbon. Fossil fuels form from the remains of living things, so they also contain carbon. Most of this carbon is in the form of hydrocarbons, which are compounds made of hydrogen and carbon. Fossil fuels can be liquids, gases, or solids. Fossil fuels include petroleum, natural gas, and coal.

Active Reading **7 Identify** As you read, underline the state of matter for each fossil fuel.

Petroleum

Petroleum, or *crude oil,* is a liquid mixture of complex hydrocarbon compounds. Crude oil is extracted from the ground by drilling then processed for use. This process, called *refining,* separates the crude oil into different products such as gasoline, kerosene, and diesel fuel. More than 35 percent of the world's energy comes from crude oil products. Crude oil is also used to make products such as ink, bubble gum, and plastics.

This crude oil will be refined into gasoline, diesel fuel, heating oil, kerosene, and other products.

Natural Gas

Natural gas is a mixture of gaseous hydrocarbons. Most natural gas is used for heating and cooking, but some is used to generate electricity. Also, some vehicles use natural gas as fuel.

Methane is the main component of natural gas. Butane and propane can also be separated from natural gas. Butane and propane are used as fuel for camp stoves and outdoor grills. Some rural homes also use propane as a heating fuel.

Natural gas is a popular fuel for cooking because it is inexpensive.

Coal

The fossil fuel most widely used for generating electrical power is a solid called coal. Coal was once used to heat homes and for transportation. In fact, many trains in the 1800s and early 1900s were pulled by coal-burning steam locomotives. Now, most people use gasoline for transportation fuel. But more than half of our nation's electricity comes from coal-burning power plants.

Coal is a fossil fuel often used to generate electricity.

How do fossil fuels form?

How might a sunny day 200 million years ago relate to your life today? If you traveled to school by bus or car, you likely used energy from sunlight that warmed Earth that long ago.

Fossil fuels form over millions of years from the buried remains of ancient organisms. Fossil fuels differ in the kinds of organisms from which they form and in how they form. This process is continuing, too. The fossil fuels forming today will be available for use in a few million years!

Petroleum and Natural Gas Form from Marine Organisms

Petroleum and natural gas form mainly from the remains of microscopic sea organisms. When these organisms die, their remains sink and settle on the ocean floor. There, the dead organisms are gradually buried by sediment. The sediment is compacted by more layers of dead organisms and sediment. Over time the sediment layers become layers of rock.

Over millions of years, heat and pressure turn the remains of the organisms into petroleum and natural gas. The petroleum and natural gas, along with groundwater, flow into pores in the rock. A rock with pores is a *permeable rock*. Permeable rocks become reservoirs where the petroleum and natural gas are trapped and concentrated over time. Humans can extract the fuels from these reservoirs.

Think Outside the Book Inquiry

8 Apply With a classmate, discuss how the process of petroleum formation might affect oil availability in the future.

Petroleum and Natural Gas Formation

❶ Microscopic marine organisms die and settle to the bottom of the sea.

❷ Layers of sediment slowly bury the dead marine organisms.

❸ Heat and pressure on these layers slowly turn the remains of these organisms into petroleum and natural gas.

❹ Petroleum and natural gas flow through permeable rocks, where they are trapped and become concentrated into reservoirs.

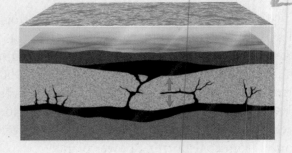

Coal Formation

1 **Peat** Partially decayed swamp plants sink and change into peat.

2 **Lignite** As sediment buries the peat, increases in temperature and pressure change peat to lignite.

3 **Bituminous Coal** As sediment builds, increased temperature and pressure change lignite to bituminous coal.

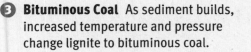

4 **Anthracite** As sediments accumulate and temperature and pressure rise, bituminous coal changes to anthracite.

Coal Forms from Plant Remains

Active Reading **9 Identify** As you read, underline the factors that convert the buried plants into coal.

Coal is formed over millions of years from the remains of swamp plants. When the plants die, they sink to the swamp floor. Low oxygen levels in the water keep many plants from decaying and allow the process of coal formation to begin. Today's swamp plants may eventually turn into coal millions of years from now.

The first step of coal formation is plant matter changing into peat. Peat is made mostly of plant material and water. Peat is not coal. In some parts of the world, peat is dried and burned for warmth or used as fuel. Peat that is buried by layers of sediment can turn into coal after millions of years.

Over time, pressure and high temperature force water and gases out of the peat. The peat gradually becomes harder, and its carbon content increases. The amount of heat and pressure determines the type of coal that forms. Lignite forms first, followed by bituminous coal and, finally, anthracite. Anthracite is highly valued because it has the highest carbon content and gives off the most energy as heat when burned.

Today, all three types of coal are mined around the world. When burned, coal releases energy as heat and pollutes the air. The greater the carbon content of the coal, the fewer pollutants are released and the cleaner the coal burns.

Visualize It!

10 Compare What is similar about the way petroleum and coal form? What is different?

_____
_____
_____
_____
_____
_____

Power Trip

How are fossil fuels used as energy sources?

Active Reading

11 Identify As you read, underline the uses of fossil fuels.

In the United States, petroleum fuels are mainly used for transportation and heating. Airplanes, trains, boats, and cars all use petroleum for energy. Some people also use petroleum as a heating fuel. There are some oil-fired power plants in the United States, but most are found in other parts of the world.

Natural gas can be used as transportation fuel but is mainly used for heating and cooking. The use of natural gas as a source of electrical power is increasing. The U.S. Department of Energy projects that most power plants in the near future will use natural gas. Today, coal is mainly used in the U.S. to generate electricity, which we use for lighting and to power appliances and technology.

Visualize It!

Burning coal heats water to produce steam. The steam turns the turbines to generate electricity. Scrubbers and filters in the smokestack help reduce air pollution.

Coal-Fired Power Plant

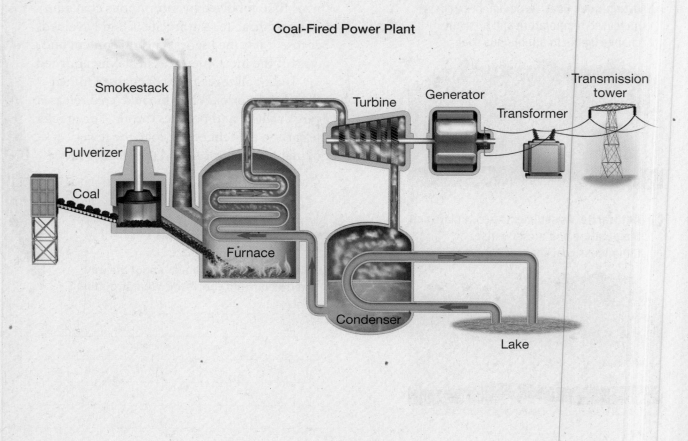

Smokestack · Pulverizer · Coal · Furnace · Turbine · Generator · Transformer · Transmission tower · Condenser · Lake

How is energy produced from nuclear fuels?

During **fission**, the nuclei of radioactive atoms are split into two or more fragments. A small particle called a neutron hits and splits an atom. This process releases large amounts of energy as heat and radiation. Fission also releases more neutrons that bombard other atoms. The process repeats as a chain reaction. Fission takes place inside a reactor core. Fuel rods containing uranium, shown in green below, provide the material for the chain reaction. Control rods that absorb neutrons are used to regulate the chain reaction. The energy is released, which is used to generate electrical power. A closed reactor system contains the radioactivity. Nuclear wastes are contained separately for disposal.

During nuclear reactions, energy in the form of heat is released, which turns water into steam. Steam turns the turbines to generate electricity.

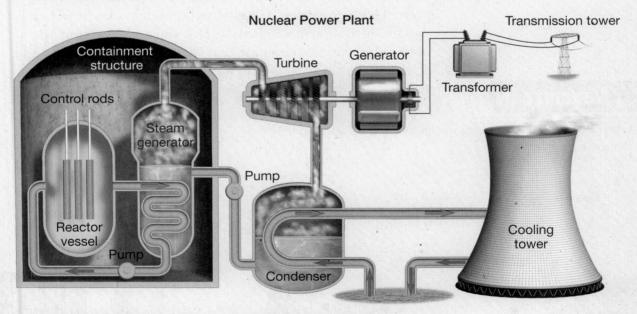

Nuclear Power Plant

12 Compare How are the two types of power plants similar? How are they different?

Similar

_____

_____

_____

_____

Different

_____

_____

_____

_____

The Pros and Cons

How can we evaluate nonrenewable energy resources?

There are advantages and disadvantages to using nonrenewable energy resources. Nonrenewable resources provide much of the energy that humans need to power transportation, warm homes, and produce electricity relatively cheaply. But the methods of obtaining and using these resources can have negative effects on the environment.

The Pros and Cons of Nuclear Fuel

Nuclear fission produces a large amount of energy and does not cause air pollution because no fuel is burned. Mining uranium also does not usually result in massive strip mines or large loss of habitats.

However, nuclear power does have drawbacks. Nuclear power plants produce dangerous wastes that remain radioactive for thousands of years. So the waste must be specially stored to prevent harm to anyone. Harmful radiation may also be released into the environment accidentally. Hot water released from the power plant can also be a problem. This heated water can disrupt aquatic ecosystems. So the hot water must be cooled before it is released into local bodies of water.

Active Reading

13 Identify As you read, underline the effects that nuclear power plants have on their surroundings.

Visualize It!

14 Infer Why do you think nuclear fuel rods are usually transported by train instead of by trucks?

_____

_____

Used nuclear fuel rods must be transported in specially built steel containers.

The Pros and Cons of Fossil Fuels

Fossil fuels are relatively inexpensive to obtain and use. However, there are problems associated with their use. Burning coal can release sulfur dioxide, which combines with moisture in the air to form acid rain. Acid rain causes damage to structures and the environment. Coal mining also disturbs habitats, lowers water tables, and pollutes water.

Environmental problems are also associated with using oil. In 2010, a blown oil well spilled an estimated 200 million gallons of crude oil in the Gulf of Mexico for 86 days. The environmental costs may continue for years.

Burning fossil fuels can cause smog, especially in cities with millions of vehicles. Smog is a brownish haze that can cause respiratory problems and contribute to acid rain. Burning fossil fuels also releases carbon dioxide into the atmosphere. Increases in atmospheric carbon dioxide can lead to global warming.

Some coal is mined by removing the tops of mountains to expose the coal. This damages habitats and can cause water pollution as well.

15 **Evaluate** In the chart below, list the advantages and disadvantages of using nuclear fuel and fossil fuels.

Type of fuel	Pros	Cons
nuclear fuel		
fossil fuels		

Visual Summary

To complete this summary, check the box that indicates true or false. Then use the key below to check your answers. You can use this page to review the main concepts of the lesson.

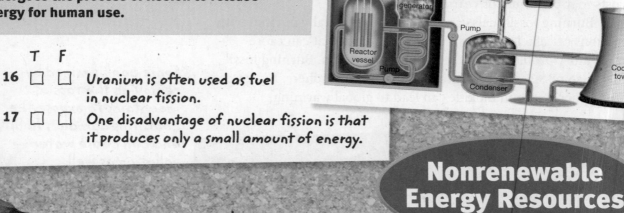

Nuclear fuel is an energy resource that undergoes the process of fission to release energy for human use.

	T	F	
16	☐	☐	Uranium is often used as fuel in nuclear fission.
17	☐	☐	One disadvantage of nuclear fission is that it produces only a small amount of energy.

Nonrenewable Energy Resources

Most of the energy used today comes from fossil fuels, which include petroleum, natural gas, and coal.

	T	F	
18	☐	☐	Natural gas forms from microscopic marine organisms.
19	☐	☐	Most transportation fuels are products of coal.
20	☐	☐	Burning fossil fuels decreases the amount of carbon dioxide in the atmosphere.

Answers: 16 True; 17 False; 18 True; 19 False; 20 False

21 **Summarize** Identify the advantages and disadvantages for both fossil fuels and nuclear fuels.

Lesson Review

Vocabulary

Fill in the blank with the term that best completes the following sentences.

1 _____ is energy in an atom's nucleus.

2 Crude oil is a liquid kind of _____

3 _____ can be renewable or nonrenewable.

4 During the process of _____, the nuclei of radioactive atoms are split into two or more smaller nuclei.

Key Concepts

5 Describe Describe how fossil fuels are converted into usable energy?

_____

_____

_____

_____

6 Sequence Which of the following sequences of processes best describes how electricity is generated in a nuclear power plant?

A fission reaction, produce steam, turn turbine, generate electricity, cool water

B produce steam, fission reaction, turn turbine, generate electricity, cool water

C cool water, fission reaction, produce steam, turn turbine, generate electricity

D produce steam, turn turbine, cool water, fission reaction, generate electricity

7 Identify Which is an example of how people use nonrenewable energy resources?

A eating a banana

B sailing a boat

C walking to school

D driving a car

Critical Thinking

8 Hypothesize Why do some places in the United States have deposits of coal but others have deposits of petroleum and natural gas?

_____

_____

_____

_____

Use the graph to answer the following questions.

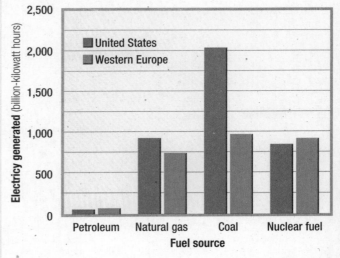

Electricity Produced from Nonrenewable Energy Resources in 2007

9 Calculate About how much more coal than petroleum is used to generate electricity in the United States and Western Europe?

_____

_____

_____

10 Analyze What patterns of energy resource use do you see in the graph?

_____

_____

_____

_____

My Notes

Renewable Energy Resources

ESSENTIAL QUESTION

How do humans use renewable energy resources?

By the end of this lesson, you should be able to describe how humans use energy resources and the role of renewable energy resources in society.

Panels such as these can turn an unused city roof into a miniature solar energy plant.

✋ **Lesson Labs**

Quick Labs
- Design a Turbine
- Understanding Solar Panels

S.T.E.M. Lab
- Modeling Geothermal Power

🧠 Engage Your Brain

1 Predict Check T or F to show whether you think each statement is true or false.

T   F

☐   ☐   Renewable energy resources can never run out.

☐   ☐   Renewable energy resources do not cause any type of pollution.

☐   ☐   Solar energy is the most widely used renewable energy resource in the United States.

☐   ☐   Renewable energy resources include solar energy, wind energy, and geothermal energy.

2 Describe Write a caption to explain how the sun's energy is being used in this photo.

_____

_____

_____

_____

_____

📖 Active Reading

3 Synthesize You can often define an unknown word if you know the meaning of its word parts. Use the word parts and sentence below to make an educated guess about the meaning of the word *geothermal*.

Word part	Meaning
geo-	Earth
therm-	heat

Example sentence
A geothermal power plant uses steam produced deep in the ground to generate electricity.

geothermal:

_____

_____

_____

Vocabulary Terms
- energy resource
- wind energy
- hydroelectric energy
- solar energy
- biomass
- geothermal energy

4 Apply As you learn the definition of each vocabulary term in this lesson, create your own definition or sketch to help you remember the meaning of the term.

Energy *Déjà Vu*

What are the two main sources of renewable energy?

An **energy resource** is a natural resource used to generate electricity and other forms of energy. Most of the energy used by humans comes from *nonrenewable resources*. These resources are used more quickly than they can be replaced. But *renewable resources* can be replaced almost as quickly as they are used. Most renewable energy resources come from the sun and some from Earth itself.

The Sun

The sun's energy is a result of nuclear fusion. Fusion is the process by which two or more nuclei fuse together to form a larger nucleus. Fusion produces a large amount of energy, which is released into space as light and heat.

Solar energy warms Earth, causing the movement of air masses. Moving air masses form winds and some ocean currents. Solar energy also fuels plant growth. Animals get energy by eating plants. Humans can harness energy from wind, moving water, plant and animal materials, and directly from the light and heat that comes from the sun.

Earth

Energy from within Earth comes from two sources. One source is the decay of radioactive elements in Earth's mantle and crust, caused by nuclear fission. Fission is the splitting of the nuclei of radioactive atoms. The second source of energy within Earth is energy stored during Earth's formation. The heat produced from these sources radiates outward toward Earth's surface. Humans can harness this heat to use as an energy source.

5 Contrast Explain how energy production in the sun differs from energy production in Earth's interior.

_____

_____

_____

_____

_____

_____

Not to scale.

Nuclear Fusion

Hydrogen nuclei

Energy

Beta particles

Helium nucleus

When atomic nuclei fuse, energy is released.

Not to scale.

Core

Earth's internal energy comes from the process of nuclear fission and the events that formed Earth.

How might a renewable energy resource become nonrenewable?

All of the energy resources you will learn about in this lesson are renewable. That doesn't mean that they can't become nonrenewable resources. Trees, for example, are a renewable resource. Some people burn wood from trees to heat their homes and cook food. However, some forests are being cut down but are not being replanted in a timely manner. Others are being cut down and replaced with buildings. If this process continues, eventually these forests will no longer be considered renewable resources.

6 Apply Read the caption below, then describe what might happen if the community uses too much of the water in the reservoir.

_____

_____

_____

_____

7 Distinguish What is the difference between nonrenewable and renewable energy resources?

_____

_____

_____

_____

Think Outside the Book

8 Apply Write an interview with a renewable resource that is afraid it might become nonrenewable. Be sure to include questions and answers.

A community uses this reservoir for water. The dam at the end of the reservoir uses moving water to produce electricity for the community.

Turn, Turn, Turn

How do humans use wind energy?

Wind is created by the sun's uneven heating of air masses in Earth's atmosphere. **Wind energy** uses the force of moving air to drive an electric generator or do other work. Wind energy is renewable because the wind will blow as long as the sun warms Earth. Wind energy is harnessed by machines called wind turbines. Electricity is generated when moving air turns turbine blades that drive an electric generator. Clusters of wind turbines, called wind farms, generate large amounts of electricity.

Although wind energy is a renewable energy resource, it has several disadvantages. Wind farms can be placed only in areas that receive large amounts of wind. The equipment required to collect and convert wind energy is also expensive to produce and maintain. And the production and maintenance of this equipment produces a small amount of pollution. The turbine blades can also be hazardous to birds.

Windmills such as these have been used for centuries to grind grain and pump surface water for irrigation.

A wind-powered water pump can pull water from deep underground when electricity is not available.

9 Infer What is the main benefit of placing these turbines in open water?

_____

_____

_____

_____

_____

Wind farms are a form of clean energy, because they do not generate air pollution as they generate electricity.

How do humans get energy from moving water?

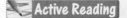

10 Identify Underline the kind of energy that is found in moving water.

Like wind, moving water has kinetic energy. People have harnessed the energy of falling or flowing water to power machines since ancient times. Some grain and saw mills still use water to power their equipment. Electrical energy produced by moving water is called **hydroelectric energy**. Hydroelectric energy is renewable because the water cycle is driven by the sun. Water that evaporates from oceans and lakes falls on higher elevations and flows downhill in streams, rivers, and waterfalls. The energy in flowing water is converted to electrical energy when it spins turbines connected to electric generators inside the dam.

Hydroelectric energy is a good source of energy only in locations where there are large, reliable amounts of flowing water. Another disadvantage of hydroelectric energy is that hydroelectric dams and their technology are expensive to build. The dams also can block the movement of fish between the sea and their spawning grounds. Special fish ladders must be built to allow fish to swim around the dam.

Visualize It!

11 Explain What is the purpose of the lake that is located behind the dam of a hydroelectric plant?

_____

_____

_____

_____

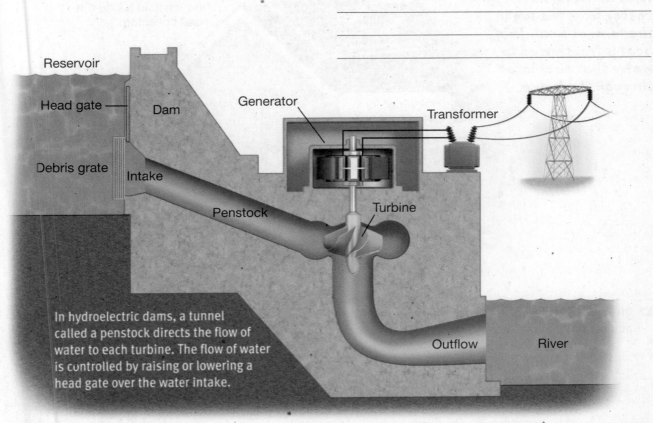

In hydroelectric dams, a tunnel called a penstock directs the flow of water to each turbine. The flow of water is controlled by raising or lowering a head gate over the water intake.

Let the Sunshine In

How do humans use solar energy?

Most forms of energy come from the sun—even fossil fuels begin with the sun as an energy resource. **Solar energy** is the energy received by Earth from the sun in the form of radiation. Solar energy can be used to warm buildings directly. Solar energy can also be converted into electricity by solar cells.

To Provide Energy as Heat

We can use liquids warmed by the sun to warm water and buildings. Some liquids, such as water, have a high capacity for absorbing and holding heat. When the heat is absorbed by the liquid in a solar collector, it can be transferred to water that circulates through a building. The hot water can be used for bathing or other household uses, or to warm the building. The only pollution generated by solar heating systems comes from the manufacture and maintenance of their equipment. Solar heating systems work best in areas with large amounts of sunlight.

Solar collectors absorb energy from the sun in the form of heat. The heat is transferred to water that circulates through the house.

Solar collector

Energy from the sun heats a fluid inside the solar collector

Hot water for household use

Cold water from the water supply is heated by hot fluid inside the pipes coming from the solar collector

Pump

Backup water heater

12 Infer Not all solar collectors use water to absorb energy from the sun. Why might a solar heating system use a liquid other than water?

_____

_____

_____

Houghton Mifflin Harcourt Publishing Company • Image Credits: ©amana images inc./Alamy Images

To Produce Electricity

Solar collectors can also be used to generate electricity. First, heated fluid is used to produce steam. Then, the steam turns a turbine connected to an electric generator.

Electricity can also be generated when sunlight is absorbed by a photovoltaic cell. A single photovoltaic cell produces a small amount of electricity. The electricity from joined photovoltaic cells can power anything from calculators to entire communities. Many cells must be joined together to form each solar panel, as shown in the solar power plant below. Solar power plants must be built in places with adequate space and abundant sunshine year-round. These requirements increase the costs of solar power.

This calculator is powered by solar cells instead of a battery.

Visualize It! Inquiry

14 **Infer** Based on this image and your reading, what might be a disadvantage to using solar energy to supply electricity to a large community?

_____

_____

❸ The inverter and transformer convert the current into the correct form and voltage for transmission to a community.

❶ Rays of sunlight strike a panel of photovoltaic cells. The energy in the sunlight causes electrons to flow, thus making an electric current.

Energy from sunlight

Photovoltaic cell

❷ The current flows along wires from the photovoltaic cells to an inverter and transformer.

How do humans get energy from living things?

Plants absorb light energy from the sun and convert it to chemical energy through *photosynthesis*. This energy is stored in leaves, stems, and roots. Chemical energy is also present in the dung of animals. These sources of energy make up biomass.

By Burning Biomass

Biomass is organic matter from plants and from animal waste that contains chemical energy. Biomass can be burned to release energy. This energy can be used to cook food, provide warmth, or power an engine. Biomass sources include trees, crops, animal waste, and peat.

Biomass is inexpensive and can usually be replaced relatively quickly, so it is considered to be a renewable resource. Some types of biomass renew more slowly than others. Peat renews so slowly in areas where it is used heavily that it is treated as a nonrenewable resource. Like fossil fuels, biomass produces pollutants when it burns.

These peat pellets will be used to generate steam in the power plant in the background. The steam will generate electricity by turning turbines.

Active Reading **15 Identify** As you read, number the steps that occur during the production of ethanol.

By Burning Alcohol

Biomass material can be used to produce a liquid fuel called ethanol, which is an alcohol. The sugars or cellulose in the plants are eaten by microbes. The microbes then give off carbon dioxide and ethanol. Over 1,000 L of ethanol can be made from 1 acre of corn. The ethanol is collected and burned as a fuel. Ethanol can also be mixed with gasoline to make a fuel called gasohol. The ethanol produced from about 40% of one corn harvest in the United States would provide only 10% of the fuel used in our cars!

16 List What are three examples of how biomass can be used for energy?

_____

_____

_____

_____

These wagons are loaded with sugar cane wastes from sugar production. The cellulose from these plant materials will be processed to produce ethanol.

Houghton Mifflin Harcourt Publishing Company • Image Credits: (t) ©Hank Morgan/Photo Researchers, Inc.; (b) ©Christian Tragni/Aurora Photos/Alamy Images

How do humans use geothermal energy?

The water in the geyser at right is heated by geothermal energy. **Geothermal energy** is energy produced by heat from Earth's interior. Geothermal energy heats rock formations deep within the ground. Groundwater absorbs this heat and forms hot springs and geysers where the water reaches Earth's surface. Geothermal energy is used to produce energy as heat and electricity.

To Provide Energy as Heat

Geothermal energy can be used to warm and cool buildings. A closed loop system of pipes runs from underground into the heating system of a home or building. Water pumped through these pipes absorbs heat from the ground and is used to warm the building. Hot groundwater can also be pumped in and used in a similar way. In warmer months, the ground is cooler than the air, so this system can also be used for cooling.

To Produce Electricity

Geothermal energy is also used to produce electricity. Wells are drilled into areas of superheated groundwater, allowing steam and hot water to escape. Geothermal power plants pump the steam or hot water from underground to spin turbines that generate electricity, as shown at right. A disadvantage of geothermal energy is pollution that occurs during production of the technology needed to capture it. The technology is also expensive to make and maintain.

Because Earth's core will be very hot for billions of years, geothermal energy will be available for a long time.

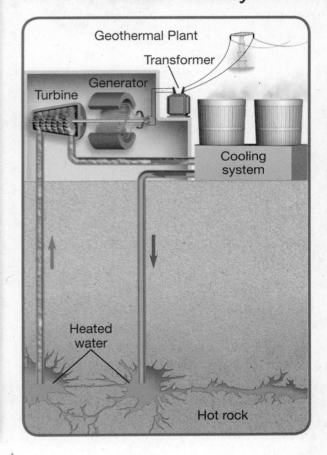

Geothermal Plant

Transformer

Generator

Turbine

Cooling system

Heated water

Hot rock

17 List What are some advantages and disadvantages to using geothermal energy?

Advantages	Disadvantages

Visual Summary

To complete this summary, fill in the blanks with the correct word or phrase. Then, use the key below to check your answers. You can use this page to review the main concepts of the lesson.

Renewable Energy Resources

The source of geothermal energy is energy from within Earth.

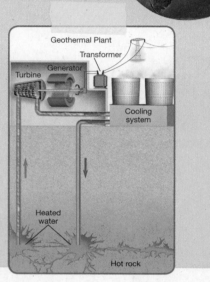

Geothermal Plant
Transformer
Generator
Turbine
Cooling system
Heated water
Hot rock

18 In geothermal power plants, hot water or _____ is pumped from within Earth's crust to produce electricity.

Most of the renewable energy resources that people use come from the sun.

Core

19 Renewable resources that come from the sun include _____ _____ _____

Answers: 18 steam; 19 biomass, solar energy, wind energy, and hydroelectric energy

20 Synthesize Which type of renewable energy resource would be best to use to provide electricity for your town? Explain your answer.

Lesson Review

Vocabulary

Fill in the blanks with the term that best completes the following sentences.

1 Organic matter that contains stored energy is called _____

2 A resource that humans can use to produce energy is a(n) _____

3 _____ is an energy resource harnessed from flowing water.

Key Concepts

4 Describe Identify a major advantage and a major disadvantage of using renewable energy resources to produce electricity.

_____

_____

_____

_____

_____

_____

5 Explain If renewable energy resources can be replaced, why do we need to conserve them? Use an example to support your answer.

_____

_____

_____

_____

_____

6 Describe What is the source of energy that powers wind and flowing water?

_____

_____

_____

_____

Critical Thinking

Use this graph to answer the following questions.

Total Renewable Energy Resources Consumed in 2009 in the United States

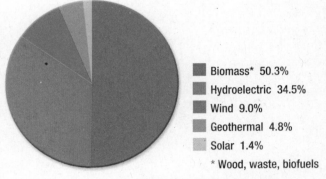

■ Biomass* 50.3%
■ Hydroelectric 34.5%
■ Wind 9.0%
■ Geothermal 4.8%
■ Solar 1.4%

* Wood, waste, biofuels

Source: Annual Energy Review 2009, U.S. Energy Information Administration

7 Evaluate Which is the most used renewable energy resource in the United States? Why do you think this is the case?

_____

_____

_____

_____

8 Evaluate Which is the least used renewable energy resource in the United States? Why do you think this is the case?

_____

_____

_____

_____

_____

_____

9 Relate How are biomass and alcohol production related to energy from the sun?

_____

_____

_____

_____

My Notes

Analyzing Technology

Skills
Identify risks
✔ Identify benefits
✔ Evaluate cost of technology
✔ Evaluate environmental impact
✔ Propose improvements
Propose risk reduction
Plan for technology failures
Compare technology
✔ Communicate results

Objectives
• Describe the effects of making paper cups on Earth's resources.
• Estimate the carbon dioxide saved by recycling paper cups.
• Propose improvements for the life cycle of a paper cup.

Analyzing the Life Cycle of a Paper Cup

A product's life cycle includes all of the phases in its "life," from getting raw materials to disposing of it once it has served its purpose. Most steps in the life cycle of a paper product affects the environment in some way.

Impact of a Paper Cup

A life cycle analysis of a paper cup shows that making it requires trees, water, ink, and plastic for a waterproof lining. The process also uses several different kinds of fuel, such as natural gas and diesel truck fuel for energy to make and transport the cups. The whole process releases about 110 grams (about ¼ pound) of carbon dioxide (KAR•buhn dy•AHK•syd) per cup into the atmosphere. This amount is 3 to 4 times the weight of a cup itself. And because of the plastic lining, paper cups are difficult to recycle.

Newspapers awaiting recycling

These paper cups probably will not be recycled.

1 **Estimate** Assume that a recycled paper cup is made up of only paper, and that paper could be recycled 5 times. About how much carbon dioxide would this prevent from being released into the atmosphere?

_____

_____

_____

_____

Recycling Paper Products

Many paper products are more easily recycled than paper cups are. Over 70% of newspaper is recycled to make various products such as cereal boxes, egg cartons, and tissue paper. Many paper products can be recycled 5 to 7 times, after which the paper fibers are too short and no longer stick together well enough to make paper. Recycling paper products not only saves trees but also saves a lot of water, electricity, and gas and reduces air pollution.

The life of a paper product starts with trees. Loggers cut the tree, and a paper mill grinds it into pulp.

Most newspapers are recycled, saving trees and energy used in logging.

The mill mixes the pulp with water and other chemicals to make paper, which is used to make paper products such as paper cups.

Most paper cups end up in a landfill.

2 Infer Most newspaper is recycled. Most paper cups are not. What is one difference in environmental impact between burial and incineration for used paper products?

_____

_____

_____

These products are used by all of us and then either recycled, incinerated, or buried in a landfill.

✋ **You Try It!** →

Now it's your turn to analyze the life cycle of a paper cup.

✋ You Try It!

Now it's your turn to analyze the life cycle of a paper cup. You'll consider things such as the benefits of paper cups and their cost in both money and environmental impact. Then you can suggest some ways to improve the cycle.

① Identify Benefits

With your class, research the benefits of making and using paper cups. List those benefits below.

Benefits

_____

② Evaluate Cost of Technology

A A paper mill uses about 16,000 gallons of water and about 400 kWh of electricity to produce one ton of paper cups. Using the information shown here, what is the cost of the water and electricity that are used to make one ton of paper cups?

_____

_____

_____

B A modern paper mill costs around $1 billion to build. How many cups would a company need to sell to pay for the cost of the plant, the water, and the electricity?

_____

_____

_____

- Water costs about $0.0007 per gallon.

- Electricity costs about $0.072/kWh.

- 33,000 cups weighs about a ton.

- One ton of cups sells for $2,000.

③ Evaluate Environmental Impact

With a partner, discuss possible impacts of the life cycle of a paper cup on the environment. Consider things such as the harvesting of trees, the use of chlorine-based chemicals to bleach the pulp, the energy required by the paper mill, problems associated with disposal of paper cups after their use, etc.

_____

_____

_____

_____

_____

④ Propose Improvements

With a partner, propose some improvements to the process of making or disposing of paper cups that might help make the life cycle of paper cups more environmentally friendly.

_____

_____

_____

_____

_____

⑤ Communicate Results

With your partner, tell the class the most important thing you have learned about the life cycle of a paper cup, and explain why you think it is important.

_____

_____

_____

_____

_____

Managing Resources

ESSENTIAL QUESTION

Why should natural resources be managed?

By the end of this lesson, you should be able to explain the consequences of society's use of natural resources and the importance of managing these resources wisely.

Bauxite is a mineral that is mined to make aluminum. The company that removed the bauxite replanted the mined area with trees. Replanting restores habitat and helps to prevent erosion.

Engage Your Brain

1 Predict Check T or F to show whether you think each statement is true or false.

T   F

☐   ☐   Renewable resources cannot be replaced at the same rate that they are used.

☐   ☐   Resource use always results in the pollution of natural areas.

☐   ☐   Placing limits on the amount of fish that can be caught can cause fish populations to increase.

☐   ☐   Recycling nonrenewable resources can cause them to be used up more quickly.

2 Describe What natural resources could be obtained from the areas in the picture?

_____

_____

_____

_____

Active Reading

3 Apply Some words have similar meanings. Use context clues to write your own definitions for the words *conservation* and *stewardship*.

Example sentence

Hotels practice water <u>conservation</u> by installing water-saving showerheads.

conservation:

_____

_____

Example sentence

Fertilizers can run off into lakes and cause algae to bloom. People who live near lakes can practice good <u>stewardship</u> of the lake by not using lawn fertilizers.

stewardship:

_____

_____

Vocabulary Terms

- natural resource
- renewable resource
- nonrenewable resource
- stewardship
- conservation

4 Identify This list shows vocabulary terms you'll learn in this lesson. As you read, underline the definition of each term.

Useful Stuff

What are the two main types of resources?

Any natural material that is used by people is a **natural resource**. Water, trees, minerals, air, and oil are just a few examples of Earth's resources. Resources can be divided into renewable and nonrenewable resources.

Renewable Resources

A natural resource that can be replaced as quickly as the resource is used is a **renewable resource**. Water, trees, and fish are examples of renewable resources. Renewable resources can become nonrenewable resources if they are used too quickly. For example, trees in a forest can become nonrenewable if they are cut down faster than new trees can grow to replace them.

Nonrenewable Resources

A natural resource that is used much faster than it can be replaced is a **nonrenewable resource**. Coal is an example of a nonrenewable resource. It takes millions of years for coal to form. Once coal is used up, it is no longer available. Minerals, oil, and natural gas are other examples of nonrenewable resources.

5 Compare How is a renewable resource different from a nonrenewable resource?

_____

_____

_____

_____

_____

_____

_____

Visualize It!

6 Identify Label each picture as a renewable resource or nonrenewable resource.

A

B
salt mine

C

_____   _____   _____

What can happen when we use resources?

Natural resources can make people's lives easier. Natural resources allow us to heat and cool buildings, produce and use electricity, transport people and goods, and make products.

While natural resources are helpful, the way they are used can cause harm. Mining and oil spills can damage ecosystems. Oil spills can also harm local fishing or tourism industries. Burning coal or other fossil fuels can cause air and water pollution. Used products can fill landfills or litter beaches and other natural areas. Overuse of resources can make them hard to find. When resources are hard to find, they become more expensive.

7 Identify As you read, underline the possible effects of resource use by people.

8 List What are three ways that natural resources are making life easier for this family?

_____

_____

_____

_____

9 Explain How can the extraction of natural resources damage the environment?

_____

_____

_____

_____

10 Describe How can human use of natural resources pollute the environment?

_____

_____

_____

_____

Best Practices

What are some effective ways to manage resources?

As human populations continue to grow, we will need more and more resources in order to survive. People can make sure that resources continue to be available by practicing stewardship and conservation. **Stewardship** is the careful and responsible management of resources. **Conservation** is the protection and wise use of natural resources.

Conserving Renewable Resources

Stewardship of renewable resources involves a variety of conservation practices. Limits on fishing or logging can increase fish populations and protect forest ecosystems. Fish can be restocked in lakes and rivers. Logged areas can be replanted with trees. Water conservation can reduce the amount of water used in an area, so that rain can renew the water supply. Reducing the use of chemicals and energy resources can reduce the amount of pollution in air and water, and on land.

Active Reading

11 Identify As you read, underline the ways that resources can be managed effectively.

Visualize It!

12 Identify Describe the ways that each activity in the picture shows stewardship of natural resources.

Ⓐ

Putting limits on the number of fish that a person keeps can help to protect fish populations.

Ⓑ

Houghton Mifflin Harcourt Publishing Company

Reducing the Use of Nonrenewable Resources

Nonrenewable resources last longer if they are used efficiently. For example, compact fluorescent light bulbs, or CFLs, use much less energy to produce the same amount of light as incandescent light bulbs do. By using less electrical energy, fewer resources like coal are needed to produce electricity. Reducing, reusing, and recycling also reduce the amount of natural resources that must be obtained from Earth. Although recycling materials requires energy, it takes much less energy to recycle an aluminum can than it does to make a new one!

You can reuse a plastic water bottle instead of buying bottled water. Reusing conserves water and oil.

13 Apply How can you reduce the use of nonrenewable resources? Write your ideas in the table below.

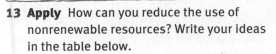

Resource	Is used to...	Ways to reduce
oil	Make plastic objects. Provide energy.	Use reusable containers. Recycle plastics. Drive less.
coal		
metal		

Compact fluorescent bulbs last longer than incandescent bulbs and use a lot less energy.

Cans, wires, and other objects made of metal can be collected and recycled into new objects.

Pluses and Minuses

What are the disadvantages and advantages of managing resources?

Managing resources has disadvantages. Developing new technologies that use fewer resources is expensive. Changing how people use resources can be difficult, because some people have a hard time breaking old habits. Recycling resources can sometimes be expensive and inconvenient.

Managing resources also has many advantages. Management can reduce the loss of a valuable resource. It can also reduce waste. Less waste means less space is needed for landfills. Many resources produce pollution as they are gathered or used, so resource management can lead to less pollution.

Visualize It!

15 Place a (–) next to each property of the hybrid electric car that is a disadvantage. Place a (+) next to each property of the car that is an advantage.

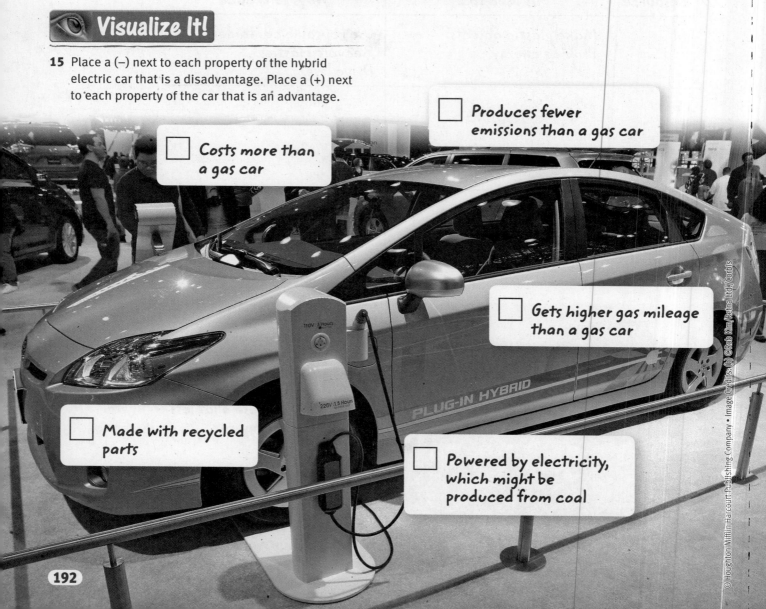

☐ Produces fewer emissions than a gas car

☐ Costs more than a gas car

☐ Gets higher gas mileage than a gas car

☐ Made with recycled parts

☐ Powered by electricity, which might be produced from coal

What kinds of changes can we make to manage resources?

Managing natural resources takes place on global, national, state, local, and individual levels. On the global level, countries make agreements to help manage international resources. For example, countries agreed to stop using chemicals called CFCs after scientists discovered that CFCs were causing damage to the ozone layer. The ozone layer is a resource that protects Earth from harmful radiation. Eliminating the use of CFCs has slowed the breakdown of the ozone layer.

Change Laws

On the national level, countries pass laws to manage resources. Many nations have laws that determine where, when, and how many trees can be harvested for timber. Laws also govern how materials must be disposed of to prevent and reduce harm to land and water. Governments spend money to promote recycling programs. In addition, government funding allows scientists to develop technologies for using resources more efficiently.

Change Habits

Think about all the things you do every day. Changing some of your habits can help to conserve resources. You can conserve water by taking shorter showers and turning off the faucet while brushing your teeth. You can use reusable lunch containers and water bottles. You can recycle disposable materials, such as plastic bottles or newspaper, instead of throwing them away. You can bike or walk instead of riding in a car. You can save energy by turning off lights or TV sets when they are not being used. Families can buy energy-efficient appliances to save even more energy.

Visualize It!

17 List What are some of the ways these students are conserving resources in their school lunchroom?

_____
_____
_____
_____
_____
_____

You can conserve resources in your school lunchroom.

ALUMINUM   MILK CARTONS   PLASTIC

Visual Summary

To complete this summary, write the answer to each question. Then use the key below to check your answers. You can use this page to review the main concepts of the lesson.

Managing Resources

Humans use natural resources to carry out daily activities.

18 What is a negative impact of resource use?

_____

_____

_____

Managing resources has advantages and disadvantages.

Managing resources can allow resources to be conserved.

19 List two ways that resources can be managed effectively.

_____

_____

_____

20 What is one advantage of developing energy-efficient technologies?

_____

_____

_____

Answers: **18** Using resources can cause pollution and damage to ecosystems; **19** Sample answers: practicing water conservation; limiting logging to protect forests; **20** a reduction in pollution

21 Apply What would a scientist need to consider when developing biofuels from plants like sugar cane and corn to use instead of fossil fuels?

Lesson Review

Vocabulary

Circle the term that best completes the following sentence.

1 *Conservation/Stewardship* is the protection and wise use of resources.

2 Anything that can be used to take care of a need is a *renewable resource/natural resource*.

3 A *renewable resource/nonrenewable resource* is used more quickly than it can be replaced.

Key Concepts

4 Identify Which of the following is a renewable resource?

A oil

B sunlight

C gold

D natural gas

5 Describe How does reusing, reducing, and recycling conserve energy?

_____

_____

_____

6 Explain How can technology be used to conserve nonrenewable resources?

_____

_____

_____

7 Compare What is the relationship between stewardship and conservation?

_____

_____

_____

_____

Critical Thinking

8 Contrast How might the management of nonrenewable resources be different from the management of renewable resources?

_____

_____

_____

_____

_____

Use the photo below to answer the following questions.

9 Predict Could the resource in the picture become nonrenewable? Explain your answer.

_____

_____

_____

10 Apply How can individuals help to conserve the resource in the picture?

_____

_____

_____

_____

My Notes

Big Idea ◁ **Humans depend on natural resources for materials and for energy.**

Lesson 1

ESSENTIAL QUESTION
How can Earth support life?

Explain how the unique properties of Earth allow life to exist.

Lesson 4

ESSENTIAL QUESTION
How do humans use renewable energy resources?

Describe how humans use energy resources and the role of renewable energy resources in society.

Lesson 2

ESSENTIAL QUESTION
What are Earth's natural resources?

Understand the types and uses of Earth's natural resources.

Lesson 5

ESSENTIAL QUESTION
Why should natural resources be managed?

Explain the consequences of society's use of natural resources and the importance of managing these resources wisely.

Lesson 3

ESSENTIAL QUESTION
How do we use nonrenewable energy resources?

Describe how humans use energy resources and the role of nonrenewable energy resources in society.

Think Outside the Book

2 **Synthesize** Choose one of these activities to help synthesize what you have learned in this unit.

☐ Using what you learned in lessons 2, 3, and 4, create a poster presentation that compares and contrasts one renewable resource and one nonrenewable resource. Include a discussion of at least one drawback for each resource type.

☐ Using what you learned in lessons 2 and 3, write a short story about a fossil fuel that follows the fuel from its formation to its use by humans.

Connect **ESSENTIAL QUESTIONS**
Lessons 2 and 5

1 **Explain** Why is it important to manage natural resources wisely?

_____

_____

_____

_____

Unit 3 Review

Name _____

Vocabulary

Check the box to show whether each statement is true or false.

T	F	
☐	☐	**1** The <u>ozone</u> layer helps insulate the Earth.
☐	☐	**2** A <u>material resource</u> is a renewable resource that is used to make objects.
☐	☐	**3** <u>Stewardship</u> is the application of various methods that use up natural resources.
☐	☐	**4** <u>Biomass</u> energy comes from organic matter such as plant material and manure.
☐	☐	**5** Rocks, water, air, minerals, forests, wildlife, and soil are all examples of a <u>natural resource</u>.

Key Concepts

Read each question below, and circle the best answer.

6 The chemical bonds in fuel are changed when the fuel is burned to move a car. What type of energy conversion is taking place in this example?

  A kinetic energy to mechanical energy

  B chemical energy to potential energy

  C potential energy to kinetic energy

  D mechanical energy to electrical energy

7 Sometimes, a renewable resource can be considered nonrenewable because it is used up faster than it can be replenished. Which of the following choices is an example of this?

  A Coal supply getting smaller because it takes millions of years to form.

  B Forests being cut down at a quicker rate than they can grow.

  C Solar energy being used to provide electricity to a home.

  D Water in streams replaced by rainfall from the atmosphere.

8 The diagram below shows the process of photosynthesis.

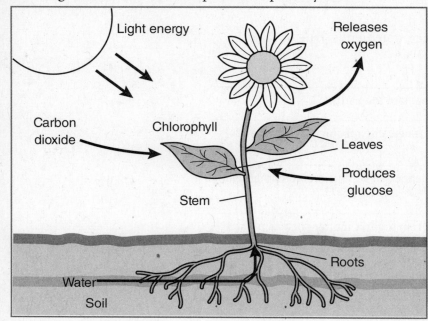

How is photosynthesis best summarized?

A The process by which oxygen enters a leaf and is converted into carbon dioxide.

B The process by which plants use the sun's energy to make chlorophyll.

C The process by which plants convert the sun's energy into energy stored as glucose.

D The process by which water enters through the roots and glucose is produced.

9 Which of the following is a disadvantage of managing resources?

A less of the natural resource is wasted

B reduction in pollution due to less manufacturing

C expense of recycling materials

D more resources extracted from Earth

10 What is a major reason solar energy is not used everywhere on a large scale?

A It is too difficult to purchase and install solar panels.

B Solar energy is not very effective at producing electricity.

C The manufacture of solar panels produces too much pollution.

D Solar panels are most efficient in places that receive lots of sunlight.

11 The chemicals released by burning petroleum in car engines contribute to what local and global effects?

A smog and global warming   **C** acid rain and fusion

B fog and radioactivity   **D** sulfur dioxide decrease and ozone buildup

12 What gas molecule found in Earth's atmosphere is made up of three oxygen atoms?

A ozone   **C** sulfur dioxide

B nitrogen   **D** carbon dioxide

13 Nuclear energy is best described as what type of energy resource?

A renewable   **C** renewable and inexhaustible

B nonrenewable   **D** nonrenewable because it is used up so rapidly

Critical Thinking

Answer the following questions in the space provided.

14 Below is an example of a technology used for alternative energy.

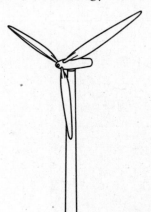

What type of energy does the equipment in the picture harness? _____

Is the type of energy harnessed by this equipment renewable or nonrenewable? Explain your answer. _____

_____

Name one advantage and one disadvantage of using this type of energy.

_____

_____

Unit 3 Review continued

15 The unique properties of Earth make life possible. What are the five basic necessities that all living things need to survive on Earth?

_____

_____

Why is the distance from Earth to the sun important for life on Earth?

_____

_____

Why is the rotation of Earth important to conditions on Earth?

_____

_____

Connect **ESSENTIAL QUESTIONS**
Lessons 3 and 5

Answer the following question in the space provided.

16 Below is a graph of the production and use of petroleum in the United States in the past, present, and likely usage in the future.

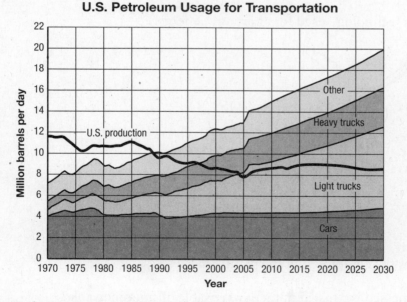

U.S. Petroleum Usage for Transportation

Summarize how current production and usage of petroleum compare.

_____

_____

Name two risks linked to offshore drilling and transporting petroleum.

_____

_____

Human Impact on the Environment

© Houghton Mifflin Harcourt Publishing Company • Image Credits: (bkgd) ©Cameron Davidson/Photographer's Choice RF/Getty Images; (br) ©David Hay Jones/Photo Researchers, Inc.

Big Idea

Humans and human population growth affect the environment.

Human actions, such as cutting down trees to build large housing developments, affect the surrounding ecosystem.

Factories cause pollution.

What do you think?

Human activities can affect Earth's air, water, and land resources in a variety of ways. What are some specific ways in which human activities affect the environment?

Unit 4
Human Impact on the Environment

Investigating Water Resources

Fresh water is an important natural resource. It is found underground and on Earth's surface. People need fresh water for many things, including drinking and household uses.

1 Think about It

A What makes fresh surface water and groundwater such valuable resources?

_____

_____

_____

B How does human activity affect the availability of fresh water?

_____

_____

_____

Rain barrels collect rainwater for home use.

② Ask A Question

Where does your water come from?

With a partner, research the source of the water used by your community. Consider contacting your local utility company for information.

Things to Consider

✔ How do our water supplies get replenished?

✔ What are the most common uses for water?

③ Make A Plan

A Describe the environment that surrounds your local water source.

_____

_____

B Describe threats to your local water supply and how your water supply can be protected.

Threats to Water Supply	Ways to Protect Water Supply

C Choose one of the ideas for protecting the water supply that you listed above. Describe how this method of protection might be implemented by your community.

_____

_____

_____

_____

Take It Home

Trace the water used in your home to its source. Use a map to determine the route by which the water you use must be transported from its source.

Human Impact on Water

ESSENTIAL QUESTION

What impact can human activities have on water resources?

By the end of this lesson, you should be able to explain the impacts that humans can have on the quality and supply of fresh water.

Humans and other organisms depend on clean water to survive. More than half of the material inside humans is water.

Engage Your Brain

1 Analyze Write a list of the reasons humans need water. Next to this list, write a list of reasons fish need water. Are there similarities between your two lists?

2 Identify Circle the word that correctly completes the following sentences.
The man in this photo is testing ~~water~~/air quality.
The flowing body of water next to the man is a ~~river~~/lake.

Active Reading

3 Synthesize You can often define an unknown word if you know the meaning of its word parts. Use the word parts and the sentence below to make an educated guess about the meaning of the word *nonrenewable*.

Word part	Meaning
renew	restore, make like new
-able	able to be
non-	not

Example sentence
Some of Earth's <u>nonrenewable</u> resources include coal and oil.

nonrenewable: *not used again*

Vocabulary Terms

- water pollution
- point-source pollution
- nonpoint-source pollution
- thermal pollution
- eutrophication
- potable
- reservoir

4 Identify This list contains the key terms you'll learn in this lesson. As you read, circle the definition of each term.

Water, Water

Close up of a mayfly larva

Organisms need clean water for life and good health. For example, young mayflies live in water, humans drink water, and brown pelicans eat fish they catch in water.

Why is water important?

Earth is the only planet with large amounts of water. Water shapes Earth's surface and affects Earth's weather and climates. Most importantly, water is vital for life. Every living thing is made mostly of water. Most life processes use water. Water is an important natural resource. For humans and other organisms, access to clean water is important for good health.

There is lots of water, so what's the problem?

About 97% of Earth's water is salty, which leaves only 3% as fresh water. However, as you can see from the graph, over two-thirds of Earth's fresh water is frozen as ice and snow. But a lot of the liquid water seeps into the ground as groundwater. That leaves much less than 1% of Earth's fresh liquid water on the surface. Water is vital for people, so this small volume of fresh surface and groundwater is a limited resource.

Areas with high densities of people, such as cities, need lots of fresh water. Cities are getting bigger, and so the need for fresh water is increasing. *Urbanization* (ER•buh•ny•zhay•shuhn) is the growth of towns and cities that results from the movement of people from rural areas into the urban areas. The greater demand for fresh water in cities is threatening the availability of water for many people. Fresh water is becoming a natural resource that cannot be replaced at the same rate at which it is used.

Distribution of Earth's Fresh Water

Icecaps and glaciers
68.7%

Groundwater
30.1%

Ground ice and permafrost
0.86%

Surface water
0.3%

Visualize It!

5 Interpret What percentage of fresh water on Earth is frozen? What percentage of fresh water is liquid?

_____

_____

Everywhere...

Where do we get fresh water?

Fresh water may fall directly as precipitation, or may melt from ice and snow. Earth's fresh liquid water is found as surface water and groundwater. *Surface water* is any body of water above the ground. It includes liquid salt or fresh water, or solid water, like snow and ice. Water may seep below the surface to become *groundwater*. Groundwater is found under Earth's surface, in spaces in rocks or in soil, where it can be liquid or frozen.

Aquifers and Groundwater

Aquifers and ground ice are forms of groundwater. An *aquifer* is a body of rock or sediment that can store a lot of water, and that allows water to flow easily through it. Aquifers store water in spaces, called *pores,* between particles of rock or sediment. Wells are dug into aquifers to reach the water. In polar regions, water is often frozen in a layer of soil called *permafrost.*

Rivers, Streams, and Lakes

Rivers, streams, and most lakes are fresh surface waters. A stream or river may flow into a bowl-shaped area, which may fill up to form a lake. Many millions of people around the world depend on fresh water that is taken from rivers and fresh water lakes.

What are water quality and supply?

Water quality is a measure of how clean or polluted water is. Water quality is important because humans and other organisms depend on clean water to survive. It is vital for living things to not only have water, but also to have clean water. Dirty, contaminated water can make us sick or even kill us.

Water supply is the availability of water. Water supply influences where and when farmers grow crops, and where people can build cities. *Water supply systems* carry water from groundwater or surface waters so people can use the water. The systems can be a network of underground pipes, or a bucket for scooping water from a well. A shortage of clean, fresh water reduces quality of life for people. Many people in developing countries do not have access to clean, fresh water.

Active Reading

6 List What are the different sources of fresh water?

_____

_____

Think Outside the Book (Inquiry)

7 Observe Keep a water diary for a day. Record every time you use water at school, at home, or elsewhere. At the end of the day, review your records. How could you reduce your water usage?

Many people do not have a water supply to their homes. Instead, they have to go to a local stream, well, or pump to gather water for cooking, cleaning, and drinking.

Under Threat

What threatens fresh water quality?

When waste or other material is added to water so that it is harmful to organisms that use it or live in it, **water pollution** (WAW•ter puh•LOO•shuhn) occurs. It is useful to divide pollution sources into two types. **Point-source pollution** comes from one specific site. For example, a major chemical spill is point-source pollution. Usually this type of pollution can be controlled once its source is found. **Nonpoint-source pollution** comes from many small sources and is more difficult to control. Most nonpoint-source pollution reaches water supplies by runoff or by seeping into groundwater. The main sources of nonpoint-source pollution are city streets, roads and drains, farms, and mines.

Active Reading

8 Identify As you read, underline the sources of water pollution.

Thermal Pollution

Any heating of natural water that results from human activity is called **thermal pollution**. For example, water that is used for cooling some power plants gets warmed up. When that water is returned to the river or lake it is at a higher temperature than the lake or river water. The warm water has less oxygen available for organisms that live in the water.

Chemical Pollution

Chemical pollution occurs when harmful chemicals are added to water supplies. Two major sources of chemical pollution are industry and agriculture. For example, refineries that process oil or metals and factories that make metal or plastic products or electronic items all produce toxic chemical waste. Chemicals used in agriculture include pesticides, herbicides, and fertilizers. These pollutants can reach water supplies by seeping into groundwater. Once in groundwater, the pollution can enter the water cycle and can be carried far from the pollution source. *Acid rain* is another form of chemical pollution. It forms when gases formed by burning fossil fuels mix with water in the air. Acid rain can harm both plants and animals. It can lower the pH of soil and water, and make them too acidic for life.

Biological Pollution

Many organisms naturally live in and around water, but they are not normally polluters. *Biological pollution* occurs when live or dead organisms are added to water supplies. Wastewater may contain disease-causing microbes from human or animal wastes. *Wastewater* is any water that has been used by people for such things as flushing toilets, showering, or washing dishes. Wastewater from feed lots and farms may also contain harmful microbes. These microbes can cause diseases such as dysentery, typhoid, or cholera.

Eutrophication

Fresh water often contains nutrients from decomposing organisms. An increase in the amount of nutrients in water is called **eutrophication** (yoo•TRAWF•ih•kay•shuhn). Eutrophication occurs naturally in water. However, *artificial eutrophication* occurs when human activity increases nutrient levels in water. Wastewater and fertilizer runoff that gets into waterways can add extra nutrients which upset the natural biology of the water. These extra nutrients cause the fast growth of algae over the water surface. An overgrowth of algae and aquatic plants can reduce oxygen levels and kill fish and other organisms in the water.

oughton Mifflin Harcourt Publishing Company

Visualize It!

Water can become polluted by human activities in many different ways.

Chemical Pollution
Sulfur in smoke and vehicle exhausts contributes to the acidification of rain, leading to acid rain. Acid rain can affect areas far from the point of pollution.

Biological pollution

Biological Pollution
Animal and human wastes can get washed into a water supply in runoff, or through leaking pipes.

Thermal pollution

Eutrophication

Chemical pollution

9 Describe How is human activity impacting water quality in this image?

_____

_____

_____

_____

10 Apply Identify one point-source and one nonpoint-source of pollution in this image.

_____

_____

_____

_____

How is water quality measured?

Before there were scientific methods of testing water, people could only look at water, taste it, and smell it to check its quality. Scientists can now test water with modern equipment, so the results are more reliable. Modern ways of testing water are especially important for finding small quantities of toxic chemicals or harmful organisms in water.

Water is a good solvent. So, water in nature usually contains dissolved solids, such as salt and other substances. Because most dissolved solids cannot be seen, it is important to measure them. Measurements of water quality include testing the levels of dissolved oxygen, pH, temperature, dissolved solids, and the number and types of microbes in the water. Quality standards depend on the intended use for the water. For example, drinking water needs to meet much stricter quality standards than environmental waters such as river or lake waters do.

Water Quality Measurement

Quality measurement	What is it?	How it relates to water quality
Dissolved solids	a measure of the amount of ions or microscopic suspended solids in water	Some dissolved solids could be harmful chemicals. Others such as calcium could cause scaling or build-up in water pipes.
pH	a measure of how acidic or alkaline water is	Aquatic organisms need a near neutral pH (approx. pH 7). Acid rain can drop the pH too low (acidic) for aquatic life to live.
Dissolved oxygen (DO)	the amount of oxygen gas that is dissolved in water	Aquatic organisms need oxygen. Animal waste and thermal pollution can decrease the amount of oxygen dissolved in water.
Turbidity	a measure of the cloudiness of water that is caused by suspended solids	High turbidity increases the chance that harmful microbes or chemicals are in the water.
Microbial load	the identification of harmful bacteria, viruses or protists in water	Microbes such as bacteria, viruses, and protists from human and animal wastes can cause diseases.

11 Predict Why might increased turbidity increase the chance of something harmful being in the water? _____

How is water treated for human use?

Active Reading 12 **Identify** As you read, number the basic steps in the water treatment process.

Natural water may be unsafe for humans to drink. So, water that is to be used as drinking water is treated to remove harmful chemicals and organisms. Screens take out large debris. Then chemicals are added that make suspended particles stick together. These particles drop out of the water in a process called *flocculation*. Flocculation also removes harmful bacteria and other microbes. Chlorine is often added to kill microbes left in the water. In some cities, fluoride is added to water supplies to help prevent tooth decay. Finally, air is bubbled through the water. Water that is suitable to drink is called **potable** water. Once water is used, it becomes wastewater. It enters the sewage system where pipes carry it to a wastewater treatment plant. There the wastewater is cleaned and filtered before being released back into the environment.

Drinking water is often mixed in large basins to help remove chemicals and harmful organisms. Paddles stir the water in the basins.

Who monitors and protects our water quality?

Active Reading 13 **Identify** As you read, underline the government agency that is responsible for enforcing water quality rules.

If a public water supply became contaminated, many people could get very sick. As a result, public water supplies are closely monitored so that any problems can be fixed quickly. The Safe Drinking Water Act is the main federal law that ensures safe drinking water for people in the United States. The act sets strict limits on the amount of heavy metals or certain types of bacteria that can be in drinking water, among other things. The Environmental Protection Agency (EPA) has the job of enforcing this law. It is responsible for setting the standards drinking water must meet before the water can be pumped into public water systems. Water quality tests can be done by trained workers or trained volunteers.

Samples of water are routinely taken to make sure the water quality meets the standards required by law.

Supply and Demand

How does water get to the faucet?

In earlier times, humans had to live near natural sources of fresh water. Over time, engineers developed ways to transport and store large amounts of water. So, humans can now live in places where fresh water is supplied by water pipes and other infrastructure. The ability to bring fresh water safely from its source to a large population has led to the urbanization of cities.

Creating Water Supply Systems

Freshwater supply is often limited, so we have found ways to store and transport water far from its source to where it is used. Surface water is collected and pumped to places where people need it. Groundwater can be found by digging wells into aquifers. Water can be lifted from a well by hand in buckets. It can be pumped into pipes that supply homes, farms, factories and cities. Piped water supply systems can deliver water over great distances to where humans need it. Water supply and storage systems are expensive to build and maintain.

Visualize It!

A public water supply includes the water source, the treatment facilities, and the pipes and pumps that send it to homes, industries, businesses, and public facilities.

Water treatment and distribution

A Water can be moved far away from its source by pumping it through pipes to large urban areas.

Intake

Lake

Tunnels

Chemicals added

Mixing basins

Settling basins

Water treatment plant

B Water is treated to make it potable.

Changing the Flow of Water

Pumping and collecting groundwater and surface waters changes how water flows in natural systems. For example, a **reservoir** (REZ•uhr•vwohr) is a body of water that usually forms behind a dam. Dams stop river waters from flowing along their natural course. The water in a reservoir would naturally have flowed to the sea. Instead, the water can be diverted into a pipeline or into artificial channels called *canals* or *aqueducts*.

What threatens our water supply?

Active Reading **14 Identify** As you read, underline the things that are a threat to water supply.

As the human use of water has increased, the demand for fresh water has also increased. Demand is greater than supply in many areas of the world, including parts of the United States. The larger a population or a city gets, the greater the demand for fresh water. Increased demand for and use of water can cause water shortages. Droughts or leaking water pipes can also cause water shortages. Water is used to keep our bodies clean and healthy. It is also used to grow crops for food. Water shortages threaten these benefits.

15 Infer Why would a larger city have a larger demand for water?

_____
_____
_____
_____
_____

C The infastructure shown here is used to supply clean water. Once water is used, it becomes wastewater. A different system, called a sewage system, carries wastewater away from urban areas to wastewater treatment plants.

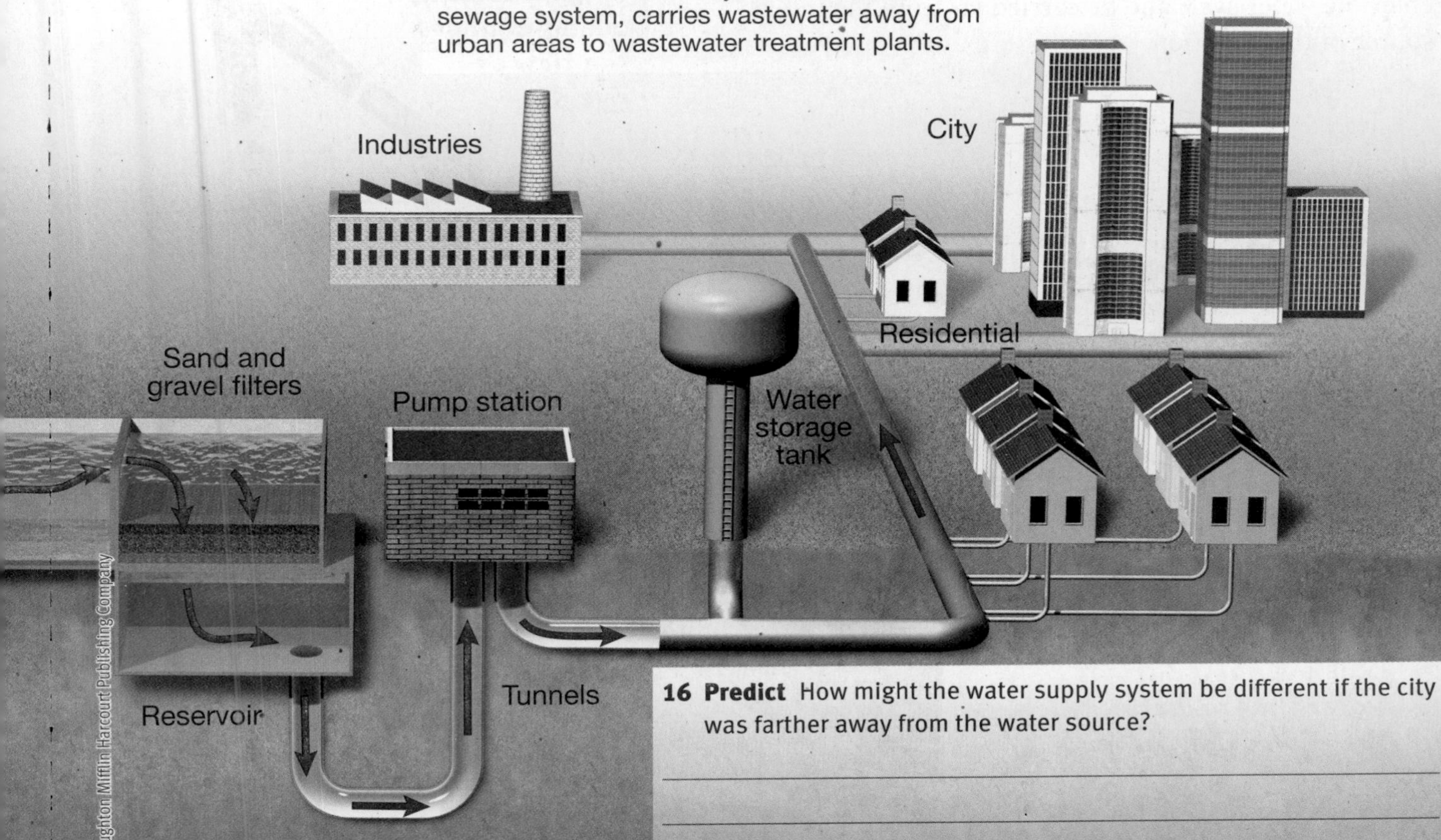

Industries

City

Residential

Sand and gravel filters

Pump station

Water storage tank

Reservoir

Tunnels

16 Predict How might the water supply system be different if the city was farther away from the water source?

_____
_____

How do efforts to supply water to humans affect the environment?

Growing urban populations place a greater demand on water supplies. Efforts to increase water supply can affect the environment. For example, building dams and irrigation canals changes the natural flow of water. The environment is physically changed by construction work. The local ecology changes too. Organisms that live in or depend on the water may lose their habitat and move away.

Aquifers are often used as freshwater sources for urban areas. When more water is taken from an aquifer than can be replaced by rain or snow, the water table can drop below the reach of existing wells. Rivers and streams may dry up and the soil that once held aquifer waters may collapse, or *subside*. In coastal areas, the overuse of groundwater can cause seawater to seep into the aquifer in a process called *saltwater intrusion*. In this way, water supplies can become contaminated with salt water.

Increasing population in an area can also affect water quality. The more people that use a water supply in one area, the greater the volume of wastewater that is produced in that area. Pollutants such as oil, pesticides, fertilizers, and heavy metals from city runoff, from industry, and from agriculture may seep into surface waters and groundwater. In this way, pollution could enter the water supply. This pollution could also enter the water cycle and be carried far from the initial source of the pollution.

Active Reading

17 Relate How can the increased demand on water affect water quality?

_____

_____

_____

_____

_____

_____

Building dams disrupts water flow and affects the ecology of the land and water.

Digging irrigation canals changes the flow of rivers.

Irrigating arid areas changes the ecology of those areas.

Death of a Sea

The Aral Sea in Central Asia was once the world's fourth-largest inland salty lake. But it has been shrinking since the 1960s. In the 1940s, the courses of the rivers that fed the lake were changed to irrigate the desert, so that crops such as cotton and rice could be grown. By 2004, the lake had shrunk to 25% of its original size. The freshwater flow into the lake was reduced and evaporation caused the lake to become so salty that most of the plants and animals in it died or left the lake.

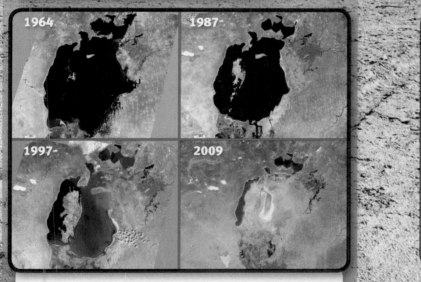

1964 1987

1997 2009

By 2007, the lake had shrunk to 10% of its original size and had split into three separate, smaller lakes.

Polluted Land

The Aral Sea is also heavily polluted by industrial wastes, pesticides, and fertilizer runoff. Salty dust that is blown from the dried seabed damages crops and pollutes drinking water. The salt- and dust-laden air cause serious public health problems in the Aral Sea region. One of the more bizarre reminders of how large the lake once was are the boats that lie abandoned on the exposed sea floor.

Extend

Inquiry

18 Identify What human activity has created the situation in the Aral Sea?

19 Apply Research the impact that of one of these two large water projects has had on people and on the environment: The Three Gorges Dam or the Columbia Basin Project.

20 Relate Research a current or past water project in the area where you live. What benefits will these projects have for people in the area? What risks might there be to the environment?

Visual Summary

To complete this summary, fill in the blanks with the correct word or phrase. Then use the key below to check your answers. You can use this page to review the main concepts of the lesson.

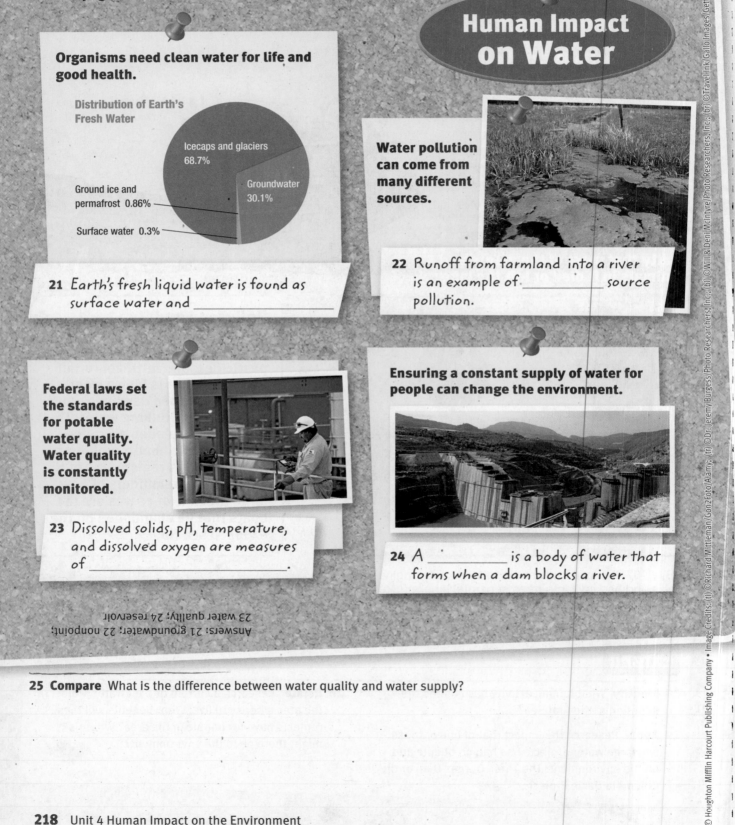

Human Impact on Water

Organisms need clean water for life and good health.

Distribution of Earth's Fresh Water

Icecaps and glaciers 68.7%

Groundwater 30.1%

Ground ice and permafrost 0.86%

Surface water 0.3%

21 Earth's fresh liquid water is found as surface water and _____

Water pollution can come from many different sources.

22 Runoff from farmland into a river is an example of _____ source pollution.

Federal laws set the standards for potable water quality. Water quality is constantly monitored.

23 Dissolved solids, pH, temperature, and dissolved oxygen are measures of _____.

Ensuring a constant supply of water for people can change the environment.

24 A _____ is a body of water that forms when a dam blocks a river.

Answers: 21 groundwater; 22 nonpoint; 23 water quality; 24 reservoir

25 Compare What is the difference between water quality and water supply?

Lesson Review

Vocabulary

Fill in the blank with the term that best completes the following sentences.

1 _____ water is a term used to describe water that is safe to drink.

2 The addition of nutrients to water by human activity is called artificial _____.

3 _____ pollution comes from many small sources.

Key Concepts

Complete the table below with the type of pollution described in each example.

Example	Type of pollution (chemical, thermal, or biological)
4 Identify A person empties an oil can into a storm drain.	
5 Identify A factory releases warm water into a local river.	
6 Identify Untreated sewage is washed into a lake during a rain storm.	

7 Describe Name two ways in which humans can affect the flow of fresh water.

_____

_____

_____

8 Explain Why does water quality need to be monitored?

_____

_____

_____

Critical Thinking

Use this graph to answer the following questions.

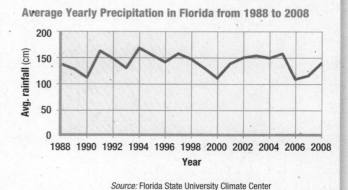

Average Yearly Precipitation in Florida from 1988 to 2008

Source: Florida State University Climate Center

9 Analyze Which year had the least precipitation?

_____

10 Infer What effect might many years of low precipitation have on water supply?

_____

_____

11 Explain Could a single person or animal be a cause of point-source pollution? Explain.

_____

_____

_____

_____

12 Apply In times of hot, dry, weather, some cities ban the use of garden sprinklers. Why do you think there is such a rule?

_____

_____

_____

_____

My Notes

Angel Montoya

CONSERVATION BIOLOGIST

In 1990, Angel Montoya was a student intern working at Laguna Atascosa National Wildlife Refuge in Texas. He became interested in the Aplomado falcon, a bird of prey that disappeared from the southwestern United States during the first half of the 20th century. Montoya decided to go looking for the raptors. He found a previously unknown population of Aplomados in Chihuahua, Mexico. His work helped to make it possible for the falcons to be reintroduced to an area near El Paso, Texas.

Restoration of the Aplomado falcon became Angel's lifework. He has monitored and researched the falcon since 1992. He helps release falcons that have been raised in captivity back into the wild and monitors falcons that have already been released. It isn't easy to keep tabs on a falcon, however. "Their first year they are pretty vulnerable, because they haven't had parents," Montoya says. "Just like juveniles, they're always getting into trouble. But I think they will do just fine."

Angel Montoya releases an Aplomado falcon back into the wild.

JOB BOARD

Environmental Engineering Technician

What You'll Do: Work closely with environmental engineers and scientists to prevent or fix environmental damage. Take care of water and wastewater treatment systems, as well as equipment used for recycling. Test water and air quality and keep good records.

Where You Might Work: In a water treatment facility, or an environmental laboratory.

Education: an associate's degree in engineering technology.

Other Job Requirements: Good communication skills and the ability to work well with others.

Agronomist

What You'll Do: Study the best ways to grow crops and work with farmers to help them use their land better, and get better yields. Agronomists are scientists who study crops and soil.

Where You Might Work: On a farm, in an agricultural business, for the U.S. Department of Agriculture or state or local government agencies, or for seed companies. Agronomists may work both in fields and in laboratories.

Education: a four-year college degree in agronomy, agriculture, or soil conservation.

PEOPLE IN SCIENCE NEWS

YUMI Someya

Fueling the Family Business

Yumi Someya's family had worked in recycling for three generations, cleaning and recycling used cooking oil. In Japan, many people enjoy fried foods. They often throw out the used cooking oil. Yumi's family business collected used oil, cleaned it, and sold it for reuse.

When Yumi traveled to Nepal, she was caught in a landslide. She learned that deforestation was one cause of the landslide and began to think about environmental issues. When she returned home, she worked with her father to find new uses for the used cooking oil. They experimented with fertilizer and soap. Then, in 1992, they learned about biodiesel—fuel made from recycled soybean oil. They thought that used cooking oil might work to fuel cars, too. With a team of researchers, they created Vegetable Diesel Fuel (VDF).

Now, VDF fuels the company's oil-collecting trucks and some Tokyo buses. Yumi hopes to eventually recycle all of the cooking oil used in Japan.

Human Impact on Land

ESSENTIAL QUESTION

What impact can human activities have on land resources?

By the end of this lesson, you should be able to identify the impact that human activity has on Earth's land.

Human activities can carve up land features. A tunnel was cut into this mountain in Zion National Park, Utah, so that people may move around easily.

Engage Your Brain

1 Predict Check T or F to show whether you think each statement is true or false.

T   F

☐ ☐ Urban areas have more open land than rural areas do.

☐ ☐ Many building materials are made from land resources.

☐ ☐ Soil provides habitat for plants but not animals.

☐ ☐ Soil can erode when trees are removed from an area.

2 Illustrate Draw a picture of an object or material that is taken from the land and that is commercially important.

Active Reading

3 Synthesize You can often define an unknown word if you know the meaning of its word parts. Use the word parts to make an educated guess about the meaning of the words *land degradation* and *deforestation*.

Word part	Meaning
degrade	to damage something
deforest	to remove trees from an area
-ation	action or process

Vocabulary Terms

- urbanization
- land degradation
- desertification
- deforestation

4 Apply As you learn the definition of each vocabulary term in this lesson, create your own definition or sketch to help you remember the meaning of the term.

land degradation:

_____

_____

deforestation:

_____

_____

Land of Plenty

Why is land important?

It is hard to imagine human life without land. Land supplies a solid surface for buildings and roads. The soil in land provides nutrients for plants and hiding places for animals. Minerals below the land's surface can be used for construction materials. Fossil fuels underground can be burned to provide energy. Land and its resources affect every aspect of human life.

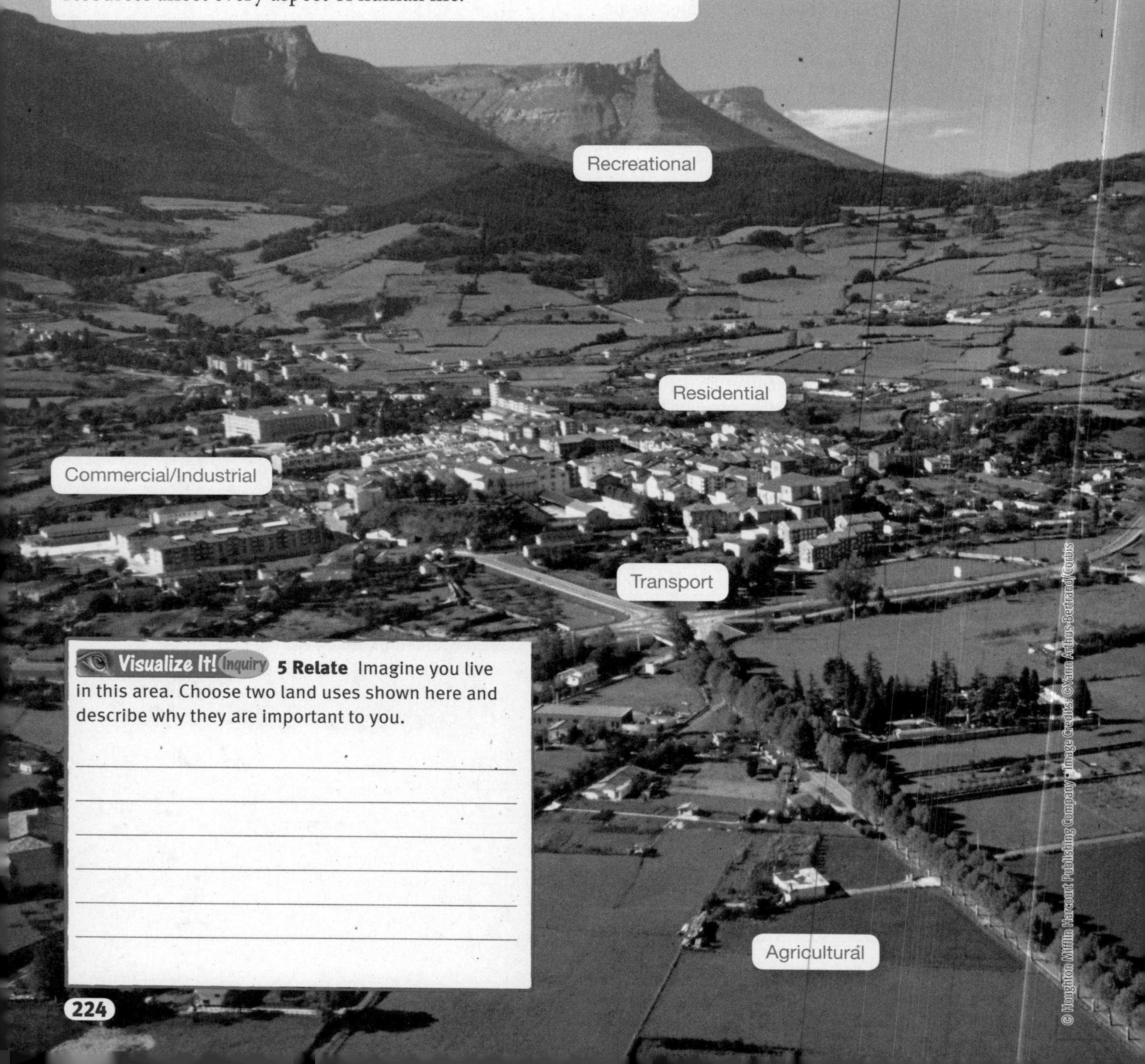

Recreational

Residential

Commercial/Industrial

Transport

Agricultural

Visualize It! (Inquiry) **5 Relate** Imagine you live in this area. Choose two land uses shown here and describe why they are important to you.

_____

_____

_____

_____

_____

_____

What are the different types of land use?

We live on land in urban or rural areas. Cities and towns are urban areas. Rural areas are open lands that may be used for farming. Humans use land in many ways. We use natural areas for *recreation*. We use roads that are built on land for *transport*. We grow crops and raise livestock on *agricultural* land. We live in *residential* areas. We build *commercial* businesses on land and extract resources such as metals and water from the land.

Recreational

Natural areas are places that humans have left alone or restored to a natural state. These wild places include forests, grasslands, and desert areas. People use natural areas for hiking, bird-watching, mountain-biking, hunting, and other fun or recreational activities.

Transport

A large network of roads and train tracks connect urban and rural areas all across the country. Roads in the U.S. highway system cover 4 million miles of land. Trucks carry goods on these highways and smaller vehicles carry passengers. Railroads carrying freight or passengers use over 120,000 miles of land for tracks. Roads and train tracks are often highly concentrated in urban areas.

Agricultural

Much of the open land in rural areas is used for agriculture. Crops such as corn, soybeans, and wheat are grown on large, open areas of land. Land is also needed to raise and feed cattle and other livestock. Agricultural land is open, but very different from the natural areas that it has replaced. Farmland generally contains only one or two types of plants, such as corn or cotton. Natural grasslands, forests, and other natural areas contain many species of plants and animals.

Active Reading 6 **Identify** As you read, underline the ways rural areas differ from urban areas.

Residential

Where do you call home? People live in both rural and urban areas. Rural areas have large areas of open land and low densities of people. Urban areas have dense human populations and small areas of open land. This means that more people live in a square km of an urban area than live in a square km of a rural area. **Urbanization** is the growth of urban areas caused by people moving into cities. When cities increase in size, the population of rural areas near the city may decrease. When an area becomes urbanized, its natural land surface is replaced by buildings, parking lots, and roads. City parks, which contain natural surfaces, may also be built in urban areas.

Commercial and Industrial

As cities or towns expand, commercial businesses are built too, and replace rural or natural areas. Industrial businesses also use land resources. For example, paper companies and furniture manufacturers use wood from trees harvested on forest land. Cement companies, fertilizer manufacturers, and steel manufacturers use minerals that are mined from below the land's surface. Commercial and industrial development usually includes development of roads or railways. Transporting goods to market forms the basis of commerce.

Active Reading

7 **Identify** What effects does urbanization have on land?

_____

_____

_____

_____

_____

_____

Why is soil important?

Soil is a mixture of mineral fragments, organic material, water, and air. Soil forms when rocks break down and dead organisms decay. There are many reasons why soil is important. Soil provides habitat for organisms such as plants, earthworms, fungi, and bacteria. Many plants get the water and nutrients they need from the soil. Because plants form the base of food webs, healthy soil is important for most land ecosystems. Healthy soil is also important for agricultural land, which supplies humans with food.

Active Reading

8 Identify As you read, underline the ways that soil is important to plants.

It Is a Habitat for Organisms

Earthworms, moles, badgers, and other burrowing animals live in soil. These animals also find food underground. *Decomposers* are organisms that break down dead animal and plant material, releasing the nutrients into the soil. Decomposers such as fungi and bacteria live in soil. Soil holds plant roots in place, providing support for the plant. In turn, plants are food for herbivores and are habitats for organisms such as birds and insects. Many animals on Earth depend on soil for shelter or food.

It Stores Water and Nutrients

Falling rain soaks into soil and is stored between soil particles. Different types of soil can store different amounts of water. Wetland soils, for example, store large amounts of water and reduce flooding. Soils are also part of the nutrient cycle. Plants take up nutrients and water stored in soil. Plants and animals that eat them die and are broken down by decomposers such as bacteria and earthworms. Nutrients are released back into the soil and the cycle starts again.

Visualize It!

Nutrients Cycle between Soil and Organisms

Earthworm

Decomposers such as earthworms break down dead organisms, releasing nutrients into the soil.

Plant roots take up nutrients, which they need to live and grow.

9 Relate A chemical spill kills many of the decomposers in the soil. How might it affect nutrient cycles in the soil?

_____

_____

Dust Bowl

In the 1930s, huge clouds of dusty soil rolled across the southern Great Plains of the United States. Areas that were once farmlands and homesteads were wiped out. What caused the soil to blow away?

Drought and Overuse

Farmers who settled in the southern Great Plains overplowed and overgrazed their land. When severe drought hit in 1931, topsoil dried out. Winds lifted the soil and carried it across the plains in huge storms that farmers called "black blizzards." The drought and dust storms continued for years.

Modern Day Dust Bowl

Today in northwest China another dust bowl is forming. Large areas of farmland were made there by clearing the natural vegetation and plowing the soil. Herds of sheep and cattle are overgrazing the land, and large dust storms are common.

Extend

Inquiry

10 Identify What type of land use by people contributed to the Dust Bowl? Does it remain a common use of land today?

11 Compare Research another area under threat from overuse that differs from the feature. What type of land use is causing the problem?

12 Illustrate Do one of the following to show how the Dust Bowl or the area you researched affected society: make a poster, write a play, write a song, or draw a cartoon strip. Present your findings to the class.

Footprints

How can human activities affect land and soil?

Human activities can have positive and negative effects on land and soil. Some activities restore land to its natural state, or increase the amount of fertile soil on land. Other activities can degrade land. **Land degradation** is the process by which human activity and natural processes damage land to the point that it can no longer support the local ecosystem. Urbanization, deforestation, and poor farming practices can all lead to land degradation.

Think Outside the Book **Inquiry**

13 **Apply** With a classmate, discuss how you could help lessen the impact of urbanization on the land in the area where you live.

Active Reading

14 **Identify** As you read, underline the effects that urbanization can have on land.

Urban Sprawl

When urbanization occurs at the edge of a city or town, it is called *urban sprawl*. Urban sprawl replaces forests, fields, and grasslands with houses, roads, schools, and shopping areas. Urban sprawl decreases the amount of farmland that is available for growing crops. It decreases the amount of natural areas that surround cities. It increases the amount of asphalt and concrete that covers the land. Rainwater runs off hard surfaces and into storm drains instead of soaking into the ground and filling aquifers. Rainwater runoff from urban areas can increase the erosion of nearby soils.

Erosion

Erosion (ih•ROH•zhuhn) is the process by which wind, water, or gravity transports soil and sediment from one place to another. Some type of erosion occurs on most land. However, erosion can speed up when land is degraded. Roots of trees and plants act as anchors to the soil. When land is cleared for farming, the trees and plants are removed and the soil is no longer protected. This exposes soil to blowing wind and running water that can wash away the soil, as shown in this photo.

Nutrient Depletion and Land Pollution

Crops use soil nutrients to grow. If the same crops are planted year after year, the same soil nutrients get used up. Plants need the right balance of nutrients to grow. Farmers can plant a different crop each year to reduce nutrient loss. Pollution from industrial activities can damage land. Mining wastes, gas and petroleum leaks, and chemical wastes can kill organisms in the soil. U.S. government programs such as Superfund help to clean up polluted land.

Desertification

When too many livestock are kept in one area, they can overgraze the area. Overgrazing removes the plants and roots that hold topsoil together. Overgrazing and other poor farming methods can cause desertification. **Desertification** (dih•zer•tuh•fih•KAY•shuhn) is the process by which land becomes more desertlike and unable to support life. Without plants, soil becomes dusty and prone to wind erosion. Deforestation and urbanization can also lead to desertification.

Deforestation

The removal of trees and other vegetation from an area is called **deforestation**. Logging for wood can cause deforestation. Surface mining causes deforestation by removing vegetation and soil to get to the minerals below. Deforestation also occurs in rain forests, as shown in the photo, when farmers cut or burn down trees so they can grow crops. Urbanization can cause deforestation when forests are replaced with buildings. Deforestation leads to increased soil erosion.

👁 Visualize It!

15 Relate How has human activity affected the forest in this photo?

_____

_____

_____

_____

_____

Visual Summary

To complete this summary, circle the correct word or phrase.
Then use the key below to check your answers. You can use this
page to review the main concepts of the lesson.

Humans use land in different ways.

16 Crops are grown on
recreational/agricultural land.

Soil is important to all organisms, including humans.

17 Decomposers/plants that live in soil
break down dead matter in the soil.

Human Impact
on Land

Human activities can affect land and soil.

18 Poor farming practices
and drought can lead to
desertification/urbanization.

Answers: 16 agricultural; 17 decomposers; 18 desertification

19 **Apply** How could concentrating human populations in cities help to
conserve agricultural and recreational lands?

Lesson Review

Vocabulary

Draw a line to connect the following terms to their definitions.

1 urbanization

2 deforestation

3 land degradation

4 desertification

A the removal of trees and other vegetation from an area

B the process by which land becomes more desertlike

C the process by which human activity can damage land

D the formation and growth of cities

Key Concepts

5 Contrast How are natural areas different from rural areas?

_____

_____

_____

_____

6 Relate How might deforestation lead to desertification?

_____

_____

_____

7 Relate Think of an animal that eats other animals. Why would soil be important to this animal?

_____

_____

_____

_____

Critical Thinking

Use this photo to answer the following questions.

8 Analyze What type of land degradation is occurring in this photo?

_____

9 Predict This type of soil damage can happen in urban areas too. Outline how urbanization could lead to this type of degradation.

_____

_____

_____

_____

_____

_____

10 Apply What kinds of land uses are around your school? Write down each type of land use. Then describe how one of these land uses might affect natural systems.

_____

_____

_____

_____

_____

_____

My Notes

Human Impact on the Atmosphere

ESSENTIAL QUESTION

How do humans impact Earth's atmosphere?

By the end of this lesson, you should be able to identify the impact that humans have had on Earth's atmosphere.

Human activities that involve burning fuels, such as driving vehicles and keeping buildings cool, can cause air pollution.

Engage Your Brain

1 Identify Check T or F to show whether you think each statement is true or false.

T　F

☐　☐　Human activities can cause air pollution.

☐　☐　Air pollution cannot affect you if you stay indoors.

☐　☐　Air pollution does not affect places outside of cities.

☐　☐　Air pollution can cause lung diseases.

2 Analyze The photo above shows the same city as the photo on the left, but on a different day. How are these photos different?

_____

_____

_____

_____

Active Reading

3 Apply Use context clues to write your own definitions for the words *contamination* and *quality*.

Example sentence
You can help prevent food <u>contamination</u> by washing your hands after touching raw meat.

contamination:

_____

_____

_____

Example sentence
The good sound <u>quality</u> coming from the stereo speakers indicated they were expensive.

quality:

_____

_____

_____

Vocabulary Terms
- greenhouse effect
- air pollution
- particulate
- smog
- acid precipitation
- air quality

4 Apply As you learn the definition of each vocabulary term in this lesson, create your own definition or sketch to help you remember the meaning of the term.

AIR
What Is It Good For?

Why is the atmosphere important?

If you were lost in a desert, you could survive a few days without food and water. But you wouldn't last more than a few minutes without air. Air is an important natural resource. The air you breathe forms part of Earth's atmosphere. The *atmosphere* (AT•muh•sfeer) is a mixture of gases that surrounds Earth. Most organisms on Earth have adapted to the natural balance of gases found in the atmosphere.

It Provides Gases That Organisms Need to Survive

Oxygen is one of the gases that make up Earth's atmosphere. It is used by most living cells to get energy from food. Every breath you take brings oxygen into your body. The atmosphere also contains carbon dioxide. Plants need carbon dioxide to make their own food through photosynthesis (foh•toh•SYN•thuh•sys).

It Absorbs Harmful Radiation

High-energy radiation from space would harm life on Earth if it were not blocked by the atmosphere. Fast-moving particles, called *cosmic rays,* enter the atmosphere every second. These particles collide with oxygen, nitrogen, and other gas molecules and are slowed down. A part of the atmosphere called the *stratosphere* contains ozone gas. The ozone layer absorbs most of the high-energy radiation from the sun, called *ultraviolet radiation* (UV), that reaches Earth.

It Keeps Earth Warm

Without the atmosphere, temperatures on Earth would not be stable. It would be too cold for life to exist. The **greenhouse effect** is the way by which certain gases in the atmosphere, such as water vapor and carbon dioxide, absorb and reradiate thermal energy. This slows the loss of energy from Earth into space. The atmosphere acts like a warm blanket that insulates the surface of Earth, preventing the sun's energy from being lost. For this reason, carbon dioxide and water vapor are called *greenhouse gases.*

Active Reading 5 **Explain** How is Earth's atmosphere similar to a warm blanket?

_____

_____

What is air pollution?

The contamination of the atmosphere by pollutants from human and natural sources is called **air pollution**. Natural sources of air pollution include volcanic eruptions, wildfires, and dust storms. In cities and suburbs, most air pollution comes from the burning of fossil fuels such as oil, gasoline, and coal. Oil refineries, chemical manufacturing plants, dry-cleaning businesses, and auto repair shops are just some potential sources of air pollution. Scientists classify air pollutants as either gases or particulates.

Active Reading

6 Identify As you read, underline sources of air pollution.

Visualize It!

7 Analyze Which one of these images could be both a natural or a human source of air pollution? Give reasons for your answer.

_____

_____

_____

_____

Factory emissions

Vehicle exhaust

Forest fires and wildfires

Gases

Gas pollutants include carbon monoxide, sulfur dioxide, nitrogen oxide, and ground-level ozone. Some of these gases occur naturally in the atmosphere. These gases are considered pollutants only when they are likely to cause harm. For example, ozone is important in the stratosphere, but at ground level it is harmful to breathe. Carbon monoxide, sulfur dioxide, and nitrogen dioxide are released from burning fossil fuels in vehicles, factories, and homes. They are a major source of air pollution.

Particulates

Particle pollutants can be easier to see than gas pollutants. A **particulate** (per•TIK•yuh•lit) is a tiny particle of solid that is suspended in air or water. Smoke contains ash, which is a particulate. The wind can pick up particulates such as dust, ash, pollen, and tiny bits of salt from the ocean and blow them far from their source. Ash, dust, and pollen are common forms of air pollution. Vehicle exhaust also contains particulates. The particulates in vehicle exhaust are a major cause of air pollution in cities.

It Stinks!

What pollutants can form from vehicle exhaust?

In urban areas, vehicle exhaust is a common source of air pollution. Gases such as carbon monoxide and particulates such as soot and ash are in exhaust fumes. Vehicle exhaust may also react with other substances in the air. When this happens, new pollutants can form. Ground-level ozone and smog are two types of pollutants that form from vehicle exhaust.

Active Reading

8 Identify As you read, underline how ground-level ozone and smog can form.

Ground-Level Ozone

Ozone in the ozone layer is necessary for life, but ground-level ozone is harmful. It is produced when sunlight reacts with vehicle exhaust and oxygen in the air. You may have heard of "Ozone Action Days" in your community. When such a warning is given, people should limit outdoor activities because ozone can damage their lungs.

Smog

Smog is another type of pollutant formed from vehicle exhaust. **Smog** forms when ground-level ozone and vehicle exhaust react in the presence of sunlight. Smog is a problem in large cities because there are more vehicles on the roads. It can cause lung damage and irritate the eyes and nose. In some cities, there can be enough smog to make a brownish haze over the city.

Visualize It!

Some compounds in smoke and exhaust are harmful by themselves. And some compounds in smoke and exhaust can react in the atmosphere to form other pollutants such as smog and acid precipitation.

Smog
Smog forms when ground-level ozone and vehicle exhaust react in the presence of sunlight.

smog

sunlight

ground-level ozone

vehicle exhaust

How does pollution from human activities produce acid precipitation?

Precipitation (prih•sip•ih•TAY•shuhn) such as rain, sleet, or snow that contains acids from air pollution is called **acid precipitation**. Burning fossil fuels releases sulfur dioxide and nitrogen oxides into the air. When these gases mix with water in the atmosphere, they form sulfuric acid and nitric acid. Precipitation is naturally slightly acidic. When carbon dioxide in the air and water mix, they form carbonic acid. Carbonic acid is a weak acid. Sulfuric acid and nitric acid are strong acids. They can make precipitation so acidic that it is harmful to the environment.

What are some effects of acid precipitation?

Acid precipitation can cause soil and water to become more acidic than normal. Plants have adapted over long periods of time to the natural acidity of the soils in which they live. When soil acidity rises, some nutrients that plants need are dissolved. These nutrients get washed away by rainwater. Bacteria and fungi that live in the soil are also harmed by acidic conditions.

Acid precipitation may increase the acidity of lakes or streams. It also releases toxic metals from soils. The increased acidity and high levels of metals in water can sicken or kill aquatic organisms. This can disrupt habitats and result in decreased biodiversity in an ecosystem. Acid precipitation can also erode the stonework on buildings and statues.

blowing winds

Smoke and fumes from factories and vehicles contain sulfur dioxide and nitrogen oxide gases, which can be blown long distances by winds.

10 Analyze Explain how pollution from one location can affect the environment far away from the source of the pollution.

_____

_____

_____

_____

Acid Precipitation
These gases dissolve in water vapor, and form sulfuric acids and nitric acids, which fall to Earth as acid precipitation.

How's the AIR?

What are measures of air quality?

Measuring how clean or polluted the air is tells us about **air quality**. Pollutants reduce air quality. Two major threats to air quality are vehicle exhausts and industrial pollutants. The air quality in cities can be poor. As more people move into cities, the cities get bigger. This leads to increased amounts of human-made pollution. Poor air circulation, such as a lack of wind, allows air pollution to stay in one area where it can build up. As pollution increases, air quality decreases.

Air Quality Index

The Air Quality Index (AQI) is a number used to describe the air quality of a location such as a city. The higher the AQI number, the more people are likely to have health problems that are linked to air pollution. Air quality is measured and given a value based on the level of pollution detected. The AQI values are divided into ranges. Each range is given a color code and a description. The Environmental Protection Agency (EPA) has AQIs for the pollutants that pose the greatest risk to public health, including ozone and particulates. The EPA can then issue advisories to avoid exposure to pollution that may harm health.

Indoor Air Pollution

The air inside a building can become more polluted than the air outside. This is because buildings are insulated to prevent outside air from entering the building. Some sources of indoor air pollution include chlorine and ammonia from household cleaners and formaldehyde from furniture. Harmful chemicals can be released from some paints and glues. Radon is a radioactive gas released when uranium decays. Radon can seep into buildings through gaps in their foundations. It can build up inside well-insulated buildings. *Ventilation,* or the mixing of indoor and outside air, can reduce indoor air pollution. Another way to reduce indoor air pollution is to limit the use of items that create the pollution.

Daily Peak Air Quality Index
Tuesday, June 21, 2009
Source: US Environmental Protection Agency

Air Quality Index (AQI) values	Levels of health concern
0–50	Good
51–100	Moderate
101–150	Unhealthy for sensitive groups
151–200	Unhealthy
201–300	Very unhealthy

Source: US Environmental Protection Agency

Color codes based on the Air Quality Index show the air quality in different areas.

Visualize It!

11 Recommend If you were a weather reporter using this map, what would you recommend for people living in areas that are colored orange?

_____

_____

_____

_____

12 Apply If this was your house, how might you decrease the sources of indoor air pollution?

Nitrogen oxides from unvented gas stove, wood stove, or kerosene heater

Chlorine and ammonia from household cleaners

Chemicals from dry cleaning

Fungi and bacteria from dirty heating and air conditioning ducts

Chemicals from paint strippers and thinners

Gasoline from car and lawn mower

Formaldehyde from furniture, carpeting, particleboard, and foam insulation

Carbon monoxide from car left running

How can air quality affect health?

Daily exposure to small amounts of air pollution can cause serious health problems. Children, elderly people, and people with asthma, allergies, lung problems, and heart problems are especially vulnerable to the effects of air pollution. The short-term effects of air pollution include coughing, headaches, and wheezing. Long-term effects, such as lung cancer and emphysema, are dangerous because they can cause death.

Think Outside the Book Inquiry

13 Evaluate Think about the community in which you live. What different things in your community and the surrounding areas might affect the air quality where you live?

Air Pollution and Your Health

Short-term effects	Long-term effects
coughing	asthma
headaches	emphysema
difficulty breathing	allergies
burning/itchy eyes	lung cancer
	chronic bronchitis

14 Identify Imagine you are walking next to a busy road where there are a lot of exhaust fumes. Circle the effects listed in the table that you are most likely to have while walking.

Things Are CHANGING

How might humans be changing Earth's climates?

The burning of fossil fuels releases greenhouse gases, such as carbon dioxide, into the atmosphere. The atmosphere today contains about 37% more carbon dioxide than it did in the mid-1700s, and that level continues to increase. Average global temperatures have also risen in recent decades.

Many people are concerned about how the greenhouse gases from human activities add to the observed trend of increasing global temperatures. Earth's atmosphere and other systems work together in complex ways, so it is hard to know exactly how much the extra greenhouse gases change the temperature. Climate scientists make computer models to understand the effects of climate change. Models predict that average global temperatures are likely to rise another 1.1 to 6.4 °C (2 to 11.5 °F) by the year 2100.

A Sunlight (radiant energy) passes through the windows of the car.

B Energy as heat is trapped inside by the windows.

C The temperature inside the car increases.

👁 **Visualize It!**

15 Synthesize How is a car with closed windows a good analogy of the atmosphere's greenhouse effect?

_____

_____

_____

What are some predicted effects of climate change?

Active Reading **16 Identify** As you read, underline some effects of an increasing average global temperature.

Scientists have already noticed many changes linked to warmer temperatures. For example, some glaciers and the Arctic sea ice are melting at the fastest rates ever recorded. A warmer Earth may lead to changes in rainfall patterns, rising sea levels, and more severe storms. These changes will have many negative impacts for life on Earth. Other predicted effects include drought in some regions and increased precipitation in others. Farming practices and the availability of food is also expected to be impacted by increased global temperatures. Such changes will likely have political and economic effects on the world, especially in developing countries.

Melt water pours from an iceberg that broke away from the Jakobshavn Glacier in West Greenland.

How is the ozone layer affected by air pollution?

In the 1980s, scientists reported an alarming discovery about Earth's protective ozone layer. Over the polar regions, the ozone layer was thinning. Chemicals called *chlorofluorocarbons* (klor•oh•flur•oh•kar•buhns) (CFCs) were causing ozone to break down into oxygen, which does not block harmful ultraviolet (UV) rays. The thinning of the ozone layer allows more UV radiation to reach Earth's surface. UV radiation is dangerous to organisms, including humans, as it causes sunburn, damages DNA (which can lead to cancer), and causes eye damage.

CFCs once had many industrial uses, such as coolants in refrigerators and air-conditioning units. CFC use has now been banned, but CFC molecules can stay in the atmosphere for about 100 years. So, CFCs released from a spray can 30 years ago are still harming the ozone layer today. However, recent studies show that breakdown of the ozone layer has slowed.

The dark blue area on this map shows the size of the ozone hole over the South Pole.

17 Infer How might these penguins near the South Pole be affected by the ozone hole?

_____

_____

_____

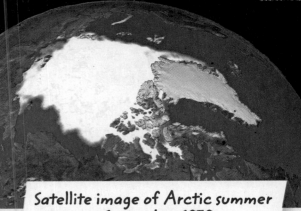

Satellite image of Arctic summer sea ice in September 1979.

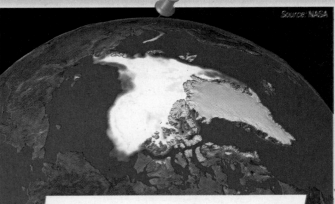

Satellite image of Arctic summer sea ice in September 2007.

Inquiry

18 Relate What effect might melting sea ice have for people who live in coastal areas?

_____

_____

© Houghton Mifflin Harcourt Publishing Company • Image Credits: (bkgd) ©Paul Souders/Corbis; (t) ©NASA/Goddard Space Flight Center Scientific Visualization Studio. Thanks to Rob Gerston (GSFC) for providing the data.; (bl) ©NASA/Goddard Space Flight Center Ozone Processing Team; (tr) Kyodo via AP Images; (bl) ©NASA/Goddard Space Flight Center Scientific Visualization Studio.

Visual Summary

To complete this summary, fill in the blanks with the correct word or phrase. Then use the key below to check your answers. You can use this page to review the main concepts of the lesson.

smog

Human activities are a major cause of air pollution.

19 Two types of air pollutants are gases and _____.

Car exhaust is a major source of air pollution in cities.

20 _____ is formed when exhausts and ozone react in the presence of sunlight.

Human Impact on the Atmosphere

Air quality and levels of pollution can be measured.

Air Quality Index (AQI) values	Levels of health concern
0–50	Good
51–100	Moderate
101–150	Unhealthy for sensitive groups
151–200	Unhealthy
201–300	Very unhealthy

21 As pollution increases, _____ decreases.

Climate change may lead to dramatic changes in global weather patterns.

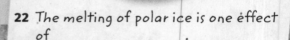

22 The melting of polar ice is one effect of _____.

Answers: 19 particulates; 20 smog; 21 air quality; 22 global warming/climate change

23 Apply Explain in your own words what the following statement means: Each of your breaths, every tree that is planted, and every vehicle on the road affects the composition of the atmosphere.

© Houghton Mifflin Harcourt Publishing Company • Image Credits: (tl) ©Steve Cole/PhotoDisc/Getty Images; (b) ©NASA/Goddard Space Flight Center Scientific Visualization Studio. Thanks to Rob Gersten (GSFC) for providing the data.

Lesson Review

Vocabulary

Draw a line to connect the following terms to their definitions.

1 Air pollution

2 Greenhouse effect

3 Air quality

4 Particulate

5 Smog

A tiny particle of solid that is suspended in air or water

B the contamination of the atmosphere by the introduction of pollutants from human and natural sources

C pollutant that forms when ozone and vehicle exhaust react with sunlight

D a measure of how clean or polluted the air is

E the process by which gases in the atmosphere, such as water vapor and carbon dioxide, absorb and release energy as heat

Key Concepts

6 Identify List three effects that an increase in urbanization can have on air quality.

_____

_____

_____

7 Relate How are ground-level ozone and smog related?

_____

_____

_____

8 Explain How can human health be affected by changes in air quality?

_____

_____

_____

Critical Thinking

Use this graph to answer the following questions.

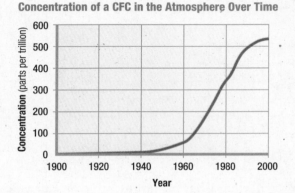

Concentration of a CFC in the Atmosphere Over Time

9 Analyze At what time in the graph did CFCs begin building up in the atmosphere?

_____

_____

10 Synthesize Since the late 1970s, the use of CFCs has been reduced, with a total ban in 2010. But CFCs can stay in the atmosphere for up to 100 years. In the space below, draw a graph showing the concentration of CFCs in the atmosphere over the next 100 years.

11 Apply Do you think it is important that humans control the amount of human-made pollution? Explain your reasoning.

_____

_____

_____

_____

_____

My Notes

Protecting Earth's Water, Land, and Air

ESSENTIAL QUESTION

How can Earth's resources be used wisely?

By the end of this lesson, you should be able to summarize the value of conserving Earth's resources and the effect that wise stewardship has on land, water, and air resources.

Picking up litter to clean streams or rivers is one way we can help preserve Earth's natural resources.

👋 **Lesson Labs**

Quick Labs
• Soil Erosion
• Investigate the Value of Recycling

Exploration Lab
• Filtering Water

🧠 Engage Your Brain

1 Predict Check T or F to show whether you think each statement is true or false.

T F

☐ ☐ Conservation is the overuse of natural resources.

☐ ☐ It is everybody's job to be a good steward of the Earth's resources.

☐ ☐ Reforestation is the planting of trees to repair degraded lands.

☐ ☐ Alternative energy sources, like solar power, increase the amount of pollution released into the air.

2 Describe Have you ever done something to protect a natural resource? Draw a picture showing what you did. Include a caption.

✏️ Active Reading

3 Synthesize You can often guess the meaning of a word from its context, or how it is used in a sentence. Use the sentence below to guess the meaning of the word *stewardship*.

Example sentence
Stewardship of water resources will ensure that there is plenty of clean water for future generations.

stewardship:

_____

_____

Vocabulary Terms

• conservation   • stewardship

4 Apply As you learn the definition of each vocabulary term in this lesson, create your own definition or sketch to help remember the meaning of the term.

Keeping It Clean

What are conservation and stewardship?

Active Reading

5 Identify As you read, underline the definitions of *conservation* and *stewardship*.

In the past, some people have used Earth's resources however they wanted, without thinking about the consequences. They thought it didn't matter if they cut down hundreds of thousands of trees or caught millions of fish. They also thought it didn't matter if they dumped trash into bodies of water. Now we know that it does matter how we use resources. Humans greatly affect the land, water, and air. If we wish to keep using our resources in the future, we need to conserve and care for them.

Conservation: Wise Use of Resources

Conservation (kahn•sur•VAY•shuhn) is the wise use of natural resources. By practicing conservation, we can help make sure that resources will still be around for future generations. It is up to everybody to conserve and protect resources. When we use energy or create waste, we can harm the environment. If we conserve whenever we can, we reduce the harm we do to the environment. We can use less energy by turning off lights, computers, and appliances. We can reuse shopping bags, as in the picture below. We can recycle whenever possible, instead of just throwing things away. By doing these things, we take fewer resources from Earth and put less pollution into the water, land, and air.

Visualize It!

6. Identify How are the people in the picture below practicing conservation?

_____

_____

_____

This old tire is being used as a planter instead of being thrown away.

Stewardship: Managing Resources

Stewardship (stoo•urd•SHIP) is the careful and responsible management of a resource. If we are not good stewards, we will use up a resource or pollute it. Stewardship of Earth's resources will ensure that the environment stays clean enough to help keep people and other living things healthy. Stewardship is everybody's job. Governments pass laws that protect water, land, and air. These laws determine how resources can be used and what materials can be released into the environment. Individuals can also act as stewards. For example, you can plant trees or help clean up a habitat in your community. Any action that helps to maintain or improve the environment is an act of stewardship.

7 Compare Fill in the Venn diagram to compare and contrast conservation and stewardship.

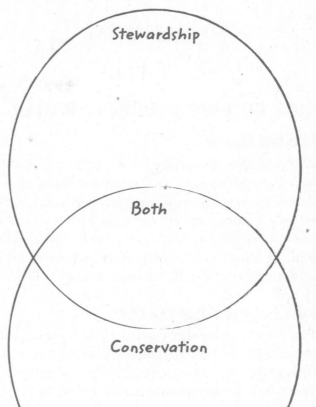

Stewardship

Both

Conservation

Turning empty lots into gardens improves the environment and provides people with healthy food.

Sea turtles are endangered. Scientists help sea turtles that have just hatched find their way to the sea.

◈ Visualize It!

8 Identify How is the person in the picture to the right practicing stewardship?

_____

_____

_____

Water Wise!

How can we preserve water resources?

Most of the Earth's surface is covered by water, so you might think there is lots of water for humans to use. However, there is actually very little fresh water on Earth, so people should use freshwater resources very carefully. People should also be careful to avoid polluting water, because the quality of water is important to the health of both humans and ecosystems. Because water is so important to our health, we need to keep it clean!

By Conserving Water

If we want to make sure there is enough water for future generations, we need to reduce the amount of water we use. In some places, if people aren't careful about using water wisely, there soon won't be enough water for everyone. There are many ways to reduce water usage. We can use low-flow toilets and showerheads. We can take shorter showers. In agriculture and landscaping, we can reduce water use by installing efficient irrigation systems. We can also use plants that don't need much water. Only watering lawns the amount they need and following watering schedules saves water. The photo below shows a simple way to use less water—just turn off the tap while brushing your teeth!

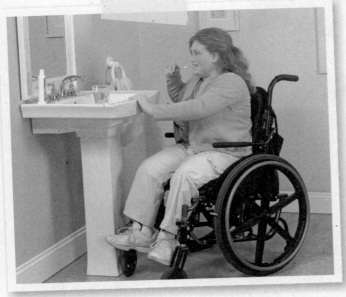

Do the Math

You Try It

9 Calculate How much fresh water is on Earth?

Solve

Each square on the grid equals 1%. Use the grid to fill in the percentage of each type of water found on Earth.

Earth's Water

■ Salt water _____

■ Ice (fresh water) _____

■ Fresh liquid water _____

10 Identify What are some ways you can reduce the amount of water you use?

- Turn off the tap when brushing my teeth.

- _____

- _____

- _____

With Water Stewardship

Humans and ecosystems need clean water. The diagram below shows how a community keeps its drinking water clean. The main way to protect drinking water is to keep pollution from entering streams, lakes, and other water sources. Laws like the Clean Water Act and Safe Drinking Water Act were passed to protect water sources. These laws indicate how clean drinking water must be and limit the types of chemicals that businesses and private citizens can release into water. These laws also help finance water treatment facilities. We can help protect water by not throwing chemicals in the trash or dumping them down the drain. We can also use nontoxic chemicals whenever possible. Reducing the amount of fertilizer we use on our gardens also reduces water pollution.

For healthy ecosystems and safe drinking water, communities need to protect water sources. The first step to protecting water sources is keeping them from becoming polluted.

Protecting Water Resources

Water testing makes sure water is safe for people to drink. It also helps us find out if there is a pollution problem that needs to be fixed.

Water treatment plants remove pollution from wastewater before it is reused or put back into the environment.

Without clean water to drink, people can get sick. Clean water is also important for agriculture and natural ecosystems.

© Houghton Mifflin Harcourt Publishing Company • Image Credits: (bkgd) ©Rich Reid/National Geographic/Getty Images; (r) ©Thinkstock/Corbis; (t) ©Flip Chalfant/The Image Bank/Getty Images

Visualize It!

11 Apply What steps should a community take to manage its water resources?

_____

_____

_____

_____

This Land Is Your Land

Active Reading

12 Identify As you read this page and the next, underline ways that we can protect land resources.

How can we preserve land resources?

People rely on land resources for recreation, agriculture, transportation, commerce, industry, and housing. If we manage land resources carefully, we can make sure that these resources will be around for generations and continue to provide resources for humans to use. We also need to make sure that there are habitats for wild animals. To do all these things, we must protect land resources from overuse and pollution. Sometimes we need to repair damage that is already done.

Through Preservation

Preservation of land resources is very important. *Preservation* means protecting land from being damaged or changed. Local, state, and national parks protect many natural areas. These parks help ensure that many species survive. Small parks can protect some species. Other species, such as predators, need larger areas. For example, wolves roam over hundreds of miles and would not be protected by small parks. By protecting areas big enough for large predators, we also protect habitats for many other species.

Yosemite National Park is one of the oldest national parks in the country. Like other national, state, and local parks, Yosemite was formed to preserve natural habitats.

Think Outside the Book

13 Apply Plant and animal species depend on land resources. Find out which endangered plant or animal species live in your area. Write a paragraph explaining how your community can help protect those species.

Through Reforestation

People use the wood from trees for many things. We use it to make paper and to build houses. We also use wood to heat homes and cook food. In many places, huge areas of forest were cut down to use the wood and nothing was done to replant the forests. Now when we cut trees down, they are often replanted, as in the picture at right. We also plant trees in areas where forests disappeared many years ago in order to help bring the forests back. The process of planting trees to reestablish forestland is called *reforestation*. Reforestation is important, but we can't cut down all forests and replant them. It is important to keep some old forests intact for the animals that need them to survive.

Through Reclamation

In order to use some resources, such as coal, metal, and minerals, the resources first have to be dug out of the ground. In the process, the land is damaged. Sometimes, large areas of land are cleared and pits are dug to reach the resource. Land can also be damaged in other ways, including by development and agriculture. *Reclamation* is the process by which a damaged land area is returned to nearly the condition it was in before people used it. Land reclamation, shown in the lower right photo, is required for mines in many states once the mines are no longer in use. Many national and state laws, such as the Surface Mining and Reclamation Act and the Resource Conservation and Recovery Act, guide land reclamation.

Reforestation

A mine being reclaimed

👁 Visualize It!

14 Compare What are the similarities between reforestation and reclamation?

_____

_____

_____

_____

Through Reducing Urban Sprawl

Urban sprawl is the outward spread of suburban areas around cities. As we build more houses and businesses across a wider area, there is less land for native plants and animals. Reducing urban sprawl helps to protect land resources. One way to reduce sprawl is to locate more people and businesses in a smaller area. A good way to do this is with vertical development—that means constructing taller buildings. Homes, businesses, and even recreational facilities can be placed within high-rise buildings. We also can reduce sprawl using mixed-use development. This development creates communities with businesses and houses very close to one another. Mixed-use communities are also better for the environment, because people can walk to work instead of driving.

Through Recycling

Recycling is one of the most important things we can do to preserve land resources. *Recycling* is the process of recovering valuable materials from waste or scrap. We can recycle many of the materials that we use. By recycling materials like metal, plastic, paper, and glass, we use fewer raw materials. Recycling aluminum cans reduces the amount of bauxite that is mined. We use bauxite in aluminum smelting. Everyone can help protect land resources by recycling. Lots of people throw away materials that can be recycled. Find out what items you can recycle!

One way to reduce urban sprawl is to locate homes and businesses close together.

Bauxite mine

15 Apply Aluminum is mined from the ground. Recycling aluminum cans decreases the need for mining bauxite. Paper can also be recycled. How does recycling paper preserve trees?

_____

_____

© Houghton Mifflin Harcourt Publishing Company • Image Credits: (tl) ©Janis Kraulis/All Canada Photos/Getty Images; (bl) ©David Young-Wolff/Stone/Getty Images; (br) ©Photoshot Holdings Ltd/Alamy

Through Using Soil Conservation Methods

Soil conservation protects soil from erosion or degradation by overuse or pollution. For example, farmers change the way they plow in order to conserve soil. Contour plowing creates ridges of soil across slopes. The small ridges keep water from eroding soils. In strip cropping, two types of crops are planted in rows next to each other to reduce erosion. Terracing is used on steep hills to prevent erosion. Areas of the hill are flattened to grow crops. This creates steps down the side of the hill. *Crop rotation* means that crops with different needs are planted in alternating seasons. This reduces the prevalence of plant diseases and makes sure there are nutrients for each crop. It also ensures that plants are growing in the soil almost year-round. In no-till farming, soils are not plowed between crop plantings. Stalks and cover crops keep water in the soils and reduce erosion by stopping soil from being blown away.

© Houghton Mifflin Harcourt Publishing Company • Image Credits: (cl) ©by marin.tomic/Flickr/Getty Images; (cr) ©NRCS/USDA; (bl) ©NRCS/USDA

Active Reading

16 Identify As you read this page, underline five methods of soil conservation.

Visualize It!

Terracing involves building leveled areas, or steps, to grow crops on.

In contour plowing, crop rows are planted in curved lines along land's natural contours.

Strip cropping prevents erosion by creating natural dams that stop water from rushing over a field.

17 Analyze Which two soil conservation techniques would be best to use on gentle slopes?

☐ contour plowing

☐ crop terracing

☐ strip cropping

18 Analyze Which soil conservation technique would be best to use on very steep slopes?

☐ contour plowing

☐ crop terracing

☐ strip cropping

Into Thin Air

19 Identify Underline the sentences that explain the relationship between burning fossil fuels and air pollution.

How can we reduce air pollution?

Polluted air can make people sick and harm organisms. Air pollution can cause the atmosphere to change in ways that are harmful to the environment and to people. There are many ways that we can reduce air pollution. We can use less energy. Also, we can develop new ways to get energy that produces less pollution. Everybody can help reduce air pollution in many different ways.

Through Energy Conservation

Energy conservation is one of the most important ways to reduce air pollution. Fossil fuels are currently the most commonly used energy resource. When they are burned, they release pollution into the air. If we use less energy, we burn fewer fossil fuels.

There are lots of ways to conserve energy. We can turn off lights when we don't need them. We can use energy-efficient lightbulbs and appliances. We can use air conditioners less in the summer and heaters less in the winter. We can unplug electronics when they are not in use. Instead of driving ourselves to places, we can use public transportation. We can also develop alternative energy sources that create less air pollution. Using wind, solar, and geothermal energy will help us burn less fossil fuel.

Using public transportation, riding a bike, sharing rides, and walking reduce the amount of air pollution produced by cars.

Many cities, such as Los Angeles, California, have air pollution problems.

Energy can be produced with very little pollution. These solar panels help us use energy from the sun and replace the use of fossil fuels.

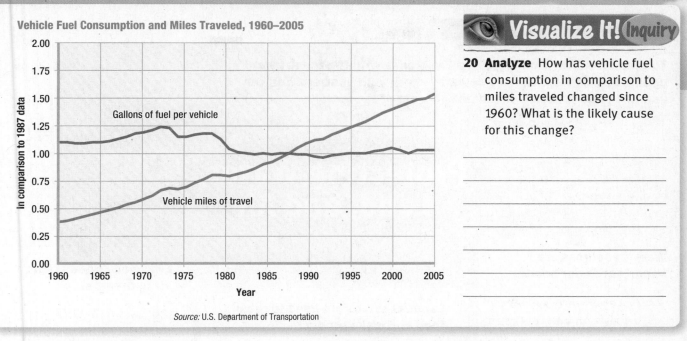

Vehicle Fuel Consumption and Miles Traveled, 1960–2005

Source: U.S. Department of Transportation

Visualize It! Inquiry

20 Analyze How has vehicle fuel consumption in comparison to miles traveled changed since 1960? What is the likely cause for this change?

_____

_____

_____

_____

_____

_____

Through Technology

There are lots of ways to generate energy without creating much air pollution. By developing these alternative energy sources, we can reduce the amount of pollution created by burning fossil fuels. Wind turbines generate clean power. So do solar panels that use energy from the sun. We also can use power created by water flowing through rivers or moving with the tides. Geothermal energy from heat in Earth's crust can be used to generate electricity. Hybrid cars get energy from their brakes and store it in batteries. They burn less gas and release less pollution. Driving smaller cars that can go farther on a gallon of gas also reduces air pollution.

New technologies, such as this compact fluorescent lightbulb (CFL), help limit air pollution. CFL bulbs use less energy to make the same amount of light.

Through Laws

Governments in many countries work independently and together to reduce air pollution. They monitor air quality and set limits on what can be released into the air. In the United States, the Clean Air Act limits the amount of toxic chemicals and other pollutants that can be released into the atmosphere by factories and vehicles. It is up to the Environmental Protection Agency to make sure that these limits are enforced. Because air isn't contained by borders, some solutions must be international. The Kyoto Protocol is a worldwide effort to limit the release of greenhouse gases— pollution that can warm the atmosphere.

21 Summarize List three ways air pollution can be reduced.

• _____

_____

• _____

_____

• _____

_____

Visual Summary

To complete this summary, fill in the blanks with the correct word or phrase. Then use the key below to check your answers. You can use this page to review the main concepts of the lesson.

Protecting Water, Land, and Air

Water resources are important to our health.

22 A community's water supply can be protected by:
- conserving water
- preventing pollution
- _____
- treating wastewater

Land resources are used to grow food and make products.

23 Land resources can be protected by:
- preservation
- reclamation and reforestation
- reducing urban sprawl
- _____
- soil conservation

Everybody needs clean air to breathe.

24 The main way to reduce air pollution is to:
- _____
- _____
- _____
- _____
- _____

Answers: 22 testing water quality; 23 recycling; 24 reduce the amount of fossil fuels burned

25 **Relate** How can you personally act as a steward of water, land, and air resources?

Lesson Review

Vocabulary

Fill in the blank with the term that best completes the following sentences.

1 _____ is the wise use of natural resources.

2 _____ is the careful and responsible management of a resource.

Key Concepts

3 Describe How can water pollution be prevented?

_____

_____

_____

Fill in the table below.

Example	Type of land resource conservation
4 Identify A county creates a park to protect a forest.	
5 Identify A mining company puts soil back in the hole and plants grass seeds on top of it.	
6 Identify A logging company plants new trees after it has cut some down.	
7 Identify A plastic milk bottle is turned into planks for a boardwalk to the beach.	
8 Identify Instead of building lots of single houses, a city builds an apartment building with a grocery store.	

9 Determine How has technology helped decrease air pollution in recent years?

_____

_____

_____

10 Explain Why is it important to protect Earth's water, land, and air resources?

_____

_____

_____

Critical Thinking

11 Explain Land reclamation can be expensive. Why might recycling materials lead to spending less money on reclamation?

_____

_____

_____

Use the graph to answer the following question.

Average Water Usage of U.S. Household

- Toilet flushes 29%
- Washing machine 21%
- Shower 21%
- Tap 12%
- Bath 9%
- Toilet leaks 5%
- Dish washing 3%

Source: U.S. Environmental Protection Agency

12 Analyze The graph above shows water use in the average U.S. household. Using the graph, identify three effective ways a household could conserve water.

_____

_____

My Notes

Unit 4 | Big Idea ▸ Humans and human population growth affect the environment.

Lesson 1
ESSENTIAL QUESTION
What impact can human activities have on water resources?
Explain the impact that humans can have on the quality and supply of fresh water.

Lesson 3
ESSENTIAL QUESTION
How do humans impact Earth's atmosphere?
Identify the impact that humans have had on Earth's atmosphere.

Lesson 2
ESSENTIAL QUESTION
What impact can human activities have on land resources?
Identify the impact that human activity has on Earth's land.

Lesson 4
ESSENTIAL QUESTION
How can Earth's resources be used wisely?
Summarize the value of conserving Earth's resources and the effect that wise stewardship has on land, water, and air resources.

Connect ESSENTIAL QUESTIONS
Lessons 1 and 2

1 Explain How does an increasing human population affect land and water resources?

_____

_____

_____

_____

Think Outside the Book

2 Synthesize Choose one of these activities to help synthesize what you have learned in this unit.

☐ Using what you learned in Lessons 1 through 4, create an informational poster that explains what steps humans can take to protect Earth's water, land, and air.

☐ Using what you learned in Lessons 1, 2, and 3, write a fable that explains how human activities can pollute water, land, or air resources. Provide a moral for your story that explains why pollution should be prevented.

Name _____

Vocabulary

Check the box to show whether each statement is true or false.

T	F	
☐	☐	1 <u>Air quality</u> is a measure of how clean or polluted the air is.
☐	☐	2 <u>Potable</u> water is suitable for drinking.
☐	☐	3 <u>Conservation</u> is the wise use of natural resources.
☐	☐	4 <u>Land degradation</u> is the process by which humans restore damaged land so that it can support the local ecosystem.
☐	☐	5 <u>Stewardship</u> of Earth's resources helps make sure that the environment remains healthy.

Key Concepts

Read each question below, and circle the best answer.

6 Smog usually forms from ground-level ozone and what other human-made pollutant?

A acid precipitation   **C** vehicle exhaust

B volcanic gases   **D** smoke from cigarettes

7 Which of the following is true about the amount of water on Earth?

A There is an ever-increasing amount of water on Earth due to rain and snowfall.

B The amount of water on Earth is replaced much faster than it is being used up.

C There is a fixed amount of water on Earth that is continuously cycled.

D The water on Earth is more than enough for the growing population.

8 Which of the following is a source of indoor air pollution?

A greenhouse gases

B steam from a hot shower

C chemicals from certain cleaning products

D radiation from sunlight entering windows

9 The graph below shows how the amount of carbon dioxide (CO_2) in our atmosphere has changed since 1960.

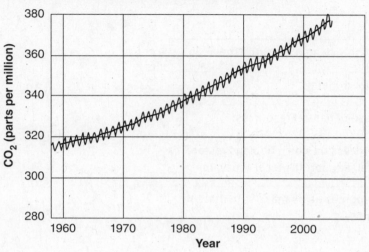

Amount of Atmospheric Carbon Dioxide per Year

Based on the information given in the graph, which of these phenomena has likely increased since 1960?

A land erosion

B coastal erosion

C ozone depletion

D greenhouse effect

10 A manufacturing plant is built on the bank of the Mississippi River. Water is diverted into the plant for use in the making of a product and is then piped back out into the river. If the water that is released back into the river is contaminated, what is this form of pollution called?

A thermal pollution

B biological pollution

C point-source pollution

D nonpoint-source pollution

11 What is the water from an artificial reservoir most likely to be reserved for?

A for future use by homes and businesses

B for recreational purposes such as swimming

C to provide a habitat for fish

D to cool hot industrial equipment

12 The picture below shows a common human activity.

What are examples of the effects this kind of pollution may cause?

A acid rain, which may cause diseases such as asthma

B global warming, which may cause diseases such as skin cancer

C respiratory diseases such as emphysema

D artificial eutrophication, harming aquatic animals

13 Humans use land in many ways. How is an area described if it contains few people, has large areas of open space, and is a mix of natural land, farmland, and parks?

A rural area   **C** natural area

B urban area   **D** industrial area

Critical Thinking

Answer the following questions in the space provided.

14 Can the atmosphere be considered a natural resource? Explain.

_____

_____

Give two examples of how the atmosphere is important to life on Earth.

_____

_____

15 The picture below is of a dam built on a river.

How does a dam affect the surrounding landscape behind and in front of the dam?

_____

_____

How does a dam affect the fish that live and breed in that river?

_____

Connect **ESSENTIAL QUESTIONS**
Lessons 1 and 2

Answer the following question in the space provided.

16 Urbanization has major effects on Earth's land and water. Natural vegetation is removed in order to make room for buildings, roads, and parking lots. How does removing vegetation affect the land?

_____

How do paved parking lots and roads with concrete or asphalt affect water flow on the land?

_____

What are three ways that urban populations can negatively affect water quality?

_____

_____

_____

How can urban populations affect a water supply?

_____

_____

Look It Up!

References

Mineral Properties

Here are five steps to take in mineral identification:

1 Determine the color of the mineral. Is it light-colored, dark-colored, or a specific color?

2 Determine the luster of the mineral. Is it metallic or non-metallic?

3 Determine the color of any powder left by its streak.

4 Determine the hardness of your mineral. Is it soft, hard, or very hard? Using a glass plate, see if the mineral scratches it.

5 Determine whether your sample has cleavage or any special properties.

TERMS TO KNOW	DEFINITION
adamantine	a non-metallic luster like that of a diamond
cleavage	how a mineral breaks when subject to stress on a particular plane
luster	the state or quality of shining by reflecting light
streak	the color of a mineral when it is powdered
submetallic	between metallic and nonmetallic in luster
vitreous	glass-like type of luster

Silicate Minerals					
Mineral	Color	Luster	Streak	Hardness	Cleavage and Special Properties
Beryl	deep green, pink, white, bluish green, or yellow	vitreous	white	7.5–8	1 cleavage direction; some varieties fluoresce in ultraviolet light
Chlorite	green	vitreous to pearly	pale green	2–2.5	1 cleavage direction
Garnet	green, red, brown, black	vitreous	white	6.5–7.5	no cleavage
Hornblende	dark green, brown, or black	vitreous	none	5–6	2 cleavage directions
Muscovite	colorless, silvery white, or brown	vitreous or pearly	white	2–2.5	1 cleavage direction
Olivine	olive green, yellow	vitreous	white or none	6.5–7	no cleavage
Orthoclase	colorless, white, pink, or other colors	vitreous	white or none	6	2 cleavage directions
Plagioclase	colorless, white, yellow, pink, green	vitreous	white	6	2 cleavage directions
Quartz	colorless or white; any color when not pure	vitreous or waxy	white or none	7	no cleavage

Nonsilicate Minerals					
Mineral	**Color**	**Luster**	**Streak**	**Hardness**	**Cleavage and Special Properties**
Native Elements					
Copper	copper-red	metallic	copper-red	2.5–3	no cleavage
Diamond	pale yellow or colorless	adamantine	none	10	4 cleavage directions
Graphite	black to gray	submetallic	black	1–2	1 cleavage direction
Carbonates					
Aragonite	colorless, white, or pale yellow	vitreous	white	3.5–4	2 cleavage directions; reacts with hydrochloric acid
Calcite	colorless or white to tan	vitreous	white	3	3 cleavage directions; reacts with weak acid; double refraction
Halides					
Fluorite	light green, yellow, purple, bluish green, or other colors	vitreous	none	4	4 cleavage directions; some varieties fluoresce
Halite	white	vitreous	white	2.0–2.5	3 cleavage directions
Oxides					
Hematite	reddish brown to black	metallic to earthy	dark red to red-brown	5.6–6.5	no cleavage; magnetic when heated
Magnetite	iron-black	metallic	black	5.5–6.5	no cleavage; magnetic
Sulfates					
Anhydrite	colorless, bluish, or violet	vitreous to pearly	white	3–3.5	3 cleavage directions
Gypsum	white, pink, gray, or colorless	vitreous, pearly, or silky	white	2.0	3 cleavage directions
Sulfides					
Galena	lead-gray	metallic	lead-gray to black	2.5–2.8	3 cleavage directions
Pyrite	brassy yellow	metallic	greenish, brownish, or black	6–6.5	no cleavage

© Houghton Mifflin Harcourt Publishing Company

References

Geologic Time Scale

Geologists developed the geologic time scale to represent the 4.6 billion years of Earth's history that have passed since Earth formed. This scale divides Earth's history into blocks of time. The boundaries between these time intervals (shown in millions of years ago or mya in the table below), represent major changes in Earth's history. Some boundaries are defined by mass extinctions, major changes in Earth's surface, and/or major changes in Earth's climate.

The four major divisions that encompass the history of life on Earth are Precambrian time, the Paleozoic era, the Mesozoic era, and the Cenozoic era. The largest divisions are eons. **Precambrian time** is made up of the first three eons, over 4 billion years of Earth's history.

The **Paleozoic era** lasted from 542 mya to 251 mya. All major plant groups, except flowering plants, appeared during this era. By the end of the era, reptiles, winged insects, and fishes had also appeared. The largest known mass extinction occurred at the end of this era.

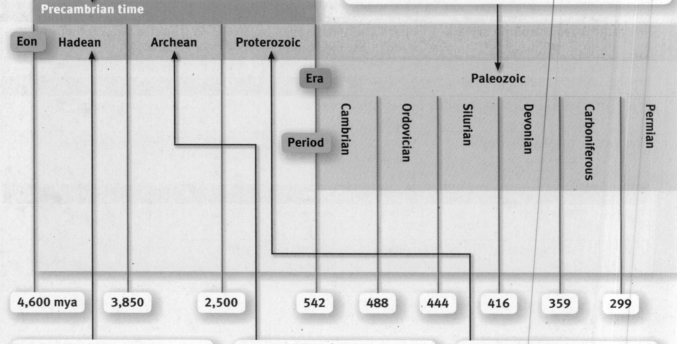

The **Hadean eon** lasted from about 4.6 billion years ago (bya) to 3.85 bya. It is described based on evidence from meterorites and rocks from the moon.

The **Archean eon** lasted from 3.85 bya to 2.5 bya. The earliest rocks from Earth that have been found and dated formed at the start of this eon.

The **Proterozoic eon** lasted from 2.5 bya to 542 mya. The first organisms, which were single-celled organisms, appeared during this eon. These organisms produced so much oxygen that they changed Earth's oceans and Earth's atmosphere.

Houghton Mifflin Harcourt Publishing Company

Divisions of Time

The divisions of time shown here represent major changes in Earth's surface and when life developed and changed significantly on Earth. As new evidence is found, the boundaries of these divisions may shift. The Phanerozoic eon is divided into three eras. The beginning of each of these eras represents a change in the types of organisms that dominated Earth. And, each era is commonly characterized by the types of organisms that dominated the era. These eras are divided into periods, and periods are divided into epochs.

The **Mesozoic era** lasted from 251 mya to 65.5 mya. During this era, many kinds of dinosaurs dominated land, and giant lizards swam in the ocean. The first birds, mammals, and flowering plants also appeared during this time. About two-thirds of all land species went extinct at the end of this era.

The **Phanerozoic eon** began 542 mya. We live in this eon.

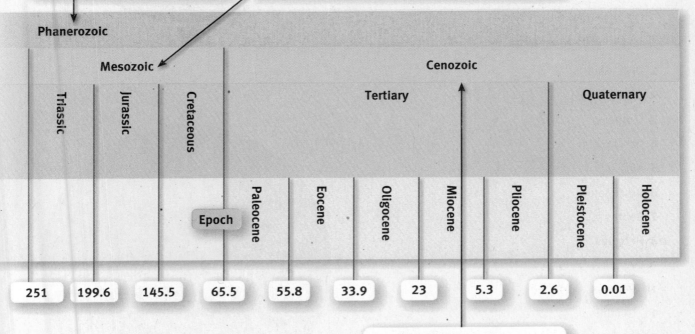

The **Cenozoic era** began 65.5 mya and continues today. Mammals dominate this era. During the Mesozoic era, mammals were small in size but grew much larger during the Cenozoic era. Primates, including humans, appeared during this era.

References

Star Charts for the Northern Hemisphere

A star chart is a map of the stars in the night sky. It shows the names and positions of constellations and major stars. Star charts can be used to identify constellations and even to orient yourself using Polaris, the North Star.

Because Earth moves through space, different constellations are visible at different times of the year. The star charts on these pages show the constellations visible during each season in the Northern Hemisphere.

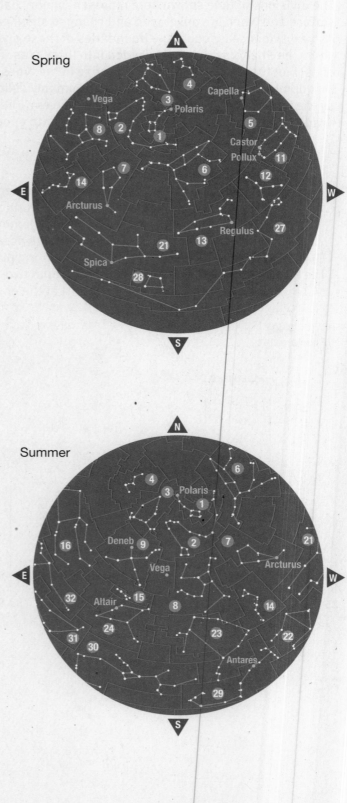

Constellations

1 Ursa Minor

2 Draco

3 Cepheus

4 Cassiopeia

5 Auriga

6 Ursa Major

7 Boötes

8 Hercules

9 Cygnus

10 Perseus

11 Gemini

12 Cancer

13 Leo

14 Serpens

15 Sagitta

16 Pegasus

17 Pisces

Houghton Mifflin Harcourt Publishing Company

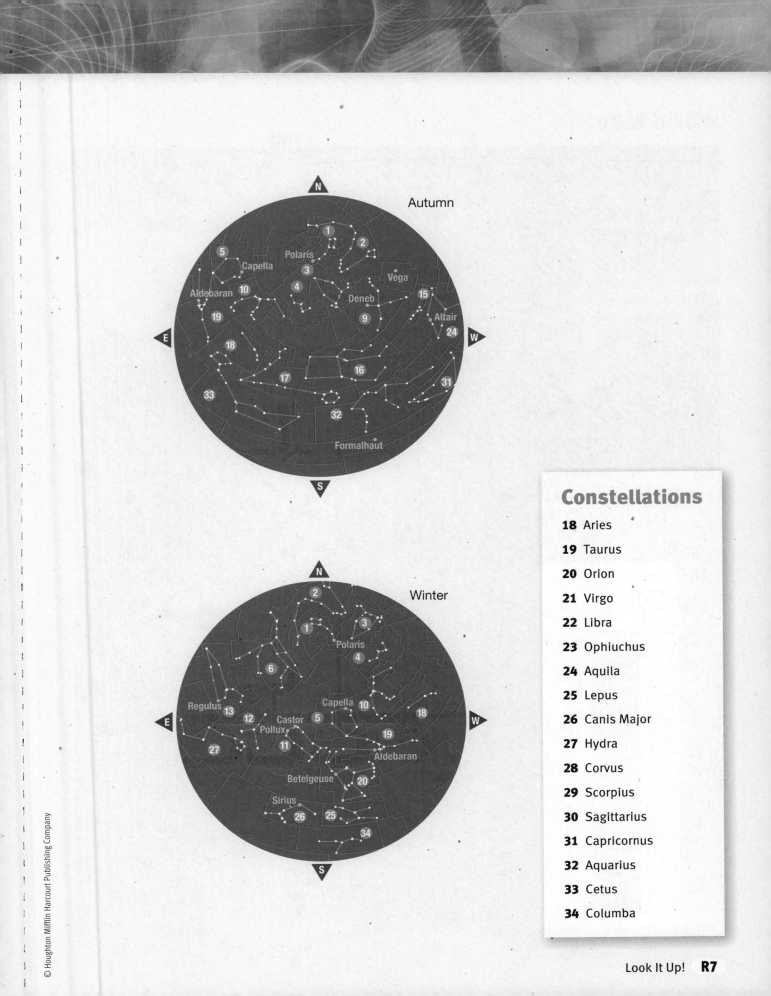

Autumn

Winter

Constellations

18 Aries

19 Taurus

20 Orion

21 Virgo

22 Libra

23 Ophiuchus

24 Aquila

25 Lepus

26 Canis Major

27 Hydra

28 Corvus

29 Scorpius

30 Sagittarius

31 Capricornus

32 Aquarius

33 Cetus

34 Columba

World Map

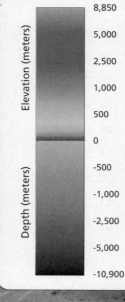

LEGEND

Boundary

 Tectonic plate boundary

Elevation and Depth

Elevation (meters)
- 8,850
- 5,000
- 2,500
- 1,000
- 500
- 0

Depth (meters)
- -500
- -1,000
- -2,500
- -5,000
- -10,900

References

Classification of Living Things

Domains and Kingdoms

All organisms belong to one of three domains: Domain Archaea, Domain Bacteria, or Domain Eukarya. Some of the groups within these domains are shown below. (Remember that genus names are italicized.)

Domain Archaea

The organisms in this domain are single-celled prokaryotes, many of which live in extreme environments.

Archaea			
Group	**Example**	**Characteristics**	
Methanogens	*Methanococcus*	produce methane gas; can't live in oxygen	
Thermophiles	*Sulpholobus*	require sulphur; can't live in oxygen	
Halophiles	*Halococcus*	live in very salty environments; most can live in oxygen	

Domain Bacteria

Organisms in this domain are single-celled prokaryotes and are found in almost every environment on Earth.

Bacteria		
Group	**Example**	**Characteristics**
Bacilli	*Escherichia*	rod shaped; some bacilli fix nitrogen; some cause disease
Cocci	*Streptococcus*	spherical shaped; some cause disease; can form spores
Spirilla	*Treponema*	spiral shaped; cause diseases such as syphilis and Lyme disease

Domain Eukarya

Organisms in this domain are single-celled or multicellular eukaryotes.

Kingdom Protista Many protists resemble fungi, plants, or animals, but are smaller and simpler in structure. Most are single celled.

Protists			
Group	**Example**	**Characteristics**	
Sarcodines	*Amoeba*	radiolarians; single-celled consumers	
Ciliates	*Paramecium*	single-celled consumers	
Flagellates	*Trypanosoma*	single-celled parasites	
Sporozoans	*Plasmodium*	single-celled parasites	
Euglenas	*Euglena*	single celled; photosynthesize	
Diatoms	*Pinnularia*	most are single celled; photosynthesize	
Dinoflagellates	*Gymnodinium*	single celled; some photosynthesize	
Algae	*Volvox*	single celled or multicellular; photosynthesize	
Slime molds	*Physarum*	single celled or multicellular; consumers or decomposers	
Water molds	powdery mildew	single celled or multicellular; parasites or decomposers	

Kingdom Fungi Most fungi are multicellular. Their cells have thick cell walls. Fungi absorb food from their environment.

Fungi		
Group	**Examples**	**Characteristics**
Threadlike fungi	bread mold	spherical; decomposers
Sac fungi	yeast; morels	saclike; parasites and decomposers
Club fungi	mushrooms; rusts; smuts	club shaped; parasites and decomposers
Lichens	British soldier	a partnership between a fungus and an alga

Kingdom Plantae Plants are multicellular and have cell walls made of cellulose. Plants make their own food through photosynthesis. Plants are classified into divisions instead of phyla.

Plants		
Group	**Examples**	**Characteristics**
Bryophytes	mosses; liverworts	no vascular tissue; reproduce by spores
Club mosses	*Lycopodium;* ground pine	grow in wooded areas; reproduce by spores
Horsetails	rushes	grow in wetland areas; reproduce by spores
Ferns	spleenworts; sensitive fern	large leaves called fronds; reproduce by spores
Conifers	pines; spruces; firs	needlelike leaves; reproduce by seeds made in cones
Cycads	*Zamia*	slow growing; reproduce by seeds made in large cones
Gnetophytes	*Welwitschia*	only three living families; reproduce by seeds
Ginkgoes	*Ginkgo*	only one living species; reproduce by seeds
Angiosperms	all flowering plants	reproduce by seeds made in flowers; fruit

Kingdom Animalia Animals are multicellular. Their cells do not have cell walls. Most animals have specialized tissues and complex organ systems. Animals get food by eating other organisms.

Animals		
Group	**Examples**	**Characteristics**
Sponges	glass sponges	no symmetry or specialized tissues; aquatic
Cnidarians	jellyfish; coral	radial symmetry; aquatic
Flatworms	planaria; tapeworms; flukes	bilateral symmetry; organ systems
Roundworms	*Trichina;* hookworms	bilateral symmetry; organ systems
Annelids	earthworms; leeches	bilateral symmetry; organ systems
Mollusks	snails; octopuses	bilateral symmetry; organ systems
Echinoderms	sea stars; sand dollars	radial symmetry; organ systems
Arthropods	insects; spiders; lobsters	bilateral symmetry; organ systems
Chordates	fish; amphibians; reptiles; birds; mammals	bilateral symmetry; complex organ systems

References

Periodic Table of the Elements

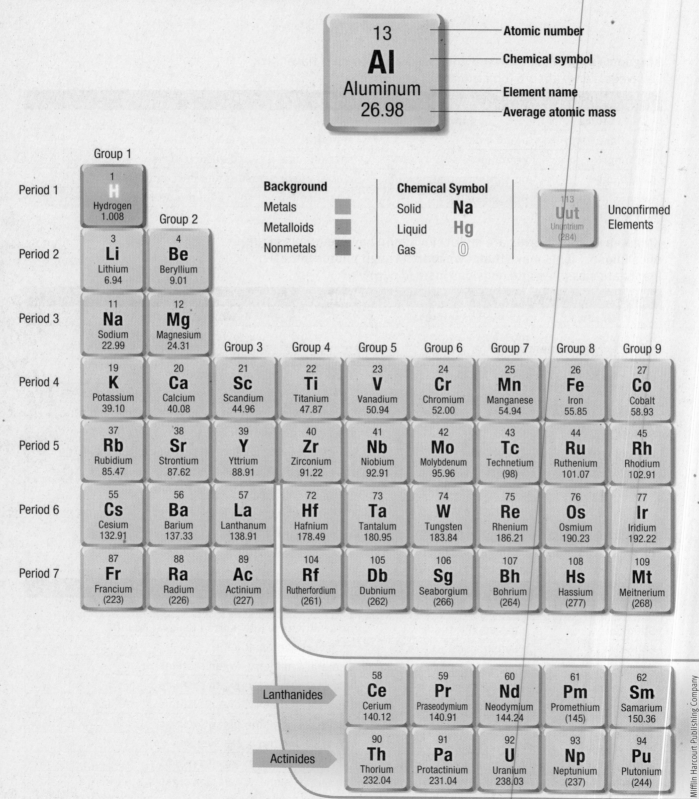

Atomic number — 13
Chemical symbol — Al
Element name — Aluminum
Average atomic mass — 26.98

Background		Chemical Symbol	
Metals		Solid	Na
Metalloids		Liquid	Hg
Nonmetals		Gas	Ⓞ

113 Uut Ununtrium (284) — Unconfirmed Elements

	Group 1	Group 2	Group 3	Group 4	Group 5	Group 6	Group 7	Group 8	Group 9
Period 1	1 **H** Hydrogen 1.008								
Period 2	3 **Li** Lithium 6.94	4 **Be** Beryllium 9.01							
Period 3	11 **Na** Sodium 22.99	12 **Mg** Magnesium 24.31							
Period 4	19 **K** Potassium 39.10	20 **Ca** Calcium 40.08	21 **Sc** Scandium 44.96	22 **Ti** Titanium 47.87	23 **V** Vanadium 50.94	24 **Cr** Chromium 52.00	25 **Mn** Manganese 54.94	26 **Fe** Iron 55.85	27 **Co** Cobalt 58.93
Period 5	37 **Rb** Rubidium 85.47	38 **Sr** Strontium 87.62	39 **Y** Yttrium 88.91	40 **Zr** Zirconium 91.22	41 **Nb** Niobium 92.91	42 **Mo** Molybdenum 95.96	43 **Tc** Technetium (98)	44 **Ru** Ruthenium 101.07	45 **Rh** Rhodium 102.91
Period 6	55 **Cs** Cesium 132.91	56 **Ba** Barium 137.33	57 **La** Lanthanum 138.91	72 **Hf** Hafnium 178.49	73 **Ta** Tantalum 180.95	74 **W** Tungsten 183.84	75 **Re** Rhenium 186.21	76 **Os** Osmium 190.23	77 **Ir** Iridium 192.22
Period 7	87 **Fr** Francium (223)	88 **Ra** Radium (226)	89 **Ac** Actinium (227)	104 **Rf** Rutherfordium (261)	105 **Db** Dubnium (262)	106 **Sg** Seaborgium (266)	107 **Bh** Bohrium (264)	108 **Hs** Hassium (277)	109 **Mt** Meitnerium (268)

Lanthanides

58 **Ce** Cerium 140.12	59 **Pr** Praseodymium 140.91	60 **Nd** Neodymium 144.24	61 **Pm** Promethium (145)	62 **Sm** Samarium 150.36

Actinides

90 **Th** Thorium 232.04	91 **Pa** Protactinium 231.04	92 **U** Uranium 238.03	93 **Np** Neptunium (237)	94 **Pu** Plutonium (244)

Houghton Mifflin Harcourt Publishing Company

The International Union of Pure and Applied Chemistry (IUPAC) has determined that, because of isotopic variance, the average atomic mass is best represented by a range of values for each of the following elements: hydrogen, lithium, boron, carbon, nitrogen, oxygen, silicon, sulfur, chlorine, and thallium. However, the values in this table are appropriate for everyday calculations.

			Group 13	Group 14	Group 15	Group 16	Group 17	Group 18
								2 **He** Helium 4.003
			5 **B** Boron 10.81	6 **C** Carbon 12.01	7 **N** Nitrogen 14.01	8 **O** Oxygen 16.00	9 **F** Fluorine 19.00	10 **Ne** Neon 20.18
Group 10	Group 11	Group 12	13 **Al** Aluminum 26.98	14 **Si** Silicon 28.09	15 **P** Phosphorus 30.97	16 **S** Sulfur 32.06	17 **Cl** Chlorine 35.45	18 **Ar** Argon 39.95
28 **Ni** Nickel 58.69	29 **Cu** Copper 63.55	30 **Zn** Zinc 65.38	31 **Ga** Gallium 69.72	32 **Ge** Germanium 72.63	33 **As** Arsenic 74.92	34 **Se** Selenium 78.96	35 **Br** Bromine 79.90	36 **Kr** Krypton 83.80
46 **Pd** Palladium 106.42	47 **Ag** Silver 107.87	48 **Cd** Cadmium 112.41	49 **In** Indium 114.82	50 **Sn** Tin 118.71	51 **Sb** Antimony 121.76	52 **Te** Tellurium 127.60	53 **I** Iodine 126.90	54 **Xe** Xenon 131.29
78 **Pt** Platinum 195.08	79 **Au** Gold 196.97	80 **Hg** Mercury 200.59	81 **Tl** Thallium 204.38	82 **Pb** Lead 207.2	83 **Bi** Bismuth 208.98	84 **Po** Polonium (209)	85 **At** Astatine (210)	86 **Rn** Radon (222)
110 **Ds** Darmstadtium (271)	111 **Rg** Roentgenium (272)	112 **Cn** Copernicium (285)	113 **Uut** Ununtrium (284)	114 **Uuq** Ununquadium (289)	115 **Uup** Ununpentium (288)	116 **Uuh** Ununhexium (292)	117 **Uus** Ununseptium (294)	118 **Uuo** Ununoctium (294)

63 **Eu** Europium 151.96	64 **Gd** Gadolinium 157.25	65 **Tb** Terbium 158.93	66 **Dy** Dysprosium 162.50	67 **Ho** Holmium 164.93	68 **Er** Erbium 167.26	69 **Tm** Thulium 168.93	70 **Yb** Ytterbium 173.05	71 **Lu** Lutetium 174.97
95 **Am** Americium (243)	96 **Cm** Curium (247)	97 **Bk** Berkelium (247)	98 **Cf** Californium (251)	99 **Es** Einsteinium (252)	100 **Fm** Fermium (257)	101 **Md** Mendelevium (258)	102 **No** Nobelium (259)	103 **Lr** Lawrencium (262)

Physical Science Refresher

Atoms and Elements

Every object in the universe is made of matter. **Matter** is anything that takes up space and has mass. All matter is made of atoms. An **atom** is the smallest particle into which an element can be divided and still be the same element. An **element**, in turn, is a substance that cannot be broken down into simpler substances by chemical means. Each element consists of only one kind of atom. An element may be made of many atoms, but they are all the same kind of atom.

Atomic Structure

Atoms are made of smaller particles called **electrons, protons**, and **neutrons**. Electrons have a negative electric charge, protons have a positive charge, and neutrons have no electric charge. Together, protons and neutrons form the **nucleus**, or small dense center, of an atom. Because protons are positively charged and neutrons are neutral, the nucleus has a positive charge. Electrons move within an area around the nucleus called the **electron cloud**. Electrons move so quickly that scientists cannot determine their exact speeds and positions at the same time.

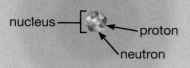

electron cloud

nucleus — proton

neutron

Atomic Number

To help distinguish one element from another, scientists use the atomic numbers of atoms. The **atomic number** is the number of protons in the nucleus of an atom. The atoms of a certain element always have the same number of protons.

When atoms have an equal number of protons and electrons, they are uncharged, or electrically neutral. The atomic number equals the number of electrons in an uncharged atom. The number of neutrons, however, can vary for a given element. Atoms of the same element that have different numbers of neutrons are called **isotopes**.

Periodic Table of the Elements

In the periodic table, each element in the table is in a separate box. And the elements are arranged from left to right in order of increasing atomic number. That is, an uncharged atom of each element has one more electron and one more proton than an uncharged atom of the element to its left. Each horizontal row of the table is called a **period**. Changes in chemical properties of elements across a period correspond to changes in the electron arrangements of their atoms.

Each vertical column of the table is known as a **group.** A group lists elements with similar physical and chemical properties. For this reason, a group is also sometimes called a family. The elements in a group have similar properties because their atoms have the same number of electrons in their outer energy level. For example, the elements helium, neon, argon, krypton, xenon, and radon all have similar properties and are known as the noble gases.

Molecules and Compounds

When two or more elements join chemically, they form a **compound**. A compound is a new substance with properties different from those of the elements that compose it. For example, water, H_2O, is a compound formed when hydrogen (H) and oxygen (O) combine. The smallest complete unit of a compound that has the properties of that compound is called a **molecule**. A chemical formula indicates the elements in a compound. It also indicates the relative number of atoms of each element in the compound. The chemical formula for water is H_2O. So, each water molecule consists of two atoms of hydrogen and one atom of oxygen. The subscript number after the symbol for an element shows how many atoms of that element are in a single molecule of the compound.

Chemical Equations

A chemical reaction occurs when a chemical change takes place. A chemical equation describes a chemical reaction using chemical formulas. The equation indicates the substances that react and the substances that are produced. For example, when carbon and oxygen combine, they can form carbon dioxide, shown in the equation below: $C + O_2 \longrightarrow CO_2$

Acids, Bases, and pH

An **ion** is an atom or group of chemically bonded atoms that has an electric charge because it has lost or gained one or more electrons. When an acid, such as hydrochloric acid, HCl, is mixed with water, it separates into ions. An **acid** is a compound that produces hydrogen ions, H^+, in water. The hydrogen ions then combine with a water molecule to form a hydronium ion, H_3O^+. A **base**, on the other hand, is a substance that produces hydroxide ions, OH^-, in water.

To determine whether a solution is acidic or basic, scientists use pH. The **pH** of a solution is a measure of the hydronium ion concentration in a solution. The pH scale ranges from 0 to 14. Acids have a pH that is less than 7. The lower the number, the more acidic the solution. The middle point, pH = 7, is neutral, neither acidic nor basic. Bases have a pH that is greater than 7. The higher the number is, the more basic the solution.

The pH of Some Common Materials

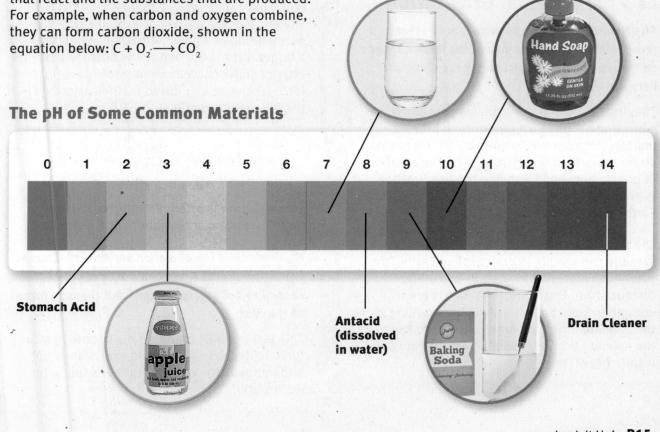

0 1 2 3 4 5 6 7 8 9 10 11 12 13 14

Stomach Acid

apple juice

Antacid (dissolved in water)

Baking Soda

Hand Soap

Drain Cleaner

References

Physical Laws and Useful Equations

Law of Conservation of Mass

Mass cannot be created or destroyed during ordinary chemical or physical changes.

The total mass in a closed system is always the same no matter how many physical changes or chemical reactions occur.

Law of Conservation of Energy

Energy can be neither created nor destroyed.

The total amount of energy in a closed system is always the same. Energy can be changed from one form to another, but all of the different forms of energy in a system always add up to the same total amount of energy, no matter how many energy conversions occur.

Law of Universal Gravitation

All objects in the universe attract each other by a force called gravity. The size of the force depends on the masses of the objects and the distance between the objects.

The first part of the law explains why lifting a bowling ball is much harder than lifting a marble. Because the bowling ball has a much larger mass than the marble does, the amount of gravity between Earth and the bowling ball is greater than the amount of gravity between Earth and the marble.

The second part of the law explains why a satellite can remain in orbit around Earth. The satellite is placed at a carefully calculated distance from Earth. This distance is great enough to keep Earth's gravity from pulling the satellite down, yet small enough to keep the satellite from escaping Earth's gravity and wandering off into space.

Newton's Laws of Motion

Newton's first law of motion states that an object at rest remains at rest, and an object in motion remains in motion at constant speed and in a straight line unless acted on by an unbalanced force.

The first part of the law explains why a football will remain on a tee until it is kicked off or until a gust of wind blows it off. The second part of the law explains why a bike rider will continue moving forward after the bike comes to an abrupt stop. Gravity and the friction of the sidewalk will eventually stop the rider.

Newton's second law of motion states that the acceleration of an object depends on the mass of the object and the amount of force applied.

The first part of the law explains why the acceleration of a 4 kg bowling ball will be greater than the acceleration of a 6 kg bowling ball if the same force is applied to both balls. The second part of the law explains why the acceleration of a bowling ball will be greater if a larger force is applied to the bowling ball. The relationship of acceleration (a) to mass (m) and force (F) can be expressed mathematically by the following equation:

$$acceleration = \frac{force}{mass}, \text{ or } a = \frac{F}{m}$$

This equation is often rearranged to read $force = mass \times acceleration$, or $F = m \times a$

Newton's third law of motion states that whenever one object exerts a force on a second object, the second object exerts an equal and opposite force on the first.

This law explains that a runner is able to move forward because the ground exerts an equal and opposite force on the runner's foot after each step.

Average speed

$$\text{average speed} = \frac{\text{total distance}}{\text{total time}}$$

Example:
A bicycle messenger traveled a distance of 136 km in 8 h. What was the messenger's average speed?

$$\frac{136 \text{ km}}{8 \text{ h}} = 17 \text{ km/h}$$

The messenger's average speed was **17 km/h**.

Average acceleration

$$\text{average acceleration} = \frac{\text{final velocity} - \text{starting velocity}}{\text{time it takes to change velocity}}$$

Example:
Calculate the average acceleration of an Olympic 100 m dash sprinter who reached a velocity of 20 m/s south at the finish line. The race was in a straight line and lasted 10 s.

$$\frac{20 \text{ m/s} - 0 \text{ m/s}}{10 \text{ s}} = 2 \text{ m/s/s}$$

The sprinter's average acceleration was **2 m/s/s south**.

Pressure

Pressure is the force exerted over a given area. The SI unit for pressure is the pascal. Its symbol is Pa.

$$\text{pressure} = \frac{\text{force}}{\text{area}}$$

Net force
Forces in the Same Direction

When forces are in the same direction, add the forces together to determine the net force.

Example:
Calculate the net force on a stalled car that is being pushed by two people. One person is pushing with a force of 13 N northwest, and the other person is pushing with a force of 8 N in the same direction.

$$13 \text{ N} + 8 \text{ N} = 21 \text{ N}$$

The net force is **21 N northwest**.

Forces in Opposite Directions

When forces are in opposite directions, subtract the smaller force from the larger force to determine the net force. The net force will be in the direction of the larger force.

Example:
Calculate the net force on a rope that is being pulled on each end. One person is pulling on one end of the rope with a force of 12 N south. Another person is pulling on the opposite end of the rope with a force of 7 N north.

$$12 \text{ N} - 7 \text{ N} = 5 \text{ N}$$

The net force is **5 N south**.

Example:
Calculate the pressure of the air in a soccer ball if the air exerts a force of 10 N over an area of 0.5 m².

$$\text{pressure} = \frac{10 \text{ N}}{0.5 \text{ m}^2} = \frac{20 \text{ N}}{\text{m}^2} = 20 \text{ Pa}$$

The pressure of the air inside the soccer ball is **20 Pa**.

Reading and Study Skills

A How-To Manual for Active Reading

This book belongs to you, and you are invited to write in it. In fact, the book won't be complete until you do. Sometimes you'll answer a question or follow directions to mark up the text. Other times you'll write down your own thoughts. And when you're done reading and writing in the book, the book will be ready to help you review what you learned and prepare for tests.

Active Reading Annotations

Before you read, you'll often come upon an Active Reading prompt that asks you to underline certain words or number the steps in a process. Here's an example.

Active Reading

12 Identify In this paragraph, number the sequence of sentences that describe replication.

Marking the text this way is called **annotating,** and your marks are called **annotations.** Annotating the text can help you identify important concepts while you read.

There are other ways that you can annotate the text. You can draw an asterisk (*) by vocabulary terms, mark unfamiliar or confusing terms and information with a question mark (?), and mark main ideas with a double underline. And you can even invent your own marks to annotate the text!

Other Annotating Opportunities

Keep your pencil, pen, or highlighter nearby as you read, so you can make a note or highlight an important point at any time. Here are a few ideas to get you started.

- Notice the headings in red and blue. The blue headings are questions that point to the main idea of what you're reading. The red headings are answers to the questions in the blue ones. Together these headings outline the content of the lesson. After reading a lesson, you could write your own answers to the questions.

- Notice the bold-faced words that are highlighted in yellow. They are highlighted so that you can easily find them again on the page where they are defined. As you read or as you review, challenge yourself to write your own sentence using the bold-faced term.

- Make a note in the margin at any time. You might
  - Ask a "What if" question
  - Comment on what you read
  - Make a connection to something you read elsewhere
  - Make a logical conclusion from the text

Use your own language and abbreviations. Invent a code, such as using circles and boxes around words to remind you of their importance or relation to each other. Your annotations will help you remember your questions for class discussions, and when you go back to the lesson later, you may be able to fill in what you didn't understand the first time you read it. Like a scientist in the field or in a lab, you will be recording your questions and observations for analysis later.

Active Reading Questions

After you read, you'll often come upon Active Reading questions that ask you to think about what you've just read. You'll write your answer underneath the question. Here's an example.

Active Reading

8 Describe Where are phosphate groups found in a DNA molecule?

_____

_____

This type of question helps you sum up what you've just read and pull out the most important ideas from the passage. In this case the question asks you to **describe** the structure of a DNA molecule that you have just read about. Other times you may be asked to do such things as **apply** a concept, **compare** two concepts, **summarize** a process, or **identify a cause-and-effect** relationship. You'll be strengthening those critical thinking skills that you'll use often in learning about science.

Reading and Study Skills

Using Graphic Organizers to Take Notes

Graphic organizers help you remember information as you read it for the first time and as you study it later. There are dozens of graphic organizers to choose from, so the first trick is to choose the one that's best suited to your purpose. Following are some graphic organizers to use for different purposes.

To remember lots of information	To relate a central idea to subordinate details	To describe a process	To make a comparison
• Arrange data in a Content Frame • Use Combination Notes to describe a concept in words and pictures	• Show relationships with a Mind Map or a Main Idea Web • Sum up relationships among many things with a Concept Map	• Use a Process Diagram to explain a procedure • Show a chain of events and results in a Cause-and-Effect Chart	• Compare two or more closely related things in a Venn Diagram

Content Frame

1 Make a four-column chart.

2 Fill the first column with categories (e.g., snail, ant, earthworm) and the first row with descriptive information (e.g., group, characteristic, appearance).

3 Fill the chart with details that belong in each row and column.

4 When you finish, you'll have a study aid that helps you compare one category to another.

Invertebrates

NAME	GROUP	CHARACTERISTICS	DRAWING
snail	mollusks	mangle	
ant	arthropods	six legs, exoskeleton	
earthworm	segmented worms	segmented body, circulatory and digestive systems	
heartworm	roundworms	digestive system	
sea star	echinoderms	spiny skin, tube feet	
jellyfish	cnidarians	stinging cells	

Combination Notes

1 Make a two-column chart.

2 Write descriptive words and definitions in the first column.

3 Draw a simple sketch that helps you remember the meaning of the term in the second column.

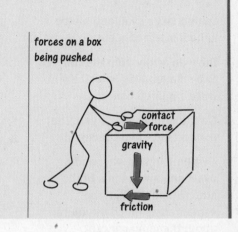

NOTES

Types of Forces
• contact force
• gravity
• friction

forces on a box being pushed

Mind Map

1 Draw an oval, and inside it write a topic to analyze.

2 Draw two or more arms extending from the oval. Each arm represents a main idea about the topic.

3 Draw lines from the arms on which to write details about each of the main ideas.

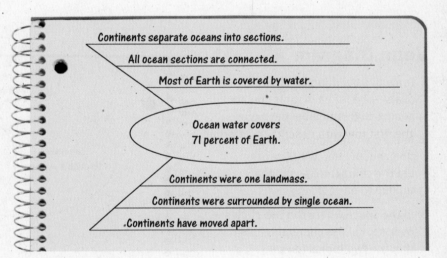

Continents separate oceans into sections.

All ocean sections are connected.

Most of Earth is covered by water.

Ocean water covers 71 percent of Earth.

Continents were one landmass.

Continents were surrounded by single ocean.

Continents have moved apart.

Main Idea Web

1 Make a box and write a concept you want to remember inside it.

2 Draw boxes around the central box, and label each one with a category of information about the concept (e.g., definition, formula, descriptive details).

3 Fill in the boxes with relevant details as you read.

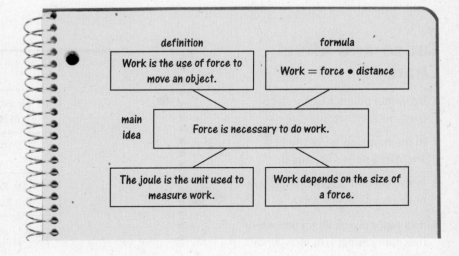

definition

Work is the use of force to move an object.

formula

Work = force • distance

main idea

Force is necessary to do work.

The joule is the unit used to measure work.

Work depends on the size of a force.

Reading and Study Skills

Concept Map

1 Draw a large oval, and inside it write a major concept.

2 Draw an arrow from the concept to a smaller oval, in which you write a related concept.

3 On the arrow, write a verb that connects the two concepts.

4 Continue in this way, adding ovals and arrows in a branching structure, until you have explained as much as you can about the main concept.

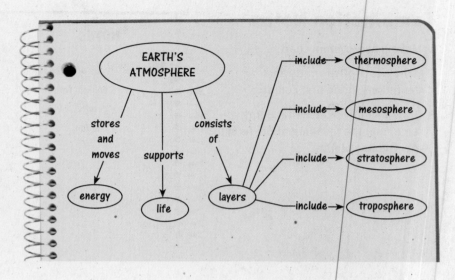

Venn Diagram

1 Draw two overlapping circles or ovals—one for each topic you are comparing—and label each one.

2 In the part of each circle that does not overlap with the other, list the characteristics that are unique to each topic.

3 In the space where the two circles overlap, list the characteristics that the two topics have in common.

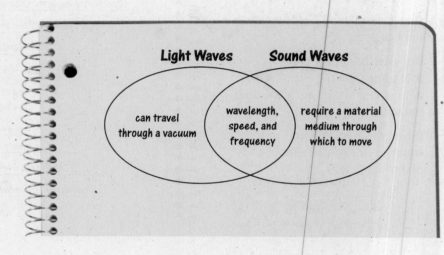

Cause-and-Effect Chart

1 Draw two boxes and connect them with an arrow.

2 In the first box, write the first event in a series (a cause).

3 In the second box, write a result of the cause (the effect).

4 Add more boxes when one event has many effects, or vice versa.

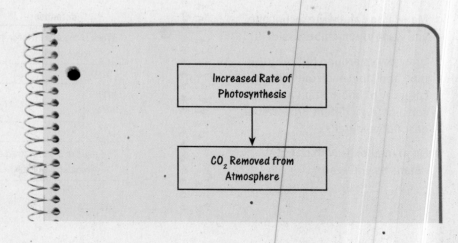

Process Diagram

A process can be a never-ending cycle. As you can see in this technology design process, engineers may backtrack and repeat steps, they may skip steps entirely, or they may repeat the entire process before a useable design is achieved.

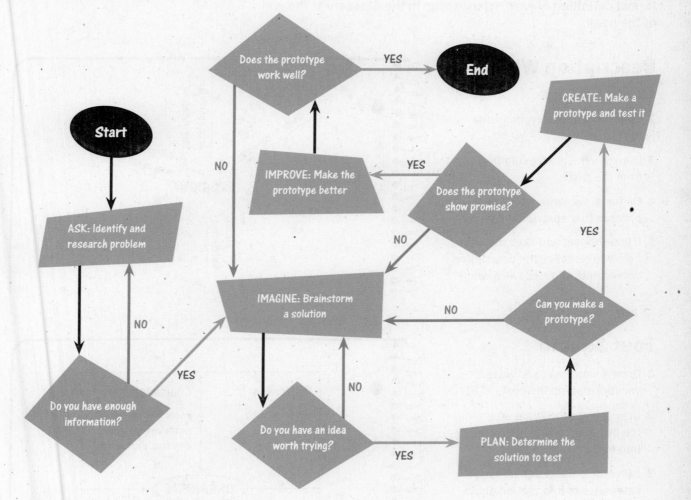

Reading and Study Skills

Using Vocabulary Strategies

Important science terms are highlighted where they are first defined in this book. One way to remember these terms is to take notes and make sketches when you come to them. Use the strategies on this page and the next for this purpose. You will also find a formal definition of each science term in the Glossary at the end of the book.

Description Wheel

1 Draw a small circle.

2 Write a vocabulary term inside the circle.

3 Draw several arms extending from the circle.

4 On the arms, write words and phrases that describe the term.

5 If you choose, add sketches that help you visualize the descriptive details or the concept as a whole.

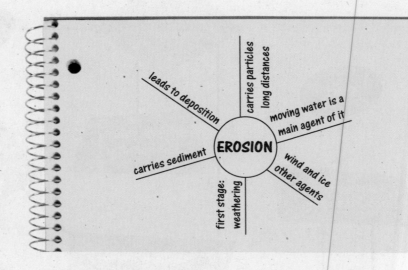

Four Square

1 Draw a small oval and write a vocabulary term inside it.

2 Draw a large rectangle around the oval, and divide the rectangle into four smaller squares.

3 Label the smaller squares with categories of information about the term, such as: definition, characteristics, examples, non-examples, appearance, and root words.

4 Fill the squares with descriptive words and drawings that will help you remember the overall meaning of the term and its essential details.

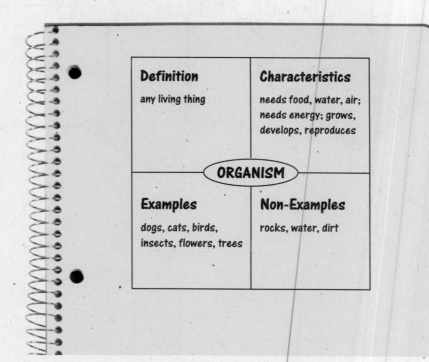

Frame Game

1 Draw a small rectangle, and write a vocabulary term inside it.

2 Draw a larger rectangle around the smaller one. Connect the corners of the larger rectangle to the corners of the smaller one, creating four spaces that frame the word.

3 In each of the four parts of the frame, draw or write details that help define the term. Consider including a definition, essential characteristics, an equation, examples, and a sentence using the term.

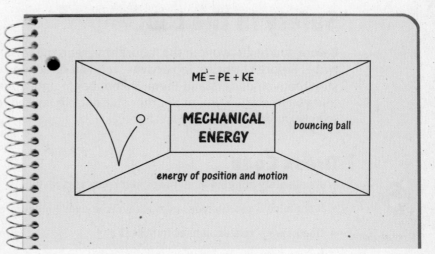

Magnet Word

1 Draw horseshoe magnet, and write a vocabulary term inside it.

2 Add lines that extend from the sides of the magnet.

3 Brainstorm words and phrases that come to mind when you think about the term.

4 On the lines, write the words and phrases that describe something essential about the term.

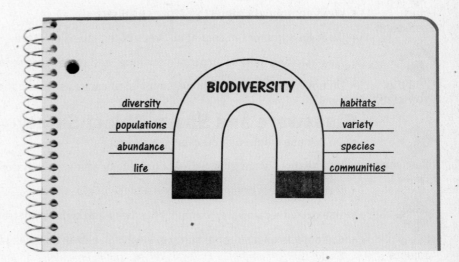

Word Triangle

1 Draw a triangle, and add lines to divide it into three parts.

2 Write a term and its definition in the bottom section of the triangle.

3 In the middle section, write a sentence in which the term is used correctly.

4 In the top section, draw a small picture to illustrate the term.

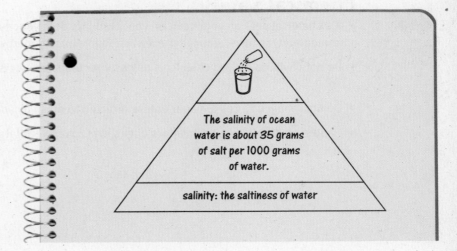

Science Skills

Safety in the Lab

Before you begin work in the laboratory, read these safety rules twice. Before starting a lab activity, read all directions and make sure that you understand them. Do not begin until your teacher has told you to start. If you or another student are injured in any way, tell your teacher immediately.

Dress Code

Eye Protection

- Wear safety goggles at all times in the lab as directed.

- If chemicals get into your eyes, flush your eyes immediately.

- Do not wear contact lenses in the lab.

- Do not look directly at the sun or any intense light source or laser.

Hand Protection

- Do not cut an object while holding the object in your hand.

- Wear appropriate protective gloves as directed.

- Wear an apron or lab coat at all times in the lab as directed.

Clothing Protection

- Tie back long hair, secure loose clothing, and remove loose jewelry.

- Do not wear open-toed shoes, sandals, or canvas shoes in the lab.

Glassware and Sharp Object Safety

Glassware Safety

- Do not use chipped or cracked glassware.

- Use heat-resistant glassware for heating or storing hot materials.

- Notify your teacher immediately if a piece of glass breaks.

Sharp Objects Safety

- Use extreme care when handling all sharp and pointed instruments.

- Cut objects on a suitable surface, always in a direction away from your body.

Chemical Safety

Chemical Safety

- If a chemical gets on your skin, on your clothing, or in your eyes, rinse it immediately (shower, faucet or eyewash fountain) and alert your teacher.

- Do not clean up spilled chemicals unless your teacher directs you to do so.

- Do not inhale any gas or vapor unless directed to do so by your teacher.

- Handle materials that emit vapors or gases in a well-ventilated area.

Electrical Safety

Electrical Safety

- Do not use equipment with frayed electrical cords or loose plugs.
- Do not use electrical equipment near water or when clothing or hands are wet.
- Hold the plug housing when you plug in or unplug equipment.

Heating and Fire Safety

Heating Safety

- Be aware of any source of flames, sparks, or heat (such as flames, heating coils, or hot plates) before working with any flammable substances.
- Know the location of lab fire extinguishers and fire-safety blankets.
- Know your school's fire-evacuation routes.
- If your clothing catches on fire, walk to the lab shower to put out the fire.
- Never leave a hot plate unattended while it is turned on or while it is cooling.
- Use tongs or appropriate insulated holders when handling heated objects.
- Allow all equipment to cool before storing it.

Wafting

Plant and Animal Safety

Plant Safety

Animal Safety

- Do not eat any part of a plant.
- Do not pick any wild plants unless your teacher instructs you to do so.
- Handle animals only as your teacher directs.
- Treat animals carefully and respectfully.
- Wash your hands thoroughly after handling any plant or animal.

Cleanup

Proper Waste Disposal

Hygienic Care

- Clean all work surfaces and protective equipment as directed by your teacher.
- Dispose of hazardous materials or sharp objects only as directed by your teacher.
- Keep your hands away from your face while you are working on any activity.
- Wash your hands thoroughly before you leave the lab or after any activity.

Science Skills

Designing, Conducting, and Reporting an Experiment

An experiment is an organized procedure to study something under specific conditions. Use the following steps of the scientific method when designing or conducting a controlled experiment.

1 Identify a Research Problem

Every day, you make observations by using your senses to gather information. Careful observations lead to good questions, and good questions can lead you to an experiment. Imagine, for example, that you pass a pond every day on your way to school, and you notice green scum beginning to form on top of it. You wonder what it is and why it seems to be growing. You list your questions, and then you do a little research to find out what is already known. A good place to start a research project is at the library. A library catalog lists all of the resources available to you at that library and often those found elsewhere. Begin your search by using:

- keywords or main topics.

- similar words, or synonyms, of your keyword.

The types of resources that will be helpful to you will depend on the kind of information you are interested in. And, some resources are more reliable for a given topic than others. Some different kinds of useful resources are:

- magazines and journals (or periodicals)—articles on a topic.

- encyclopedias—a good overview of a topic.

- books on specific subjects—details about a topic.

- newspapers—useful for current events.

The Internet can also be a great place to find information. Some of your library's reference materials may even be online. When using the Internet, however, it is especially important to make sure you are using appropriate and reliable sources. Websites of universities and government agencies are usually more accurate and reliable than websites created by individuals or businesses. Decide which sources are relevant and reliable for your topic. If in doubt, check with your teacher.

Take notes as you read through the information in these resources. You will probably come up with many questions and ideas for which you can do more research as needed. Once you feel you have enough information, think about the questions you have on the topic. Then, write down the problem that you want to investigate. Your notes might look like these.

Research Questions	Research Problem	Library and Internet Resources
• How do algae grow? • How do people measure algae? • What kind of fertilizer would affect the growth of algae? • Can fertilizer and algae be used safely in a lab? How?	How does fertilizer affect the algae in a pond?	Pond fertilization: initiating an algal bloom – from University of California Davis website. Blue-Green algae in Wisconsin waters-from the Department of Natural Resources of Wisconsin website.

As you gather information from reliable sources, record details about each source, including author name(s), title, date of publication, and/or web address. Make sure to also note the specific information that you use from each source. Staying organized in this way will be important when you write your report and create a bibliography or works cited list. Recording this information and staying organized will help you credit the appropriate author(s) for the information that you have gathered.

Representing someone else's ideas or work as your own, (without giving the original author credit), is known as plagiarism. Plagiarism can be intentional or unintentional. The best way to make sure that you do not commit plagiarism is to always do your own work and to always give credit to others when you use their words or ideas.

Current scientific research is built on scientific research and discoveries that have happened in the past. This means that scientists are constantly learning from each other and combining ideas to learn more about the natural world through investigation. But, a good scientist always credits the ideas and research that they have gathered from other people to those people. There are more details about crediting sources and creating a bibliography under step 9.

2 Make a Prediction

A prediction is a statement of what you expect will happen in your experiment. Before making a prediction, you need to decide in a general way what you will do in your procedure. You may state your prediction in an if-then format.

Prediction

If the amount of fertilizer in the pond water is increased, then the amount of algae will also increase.

© Houghton Mifflin Harcourt Publishing Company

Science Skills

3 Form a Hypothesis

Many experiments are designed to test a hypothesis. A hypothesis is a tentative explanation for an expected result. You have predicted that additional fertilizer will cause additional algae growth in pond water; your hypothesis should state the connection between fertilizer and algal growth.

> **Hypothesis**
>
> The addition of fertilizer to pond water will affect the amount of algae in the pond.

4 Identify Variables to Test the Hypothesis

The next step is to design an experiment to test the hypothesis. The experimental results may or may not support the hypothesis. Either way, the information that results from the experiment may be useful for future investigations.

Experimental Group and Control Group

An experiment to determine how two factors are related has a control group and an experimental group. The two groups are the same, except that the investigator changes a single factor in the experimental group and does not change it in the control group.

> **Experimental Group:** two containers of pond water with one drop of fertilizer solution added to each
>
> **Control Group:** two containers of the same pond water sampled at the same time but with no fertilizer solution added

Variables and Constants

In a controlled experiment, a variable is any factor that can change. Constants are all of the variables that are kept the same in both the experimental group and the control group.

The independent variable is the factor that is manipulated or changed in order to test the effect of the change on another variable. The dependent variable is the factor the investigator measures to gather data about the effect.

Independent Variable	Dependent Variable	Constants
Amount of fertilizer in pond water	Growth of algae in the pond water	• Where and when the pond water is obtained • The type of container used • Light and temperature conditions where the water is stored

5 Write a Procedure

Write each step of your procedure. Start each step with a verb, or action word, and keep the steps short. Your procedure should be clear enough for someone else to use as instructions for repeating your experiment.

Procedure

1. Use the masking tape and the marker to label the containers with your initials, the date, and the identifiers "Jar 1 with Fertilizer," "Jar 2 with Fertilizer," "Jar 1 without Fertilizer," and "Jar 2 without Fertilizer."

2. Put on your gloves. Use the large container to obtain a sample of pond water.

3. Divide the water sample equally among the four smaller containers.

4. Use the eyedropper to add one drop of fertilizer solution to the two containers labeled, "Jar 1 with Fertilizer," and "Jar 2 with Fertilizer".

5. Cover the containers with clear plastic wrap. Use the scissors to punch ten holes in each of the covers.

6. Place all four containers on a window ledge. Make sure that they all receive the same amount of light.

7. Observe the containers every day for one week.

8. Use the ruler to measure the diameter of the largest clump of algae in each container, and record your measurements daily.

Science Skills

6 Experiment and Collect Data

Once you have all of your materials and your procedure has been approved, you can begin to experiment and collect data. Record both quantitative data (measurements) and qualitative data (observations), as shown below.

Algal Growth and Fertilizer

Date and Time	Experimental Group		Control Group		Observations
	Jar 1 with Fertilizer (diameter of algal clump in mm)	Jar 2 with Fertilizer (diameter of algal clump in mm)	Jar 1 without Fertilizer (diameter of algal clump in mm)	Jar 2 without Fertilizer (diameter of algal clump in mm)	
5/3 4:00 p.m.	0	0	0	0	condensation in all containers
5/4 4:00 p.m.	0	3	0	0	tiny green blobs in Jar 2 with fertilizer
5/5 4:15 p.m.	4	5	0	3	green blobs in Jars 1 and 2 with fertilizer and Jar 2 without fertilizer
5/6 4:00 p.m.	5	6	0	4	water light green in Jar 2 with fertilizer
5/7 4:00 p.m.	8	10	0	6	water light green in Jars 1 and 2 with fertilizer and Jar 2 without fertilizer
5/8 3:30 p.m.	10	18	0	6	cover off of Jar 2 with fertilizer
5/9 3:30 p.m.	14	23	0	8	drew sketches of each container

Drawings of Samples Viewed Under Microscope on 5/9 at 100x

Jar 1 with Fertilizer

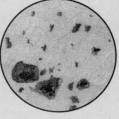
Jar 2 with Fertilizer

Jar 1 without Fertilizer

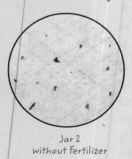
Jar 2 without Fertilizer

7 Analyze Data

After you complete your experiment, you must analyze all of the data you have gathered. Tables, statistics, and graphs are often used in this step to organize and analyze both the qualitative and quantitative data. Sometimes, your qualitative data are best used to help explain the relationships you see in your quantitative data.

Computer graphing software is useful for creating a graph from data that you have collected. Most graphing software can make line graphs, pie charts, or bar graphs from data that has been organized in a spreadsheet. Graphs are useful for understanding relationships in the data and for communicating the results of your experiment.

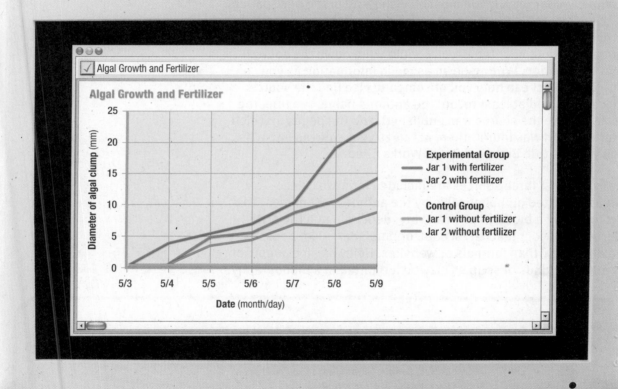

Science Skills

8 Make Conclusions

To draw conclusions from your experiment, first, write your results. Then, compare your results with your hypothesis. Do your results support your hypothesis? What have you learned?

Conclusion

More algae grew in the pond water to which fertilizer had been added than in the pond water to which fertilizer had not been added. My hypothesis was supported. I conclude that it is possible that the growth of algae in ponds can be influenced by the input of fertilizer.

9 Create a Bibliography or Works Cited List

To complete your report, you must also show all of the newspapers, magazines, journals, books, and online sources that you used at every stage of your investigation. Whenever you find useful information about your topic, you should write down the source of that information. Writing down as much information as you can about the subject can help you or someone else find the source again. You should at least record the author's name, the title, the date and where the source was published, and the pages in which the information was found. Then, organize your sources into a list, which you can title Bibliography or Works Cited.

Usually, at least three sources are included in these lists. Sources are listed alphabetically, by the authors' last names. The exact format of a bibliography can vary, depending on the style preferences of your teacher, school, or publisher. Also, books are cited differently than journals or websites. Below is an example of how different kinds of sources may be formatted in a bibliography.

BOOK: Hauschultz, Sara. Freshwater Algae. Brainard, Minnesota: Northwoods Publishing, 2011.

ENCYCLOPEDIA: Lasure, Sedona. "Algae is not all just pond scum." Encyclopedia of Algae. 2009.

JOURNAL: Johnson, Keagan. "Algae as we know it." Sci Journal, vol 64. (September 2010): 201-211.

WEBSITE: Dout, Bill. "Keeping algae scum out of birdbaths." Help Keep Earth Clean. News. January 26, 2011. <www.SaveEarth.org>.

Using a Microscope

Scientists use microscopes to see very small objects that cannot easily be seen with the eye alone. A microscope magnifies the image of an object so that small details may be observed. A microscope that you may use can magnify an object 400 times—the object will appear 400 times larger than its actual size.

Body The body separates the lens in the eyepiece from the objective lenses below.

Nosepiece The nosepiece holds the objective lenses above the stage and rotates so that all lenses may be used.

High-Power Objective Lens This is the largest lens on the nosepiece. It magnifies an image approximately 40 times.

Stage The stage supports the object being viewed.

Diaphragm The diaphragm is used to adjust the amount of light passing through the slide and into an objective lens.

Mirror or Light Source Some microscopes use light that is reflected through the stage by a mirror. Other microscopes have their own light sources.

Eyepiece Objects are viewed through the eyepiece. The eyepiece contains a lens that commonly magnifies an image ten times.

Coarse Adjustment This knob is used to focus the image of an object when it is viewed through the low-power lens.

Fine Adjustment This knob is used to focus the image of an object when it is viewed through the high-power lens.

Low-Power Objective Lens This is the smallest lens on the nosepiece. It magnifies images about 10 times.

Arm The arm supports the body above the stage. Always carry a microscope by the arm and base.

Stage Clip The stage clip holds a slide in place on the stage.

Base The base supports the microscope.

© Houghton Mifflin Harcourt Publishing Company

Science Skills

Measuring Accurately

Precision and Accuracy

When you do a scientific investigation, it is important that your methods, observations, and data be both precise and accurate.

Low precision: The darts did not land in a consistent place on the dartboard.

Precision, but not accuracy: The darts landed in a consistent place, but did not hit the bull's eye.

Prescision and accuracy: The darts landed consistently on the bull's eye.

Precision

In science, *precision* is the exactness and consistency of measurements. For example, measurements made with a ruler that has both centimeter and millimeter markings would be more precise than measurements made with a ruler that has only centimeter markings. Another indicator of precision is the care taken to make sure that methods and observations are as exact and consistent as possible. Every time a particular experiment is done, the same procedure should be used. Precision is necessary because experiments are repeated several times and if the procedure changes, the results might change.

Example

Suppose you are measuring temperatures over a two-week period. Your precision will be greater if you measure each temperature at the same place, at the same time of day, and with the same thermometer than if you change any of these factors from one day to the next.

Accuracy

In science, it is possible to be precise but not accurate. *Accuracy* depends on the difference between a measurement and an actual value. The smaller the difference, the more accurate the measurement.

Example

Suppose you look at a stream and estimate that it is about 1 meter wide at a particular place. You decide to check your estimate by measuring the stream with a meter stick, and you determine that the stream is 1.32 meters wide. However, because it is difficult to measure the width of a stream with a meter stick, it turns out that your measurement was not very accurate. The stream is actually 1.14 meters wide. Therefore, even though your estimate of about 1 meter was less precise than your measurement, your estimate was actually more accurate.

Graduated Cylinders

How to Measure the Volume of a Liquid with a Graduated Cylinder

- Be sure that the graduated cylinder is on a flat surface so that your measurement will be accurate.

- When reading the scale on a graduated cylinder, be sure to have your eyes at the level of the surface of the liquid.

- The surface of the liquid will be curved in the graduated cylinder. Read the volume of the liquid at the bottom of the curve, or meniscus (muh-NIHS-kuhs).

- You can use a graduated cylinder to find the volume of a solid object by measuring the increase in a liquid's level after you add the object to the cylinder.

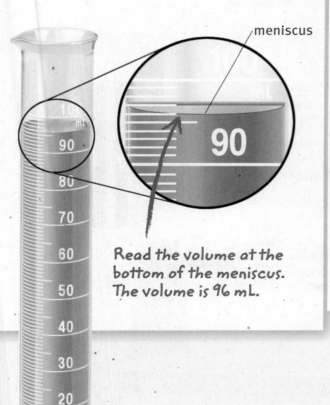

meniscus

Read the volume at the bottom of the meniscus. The volume is 96 mL.

Metric Rulers

How to Measure the Length of a Leaf with a Metric Ruler

1 Lay a ruler flat on top of the leaf so that the 1-centimeter mark lines up with one end. Make sure the ruler and the leaf do not move between the time you line them up and the time you take the measurement.

2 Look straight down on the ruler so that you can see exactly how the marks line up with the other end of the leaf.

3 Estimate the length by which the leaf extends beyond a marking. For example, the leaf below extends about halfway between the 4.2-centimeter and 4.3-centimeter marks, so the apparent measurement is about 4.25 centimeters.

4 Remember to subtract 1 centimeter from your apparent measurement, since you started at the 1-centimeter mark on the ruler and not at the end. The leaf is about 3.25 centimeters long (4.25 cm − 1 cm = 3.25 cm).

Triple Beam Balance

This balance has a pan and three beams with sliding masses, called riders. At one end of the beams is a pointer that indicates whether the mass on the pan is equal to the masses shown on the beams.

How to Measure the Mass of an Object

1 Make sure the balance is zeroed before measuring the mass of an object. The balance is zeroed if the pointer is at zero when nothing is on the pan and the riders are at their zero points. Use the adjustment knob at the base of the balance to zero it.

2 Place the object to be measured on the pan.

3 Move the riders one notch at a time away from the pan. Begin with the largest rider. If moving the largest rider one notch brings the pointer below zero, begin measuring the mass of the object with the next smaller rider.

4 Change the positions of the riders until they balance the mass on the pan and the pointer is at zero. Then add the readings from the three beams to determine the mass of the object.

300 g	position of largest rider
90 g	position of middle rider
+ 3 g	position of smallest rider
393 g	mass of beaker and water

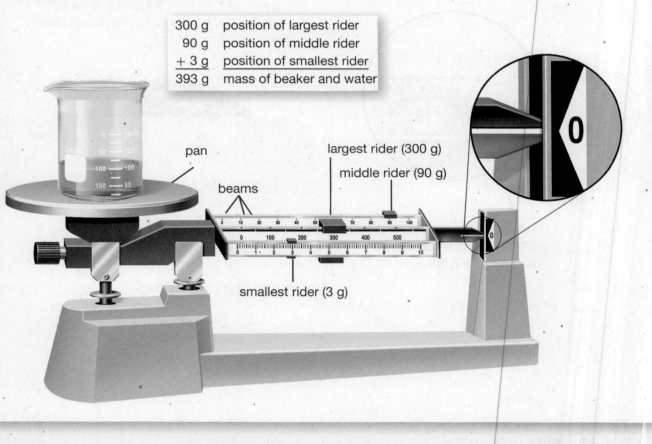

pan

beams

largest rider (300 g)

middle rider (90 g)

smallest rider (3 g)

Using the Metric System and SI Units

Scientists use International System (SI) units for measurements of distance, volume, mass, and temperature. The International System is based on powers of ten and the metric system of measurement.

Basic SI Units		
Quantity	Name	Symbol
length	meter	m
volume	liter	L
mass	gram	g
temperature	kelvin	K

SI Prefixes		
Prefix	Symbol	Power of 10
kilo-	k	1000
hecto-	h	100
deca-	da	10
deci-	d	0.1 or $\frac{1}{10}$
centi-	c	0.01 or $\frac{1}{100}$
milli-	m	0.001 or $\frac{1}{1000}$

Changing Metric Units

You can change from one unit to another in the metric system by multiplying or dividing by a power of 10.

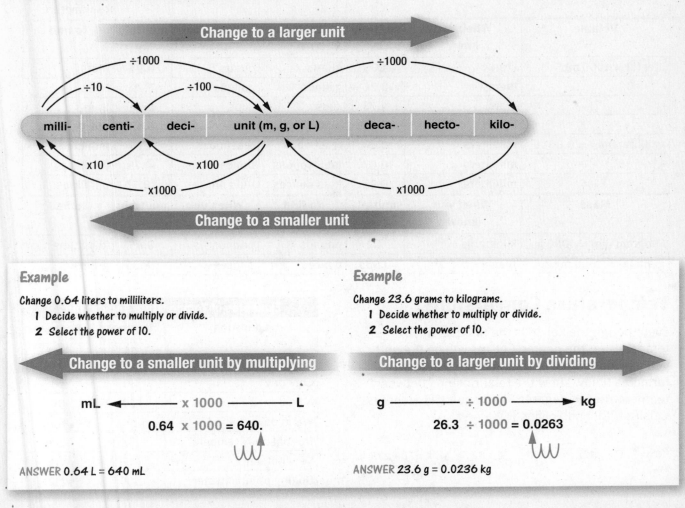

Change to a larger unit

÷1000   ÷10   ÷100   ÷1000

milli- centi- deci- unit (m, g, or L) deca- hecto- kilo-

x10   x100   x1000   x1000

Change to a smaller unit

Example

Change 0.64 liters to milliliters.
1 Decide whether to multiply or divide.
2 Select the power of 10.

Change to a smaller unit by multiplying

mL ◄——— x 1000 ——— L

0.64 × 1000 = 640.

ANSWER 0.64 L = 640 mL

Example

Change 23.6 grams to kilograms.
1 Decide whether to multiply or divide.
2 Select the power of 10.

Change to a larger unit by dividing

g ——— ÷ 1000 ——► kg

26.3 ÷ 1000 = 0.0263

ANSWER 23.6 g = 0.0236 kg

Science Skills

Converting Between SI and U.S. Customary Units

Use the chart below when you need to convert between SI units and U.S. customary units.

SI Unit	From SI to U.S. Customary			From U.S. Customary to SI		
Length	**When you know**	**multiply by**	**to find**	**When you know**	**multiply by**	**to find**
kilometer (km) = 1000 m	kilometers	0.62	miles	miles	1.61	kilometers
meter (m) = 100 cm	meters	3.28	feet	feet	0.3048	meters
centimeter (cm) = 10 mm	centimeters	0.39	inches	inches	2.54	centimeters
millimeter (mm) = 0.1 cm	millimeters	0.04	inches	inches	25.4	millimeters
Area	**When you know**	**multiply by**	**to find**	**When you know**	**multiply by**	**to find**
square kilometer (km²)	square kilometers	0.39	square miles	square miles	2.59	square kilometers
square meter (m²)	square meters	1.2	square yards	square yards	0.84	square meters
square centimeter (cm²)	square centimeters	0.155	square inches	square inches	6.45	square centimeters
Volume	**When you know**	**multiply by**	**to find**	**When you know**	**multiply by**	**to find**
liter (L) = 1000 mL	liters	1.06	quarts	quarts	0.95	liters
	liters	0.26	gallons	gallons	3.79	liters
	liters	4.23	cups	cups	0.24	liters
	liters	2.12	pints	pints	0.47	liters
milliliter (mL) = 0.001 L	milliliters	0.20	teaspoons	teaspoons	4.93	milliliters
	milliliters	0.07	tablespoons	tablespoons	14.79	milliliters
	milliliters	0.03	fluid ounces	fluid ounces	29.57	milliliters
Mass	**When you know**	**multiply by**	**to find**	**When you know**	**multiply by**	**to find**
kilogram (kg) = 1000 g	kilograms	2.2	pounds	pounds	0.45	kilograms
gram (g) = 1000 mg	grams	0.035	ounces	ounces	28.35	grams

Temperature Conversions

Even though the kelvin is the SI base unit of temperature, the degree Celsius will be the unit you use most often in your science studies. The formulas below show the relationships between temperatures in degrees Fahrenheit (°F), degrees Celsius (°C), and kelvins (K).

$$°C = \frac{5}{9}\ (°F - 32) \qquad °F = \frac{9}{5}\ °C + 32 \qquad K = °C + 273$$

Examples of Temperature Conversions		
Condition	**Degrees Celsius**	**Degrees Fahrenheit**
Freezing point of water	0	32
Cool day	10	50
Mild day	20	68
Warm day	30	86
Normal body temperature	37	98.6
Very hot day	40	104
Boiling point of water	100	212

Math Refresher

Performing Calculations

Science requires an understanding of many math concepts. The following pages will help you review some important math skills.

Mean

The mean is the sum of all values in a data set divided by the total number of values in the data set. The mean is also called the *average*.

Example

Find the mean of the following set of numbers: 5, 4, 7, and 8.

Step 1   Find the sum.

5 + 4 + 7 + 8 = 24

Step 2   Divide the sum by the number of numbers in your set. Because there are four numbers in this example, divide the sum by 4.

24 ÷ 4 = 6

Answer The average, or mean, is 6.

Median

The median of a data set is the middle value when the values are written in numerical order. If a data set has an even number of values, the median is the mean of the two middle values.

Example

To find the median of a set of measurements, arrange the values in order from least to greatest. The median is the middle value.

13 mm   14 mm   16 mm   21 mm   23 mm

Answer The median is 16 mm.

Mode

The mode of a data set is the value that occurs most often.

Example

To find the mode of a set of measurements, arrange the values in order from least to greatest and determine the value that occurs most often.

13 mm, 14 mm, 14 mm, 16 mm,
21 mm, 23 mm, 25 mm

Answer The mode is 14 mm.

A data set can have more than one mode or no mode. For example, the following data set has modes of 2 mm and 4 mm:

2 mm   2 mm   3 mm   4 mm   4 mm

The data set below has no mode, because no value occurs more often than any other.

2 mm   3 mm   4 mm   5 mm

Math Refresher

Ratios

A **ratio** is a comparison between numbers, and it is usually written as a fraction.

Example

Find the ratio of thermometers to students if you have 36 thermometers and 48 students in your class.

Step 1 Write the ratio.

$$\frac{36 \text{ thermometers}}{48 \text{ students}}$$

Step 2 Simplify the fraction to its simplest form.

$$\frac{36}{48} = \frac{36 \div 12}{48 \div 12} = \frac{3}{4}$$

The ratio of thermometers to students is 3 to 4 or 3:4.

Proportions

A **proportion** is an equation that states that two ratios are equal.

$$\frac{3}{1} = \frac{12}{4}$$

To solve a proportion, you can use cross-multiplication. If you know three of the quantities in a proportion, you can use cross-multiplication to find the fourth.

Example

Imagine that you are making a scale model of the solar system for your science project. The diameter of Jupiter is 11.2 times the diameter of the Earth. If you are using a plastic-foam ball that has a diameter of 2 cm to represent the Earth, what must the diameter of the ball representing Jupiter be?

$$\frac{11.2}{1} = \frac{x}{2 \text{ cm}}$$

Step 1 Cross-multiply.

$$\frac{11.2}{1} = \frac{x}{2}$$

$$11.2 \times 2 = x \times 1$$

Step 2 Multiply.

$$22.4 = x \times 1$$

$$x = 22.4 \text{ cm}$$

You will need to use a ball that has a diameter of 22.4 cm to represent Jupiter.

Rates

A **rate** is a ratio of two values expressed in different units. A unit rate is a rate with a denominator of 1 unit.

Example

A plant grew 6 centimeters in 2 days. The plant's rate of growth was $\frac{6 \text{ cm}}{2 \text{ days}}$.

To describe the plant's growth in centimeters per day, write a unit rate.

Divide numerator and denominator by 2:

$$\frac{6 \text{ cm}}{2 \text{ days}} = \frac{6 \text{ cm} \div 2}{2 \text{ days} \div 2}$$

Simplify:

$$= \frac{3 \text{ cm}}{1 \text{ day}}$$

Answer The plant's rate of growth is 3 centimeters per day.

Percent

A **percent** is a ratio of a given number to 100. For example, 85% = 85/100. You can use percent to find part of a whole.

Example
What is 85% of 40?

Step 1   Rewrite the percent as a decimal by moving the decimal point two places to the left.

$$0.85$$

Step 2   Multiply the decimal by the number that you are calculating the percentage of.

$$0.85 \times 40 = 34$$

85% of 40 is 34.

Decimals

To **add** or **subtract decimals**, line up the digits vertically so that the decimal points line up. Then, add or subtract the columns from right to left. Carry or borrow numbers as necessary.

Example
Add the following numbers: 3.1415 and 2.96.

Step 1   Line up the digits vertically so that the decimal points line up.

$$\begin{array}{r} 3.1415 \\ + 2.96 \\ \hline \end{array}$$

Step 2   Add the columns from right to left, and carry when necessary.

$$\begin{array}{r} 3.1415 \\ + 2.96 \\ \hline 6.1015 \end{array}$$

The sum is 6.1015.

Fractions

A **fraction** is a ratio of two nonzero whole numbers.

Example
Your class has 24 plants. Your teacher instructs you to put 5 plants in a shady spot. What fraction of the plants in your class will you put in a shady spot?

Step 1   In the denominator, write the total number of parts in the whole.

$$\frac{?}{24}$$

Step 2   In the numerator, write the number of parts of the whole that are being considered.

$$\frac{5}{24}$$

So, $\frac{5}{24}$ of the plants will be in the shade.

Math Refresher

Simplifying Fractions

It is usually best to express a fraction in its simplest form. Expressing a fraction in its simplest form is called **simplifying a fraction**.

Example

Simplify the fraction $\frac{30}{45}$ to its simplest form.

Step 1 Find the largest whole number that will divide evenly into both the numerator and denominator. This number is called the greatest common factor (GCF).

Factors of the numerator 30:
1, 2, 3, 5, 6, 10, **15**, 30

Factors of the denominator 45:
1, 3, 5, 9, **15**, 45

Step 2 Divide both the numerator and the denominator by the GCF, which in this case is 15.

$$\frac{30}{45} = \frac{30 \div 15}{45 \div 15} = \frac{2}{3}$$

Thus, $\frac{30}{45}$ written in its simplest form is $\frac{2}{3}$.

Adding and Subtracting Fractions

To **add** or **subtract fractions** that have the same denominator, simply add or subtract the numerators.

Examples

$\frac{3}{5} + \frac{1}{5} = ?$ and $\frac{3}{4} - \frac{1}{4} = ?$

Step 1 Add or subtract the numerators.

$$\frac{3}{5} + \frac{1}{5} = \frac{4}{} \text{ and } \frac{3}{4} - \frac{1}{4} = \frac{2}{}$$

Step 2 Write in the common denominator, which remains the same.

$$\frac{3}{5} + \frac{1}{5} = \frac{4}{5} \text{ and } \frac{3}{4} - \frac{1}{4} = \frac{2}{4}$$

Step 3 If necessary, write the fraction in its simplest form.

$\frac{4}{5}$ cannot be simplified, and $\frac{2}{4} = \frac{1}{2}$.

To **add** or **subtract** fractions that have **different denominators**, first find the least common denominator (LCD).

Examples

$\frac{1}{2} + \frac{1}{6} = ?$ and $\frac{3}{4} - \frac{2}{3} = ?$

Step 1 Write the equivalent fractions that have a common denominator.

$$\frac{3}{6} + \frac{1}{6} = ? \text{ and } \frac{9}{12} - \frac{8}{12} = ?$$

Step 2 Add or subtract the fractions.

$$\frac{3}{6} + \frac{1}{6} = \frac{4}{6} \text{ and } \frac{9}{12} - \frac{8}{12} = \frac{1}{12}$$

Step 3 If necessary, write the fraction in its simplest form.

$\frac{4}{6} = \frac{2}{3}$, and $\frac{1}{12}$ cannot be simplifed.

Multiplying Fractions

To **multiply fractions**, multiply the numerators and the denominators together, and then simplify the fraction to its simplest form.

Example

$\frac{5}{9} \times \frac{7}{10} = ?$

Step 1 Multiply the numerators and denominators.

$$\frac{5}{9} \times \frac{7}{10} = \frac{5 \times 7}{9 \times 10} = \frac{35}{90}$$

Step 2 Simplify the fraction.

$$\frac{35}{90} = \frac{35 \div 5}{90 \div 5} = \frac{7}{18}$$

Dividing Fractions

To **divide fractions,** first rewrite the divisor (the number you divide by) upside down. This number is called the reciprocal of the divisor. Then multiply and simplify if necessary.

Example

$$\frac{5}{8} \div \frac{3}{2} = ?$$

Step 1 Rewrite the divisor as its reciprocal.

$$\frac{3}{2} \longrightarrow \frac{2}{3}$$

Step 2 Multiply the fractions.

$$\frac{5}{8} \times \frac{2}{3} = \frac{5 \times 2}{8 \times 3} = \frac{10}{24}$$

Step 3 Simplify the fraction.

$$\frac{10}{24} = \frac{10 \div 2}{24 \div 2} = \frac{5}{12}$$

Using Significant Figures

The **significant figures** in a decimal are the digits that are warranted by the accuracy of a measuring device.

When you perform a calculation with measurements, the number of significant figures to include in the result depends in part on the number of significant figures in the measurements. When you multiply or divide measurements, your answer should have only as many significant figures as the measurement with the fewest significant figures.

Examples

Using a balance and a graduated cylinder filled with water, you determined that a marble has a mass of 8.0 grams and a volume of 3.5 cubic centimeters. To calculate the density of the marble, divide the mass by the volume.

Write the formula for density: $\text{Density} = \frac{\text{mass}}{\text{volume}}$

Substitute measurements: $= \frac{8.0 \text{ g}}{3.5 \text{ cm}^3}$

Use a calculator to divide: $\approx 2.285714286 \text{ g/cm}^3$

Answer Because the mass and the volume have two significant figures each, give the density to two significant figures. The marble has a density of 2.3 grams per cubic centimeter.

Using Scientific Notation

Scientific notation is a shorthand way to write very large or very small numbers. For example, 73,500,000,000,000,000,000,000 kg is the mass of the moon. In scientific notation, it is 7.35×10^{22} kg. A value written as a number between 1 and 10, times a power of 10, is in scientific notation.

Examples

You can convert from standard form to scientific notation.

Standard Form	Scientific Notation
720,000	7.2×10^5
5 decimal places left	Exponent is 5.
0.000291	2.91×10^{-4}
4 decimal places right	Exponent is −4.

You can convert from scientific notation to standard form.

Scientific Notation	Standard Form
4.63×10^7	46,300,000
Exponent is 7.	7 decimal places right
1.08×10^{-6}	0.00000108
Exponent is −6.	6 decimal places left

Math Refresher

Making and Interpreting Graphs

Circle Graph

A circle graph, or pie chart, shows how each group of data relates to all of the data. Each part of the circle represents a category of the data. The entire circle represents all of the data. For example, a biologist studying a hardwood forest in Wisconsin found that there were five different types of trees. The data table at right summarizes the biologist's findings.

Wisconsin Hardwood Trees	
Type of tree	**Number found**
Oak	600
Maple	750
Beech	300
Birch	1,200
Hickory	150
Total	3,000

How to Make a Circle Graph

1 To make a circle graph of these data, first find the percentage of each type of tree. Divide the number of trees of each type by the total number of trees, and multiply by 100%.

$$\frac{600 \text{ oak}}{3,000 \text{ trees}} \times 100\% = 20\%$$

$$\frac{750 \text{ maple}}{3,000 \text{ trees}} \times 100\% = 25\%$$

$$\frac{300 \text{ beech}}{3,000 \text{ trees}} \times 100\% = 10\%$$

$$\frac{1,200 \text{ birch}}{3,000 \text{ trees}} \times 100\% = 40\%$$

$$\frac{150 \text{ hickory}}{3,000 \text{ trees}} \times 100\% = 5\%$$

2 Now, determine the size of the wedges that make up the graph. Multiply each percentage by 360°. Remember that a circle contains 360°.

$$20\% \times 360° = 72° \qquad 25\% \times 360° = 90°$$

$$10\% \times 360° = 36° \qquad 40\% \times 360° = 144°$$

$$5\% \times 360° = 18°$$

3 Check that the sum of the percentages is 100 and the sum of the degrees is 360.

$$20\% + 25\% + 10\% + 40\% + 5\% = 100\%$$

$$72° + 90° + 36° + 144° + 18° = 360°$$

4 Use a compass to draw a circle and mark the center of the circle.

5 Then, use a protractor to draw angles of 72°, 90°, 36°, 144°, and 18° in the circle.

6 Finally, label each part of the graph, and choose an appropriate title.

A Community of Wisconsin Hardwood Trees

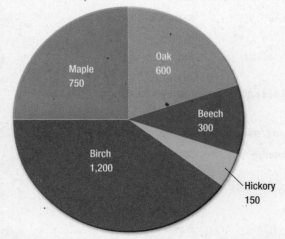

Line Graphs

Line graphs are most often used to demonstrate continuous change. For example, Mr. Smith's students analyzed the population records for their hometown, Appleton, between 1910 and 2010. Examine the data at right.

Because the year and the population change, they are the variables. The population is determined by, or dependent on, the year. Therefore, the population is called the **dependent variable,** and the year is called the **independent variable**. Each year and its population make a **data pair**. To prepare a line graph, you must first organize data pairs into a table like the one at right.

Population of Appleton, 1910–2010	
Year	**Population**
1910	1,800
1930	2,500
1950	3,200
1970	3,900
1990	4,600
2010	5,300

How to Make a Line Graph

1 Place the independent variable along the horizontal (x) axis. Place the dependent variable along the vertical (y) axis.

2 Label the x-axis "Year" and the y-axis "Population." Look at your greatest and least values for the population. For the y-axis, determine a scale that will provide enough space to show these values. You must use the same scale for the entire length of the axis. Next, find an appropriate scale for the x-axis.

3 Choose reasonable starting points for each axis.

4 Plot the data pairs as accurately as possible.

5 Choose a title that accurately represents the data.

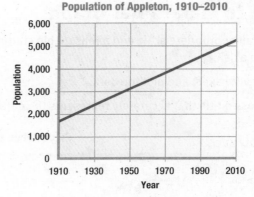

How to Determine Slope

Slope is the ratio of the change in the y-value to the change in the x-value, or "rise over run."

1 Choose two points on the line graph. For example, the population of Appleton in 2010 was 5,300 people. Therefore, you can define point A as (2010, 5,300). In 1910, the population was 1,800 people. You can define point B as (1910, 1,800).

2 Find the change in the y-value.
(y at point A) − (y at point B) =
5,300 people − 1,800 people =
3,500 people

3 Find the change in the x-value.
(x at point A) − (x at point B) =
2010 − 1910 = 100 years

4 Calculate the slope of the graph by dividing the change in y by the change in x.

$$slope = \frac{change\ in\ y}{change\ in\ x}$$

$$slope = \frac{3,500\ people}{100\ years}$$

$$slope = 35\ people\ per\ year$$

In this example, the population in Appleton increased by a fixed amount each year. The graph of these data is a straight line. Therefore, the relationship is **linear**. When the graph of a set of data is not a straight line, the relationship is **nonlinear**.

Math Refresher

Bar Graphs

Bar graphs can be used to demonstrate change that is not continuous. These graphs can be used to indicate trends when the data cover a long period of time. A meteorologist gathered the precipitation data shown here for Summerville for April 1–15 and used a bar graph to represent the data.

Precipitation in Summerville, April 1–15			
Date	Precipitation (cm)	Date	Precipitation (cm)
April 1	0.5	April 9	0.25
April 2	1.25	April 10	0.0
April 3	0.0	April 11	1.0
April 4	0.0	April 12	0.0
April 5	0.0	April 13	0.25
April 6	0.0	April 14	0.0
April 7	0.0	April 15	6.50
April 8	1.75		

How to Make a Bar Graph

1 Use an appropriate scale and a reasonable starting point for each axis.

2 Label the axes, and plot the data.

3 Choose a title that accurately represents the data.

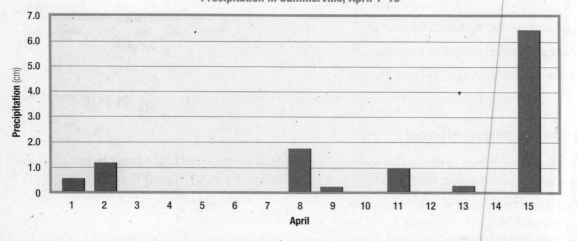

Precipitation in Summerville, April 1–15

Glossary

Pronunciation Key							
Sound	**Symbol**	**Example**	**Respelling**	**Sound**	**Symbol**	**Example**	**Respelling**
ă	a	pat	PAT	ŏ	ah	bottle	BAHT'l
ā	ay	pay	PAY	ō	oh	toe	TOH
âr	air	care	KAIR	ô	aw	caught	KAWT
ä	ah	father	FAH•ther	ôr	ohr	roar	ROHR
är	ar	argue	AR•gyoo	oi	oy	noisy	NOYZ•ee
ch	ch	chase	CHAYS	ŏŏ	u	book	BUK
ě	e	pet	PET	ōō	oo	boot	BOOT
ě (at end of a syllable)	eh	settee lessee	seh•TEE leh•SEE	ou	ow	pound	POWND
ěr	ehr	merry	MEHR•ee	s	s	center	SEN•ter
ē	ee	beach	BEECH	sh	sh	cache	CASH
g	g	gas	GAS	ŭ	uh	flood	FLUHD
ĭ	i	pit	PIT	ûr	er	bird	BERD
ĭ (at end of a syllable)	ih	guitar	gih•TAR	z	z	xylophone	ZY•luh•fohn
ī	y eye (only for a complete syllable)	pie island	PY EYE•luh'nd	z	z	bags	BAGZ
				zh	zh	decision	dih•SIZH•uhn
îr	ir	hear	HIR	ə	uh	around broken focus	uh•ROWND BROH•kuhn FOH•kuhs
j	j	germ	JERM	ər	er	winner	WIN•er
k	k	kick	KIK	th	th	thin they	THIN THAY
ng	ng	thing	THING	w	w	one	WUHN
ngk	ngk	bank	BANGK	wh	hw	whether	HWETH•er

A

abiotic factor (ay·by·AHT·ik FAK·ter) an environmental factor that is not associated with the activities of living organisms (7)

factor abiótico un factor ambiental que no está asociado con las actividades de los seres vivos

acid precipitation (AS·id prih·sip·ih·TAY·shuhn) rain, sleet, or snow that contains a high concentration of acids (237)

precipitación ácida lluvia, aguanieve, o nieve que contiene una alta concentración de ácidos

air pollution (AIR puh·LOO·shuhn) the contamination of the atmosphere by the introduction of pollutants from human and natural sources (235)

contaminación del aire la contaminación de la atmósfera debido a la introducción de contaminantes provenientes de fuentes humanas y naturales

air quality (AIR KWAHL·ih·tee) a measure of the pollutants in the air that is used to express how clean or polluted the air is (238)

calidad de aire una medida de los contaminantes presentes en el aire que se usa para expresar el nivel de pureza o contaminación del aire

atmosphere (AT·muh·sfir) a mixture of gases that surrounds a planet, moon, or other celestial body (142)

atmósfera una mezcla de gases que rodea un planeta, una luna, u otras cuerpos celestes

B

biodiversity (by·oh·dih·VER·sih·tee) the number and variety of organisms in a given area during a specific period of time (106, 117)

biodiversidad el número y la variedad de organismos que se encuentran en un área determinada durante un período específico de tiempo

biomass (BY·oh·mas) plant material, manure, or any other organic matter that is used as an energy source (178)

biomasa materia vegetal, estiércol o cualquier otra materia orgánica que se usa como fuente de energía

biome (BY·ohm) a large region characterized by a specific type of climate and certain types of plant and animal communities (10, 64)

bioma una región extensa caracterizada por un tipo de clima específico y ciertos tipos de comunidades de plantas y animales

biotic factor (by·AHT·ik FAK·ter) an environmental factor that is associated with or results from the activities of living organisms (6)

factor biótico un factor ambiental que está asociado con las actividades de los seres vivos o que resulta de ellas

C

carbon cycle (KAR·buhn SY·kuhl) the movement of carbon from the nonliving environment into living things and back (96)

ciclo del carbono el movimiento del carbono del ambiente sin vida a los seres vivos y de los seres vivos al ambiente

carnivore (KAR·nuh·vohr) an organism that eats animals (21)

carnívoro un organismo que se alimenta de animales

carrying capacity (KAIR·ee·ing kuh·PAS·ih·tee) the largest population that an environment can support at any given time (34)

capacidad de carga la población más grande que un ambiente puede sostener en cualquier momento dado

commensalism (kuh·MEN·suh·liz·uhm) a relationship between two organisms in which one organism benefits and the other is unaffected (46)

comensalismo una relación entre dos organismos en la que uno se beneficia y el otro no es afectado

community (kuh·MYOO·nih·tee) all of the populations of species that live in the same habitat and interact with each other (9)

comunidad todas las poblaciones de especies que viven en el mismo hábitat e interactúan entre sí

competition (kahm·pih·TISH·uhn) ecological relationship in which two or more organisms depend on the same limited resource (38, 48)

competencia la relación ecológica en la que dos o más organismos dependen del mismo recurso limitado

coniferous tree (kuh·NIF·er·uhs TREE) cone-bearing trees that usually keep their leaves or needles during all the seasons of the year (67)

árbol conifero los árboles que producen conos o piñas y que generalmente conservan sus hojas o agujas durante todas las estaciones del año

conservation (kahn·ser·VAY·shuhn) the wise use of and preservation of natural resources (123, 190, 246)

conservación el uso inteligente y la preservación de los recursos naturales

consumer (kuhn·SOO·mer) an organism that eats other organisms or organic matter (21)

consumidor un organismo que se alimenta de otros organismos o de materia orgánica

cooperation (koh·ahp·uh·RAY·shuhn) an interaction between two or more living things in which they are said to work together (39)

cooperación la interacción entre dos o más organismos vivos en la cual se dice que trabajan juntos

D

deciduous tree (dih·SIJ·oo·uhs TREE) trees that lose their leaves at the end of the growing season (70)
árbol caducifolio los árboles que pierden sus hojas al final de una estación de crecimiento

decomposer (dee·kuhm·POH·zer) an organism that gets energy by breaking down the remains of dead organisms or animal wastes and consuming or absorbing the nutrients (20)
descomponedor un organismo que, para obtener energía, desintegra los restos de organismos muertos o los desechos de animales y consume o absorbe los nutrientes

deforestation (dee·fohr·ih·STAY·shuhn) the removal of trees and other vegetation from an area (229)
deforestación la remoción de árboles y demás vegetación de un área

desert (DEZ·ert) a region characterized by a very dry climate and extreme temperatures (68)
desierto una región que se caracteriza por tener un clima muy seco y temperaturas extremas

desertification (dih·zer·tuh·fih·KAY·shuhn) the process by which human activities or climatic changes make arid or semiarid areas more desertlike (229)
desertificación el proceso por medio del cual las actividades humanas o los cambios climáticos hacen que un área árida o semiárida se vuelva más parecida a un desierto

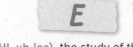

E

ecology (ee·KAHL·uh·jee) the study of the interactions of living organisms with one another and with their environment (6)
ecología el estudio de las interacciones de los seres vivos entre sí mismos y entre sí mismos y su ambiente

ecosystem (EE·koh·sis·tuhm) a community of organisms and their abiotic, or nonliving, environment (9)
ecosistema una comunidad de organismos y su ambiente abiótico o no vivo

energy (EN·er·jee) the ability to cause change (90)
energía la capacidad de producir un cambio

energy pyramid (EN·er·jee PIR·uh·mid) a triangular diagram that shows an ecosystem's loss of energy, which results as energy passes through the ecosystem's food chain; each row in the pyramid represents a trophic (feeding) level in an ecosystem, and the area of a row represents the energy stored in that trophic level (92)
pirámide de energía un diagrama con forma de triángulo que muestra la pérdida de energía que ocurre en un ecosistema a medida que la energía pasa a través de la cadena alimenticia del ecosistema; cada hilera de la pirámide representa un nivel trófico (de alimentación) en el ecosistema, y el área de la hilera representa la energía almacenada en ese nivel trófico

energy resource (EN·er·jee REE·sohrs) a natural resource that humans use to generate energy (152, 160, 172)
recurso energético un recurso natural que utilizan los humanos para generar energía

estuary (ES·choo·ehr·ee) an area where fresh water mixes with salt water from the ocean (80)
estuario un área donde el agua dulce de los ríos se mezcla con el agua salada del océano

eutrophication (yoo·trohf·ih·KAY·shuhn) an increase in the amount of nutrients, such as nitrates, in a marine or aquatic ecosystem (102, 120, 210)
eutrofización un aumento en la cantidad de nutrientes, tales como nitratos, en un ecosistema marino o acuático

F

fission (FISH·uhn) the process by which a nucleus splits into two or more fragments and releases neutrons and energy (165)
fisión el proceso por medio del cual un núcleo se divide en dos o más fragmentos y libera neutrones y energía

food chain (FOOD CHAYN) the pathway of energy transfer through various stages as a result of the feeding patterns of a series of organisms (23)
cadena alimenticia la vía de transferencia de energía través de varias etapas, que ocurre como resultado de los patrones de alimentación de una serie de organismos

food web (FOOD WEB) a diagram that shows the feeding relationships between organisms in an ecosystem (24)
red alimenticia un diagrama que muestra las relaciones de alimentación entre los organismos de un ecosistema

fossil fuel (FAHS·uhl FYOO·uhl) a nonrenewable energy resource formed from the remains of organisms that lived long ago; examples include oil, coal, and natural gas (149, 160)
combustible fósil un recurso energético no renovable formado a partir de los restos de organismos que vivieron hace mucho tiempo; algunos ejemplos incluyen el petróleo, el carbón, y el gas natural

geothermal energy (jee·oh·THER·muhl EN·er·jee) the energy produced by heat within Earth (179)
energía geotérmica la energía producida por el calor del interior de la Tierra

grassland (GRAS·land) a region that is dominated by grasses, that has few woody shrubs and trees, that has fertile soils, and that receives moderate amounts of seasonal rainfall (69)
pradera una región en la que predomina la hierba, tiene algunos arbustos leñosos y árboles, y suelos fértiles, y recibe cantidades moderadas de precipitaciones estacionales

greenhouse effect (GREEN·hows ih·FEKT) the warming of the surface and lower atmosphere of Earth that occurs when water vapor, carbon dioxide, and other gases absorb and reradiate thermal energy (234)
efecto invernadero el calentamiento de la superficie y de la parte más baja de la atmósfera, el cual se produce cuando el vapor de agua, el dióxido de carbono, y otros gases absorben y vuelven a irradiar la energía térmica

habitat (HAB·ih·tat) the place where an organism usually lives (12)
hábitat el lugar donde generalmente vive un organismo

herbivore (HER·buh·vohr) an organism that eats only plants (21)
herbívoro un organismo que sólo come plantas

hydroelectric energy (hy·droh·ee·LEK·trik EN·er·jee) electrical energy produced by the flow of water (175)
energía hidroeléctrica energía eléctrica producida por el flujo del agua

land degradation (LAND deg·ruh·DAY·shuhn) the process by which human activity and natural processes damage land to the point that it can no longer support the local ecosystem (228)
degradación del suelo el proceso por el cual la actividad humana y los procesos naturales dañan el suelo de modo que el ecosistema local no puede subsistir

law of conservation of energy (LAW UHV kahn·suhr·VAY·shuhn UHV EN·er·jee) the law that states that energy cannot be created or destroyed but can be changed from one form to another (91)
ley de la conservación de la energía la ley que establece que la energía ni se crea ni se destruye, sólo se transforma de una forma a otra

law of conservation of mass (LAW UHV kahn·suhr·VAY·shuhn UHV MAS) the law that states that mass cannot be created or destroyed in ordinary chemical and physical changes (91)
ley de la conservación de la masa la ley que establece que la masa no se crea ni se destruye por cambios químicos o físicos comunes

limiting factor (LIM·ih·ting FAK·ter) an environmental factor that prevents an organism or population from reaching its full potential of size or activity (36)
factor limitante un factor ambiental que impide que un organismo o población alcance su máximo potencial de distribución o de actividad

material resource (muh·TIR·ee·uhl REE·sohrs) a natural resource that humans use to make objects or to consume as food and drink (150)
recurso material un recurso natural que utilizan los seres humanos para fabricar objetos o para consumir como alimento o bebida

matter (MAT·er) anything that has mass and takes up space (90)
materia cualquier cosa que tiene masa y ocupa un lugar en el espacio

mutualism (MYOO·choo·uh·liz·uhm) a relationship between two species in which both species benefit (46)
mutualismo una relación entre dos especies en la que ambas se benefician

natural resource (NACH·uh·ruhl REE·sohrs) any natural material that is used by humans, such as water, petroleum, minerals, forests, and animals (148, 188)
recurso natural cualquier material natural que es utilizado por los seres humanos, como agua, petróleo, minerales, bosques, y animales

niche (NICH) the role of a species in its community, including use of its habitat and its relationships with other species (12)
nicho el papel que juega una especie en su comunidad, incluidos el uso de su hábitat y su relación con otras especies

nitrogen cycle (NY·truh·juhn SY·kuhl) the cycling of nitrogen between organisms, soil, water, and the atmosphere (95)
ciclo del nitrógeno el ciclado del nitrógeno entre los organismos, el suelo, el agua y la atmósfera

nonpoint-source pollution · (nahn·POYNT SOHRS puh·LOO·shuhn) pollution that comes from many sources rather than from a single specific site; an example is pollution that reaches a body of water from streets and storm sewers (210)
contaminación no puntual contaminación que proviene de muchas fuentes, en lugar de provenir de un solo sitio específico; un ejemplo es la contaminación que llega a una masa de agua a partir de las calles y los drenajes

nonrenewable resource (nahn·rih·NOO·uh·buhl REE·sohrs) a resource that forms at a rate that is much slower than the rate at which the resource is consumed (149, 188)
recurso no renovable un recurso que se forma a una tasa que es mucho más lenta que la tasa a la que se consume

nuclear energy (NOO·klee·er EN·er·jee) the energy released by a fission or fusion reaction; the binding energy of the atomic nucleus (160)
energía nuclear la energía liberada por una reacción de fisión o fusión; la energía de enlace del núcleo atómico

omnivore (AHM·nuh·vohr) an organism that eats both plants and animals (21)
omnívoro un organismo que come tanto plantas como animales

ozone (OH·zohn) a gas molecule that is made up of three oxygen atoms (143)
ozono una molécula de gas que está formada por tres átomos de oxígeno

parasitism (PAIR·uh·sih·tiz·uhm) a relationship between two species in which one species, the parasite, benefits from the other species, the host, which is harmed (47)
parasitismo una relación entre dos especies en la que una, el parásito, se beneficia de la otra, el huésped, que resulta perjudicada

particulate (par·TIK·yuh·lit) a tiny particle of solid that is suspended in air or water (235)
material particulado una pequeña partícula de material sólido que se encuentra suspendida en el aire o el agua

photosynthesis (foh·toh·SIN·thih·sis) the process by which plants, algae, and some bacteria use sunlight, carbon dioxide, and water to make food (138)
fotosíntesis el proceso por medio del cual las plantas, las algas, y algunas bacterias utilizan la luz solar, el dióxido de carbono, y el agua para producir alimento

pioneer species (py·uh·NIR SPEE·sheez) a species that colonizes an uninhabited area and that starts a process of succession (104)
especie pionera una especie que coloniza un área deshabitada y empieza un proceso de sucesión

point-source pollution (POYNT SOHRS puh·LOO·shuhn) pollution that comes from a specific site (210)
contaminación puntual contaminación que proviene de un lugar específico

population (pahp·yuh·LAY·shuhn) a group of organisms of the same species that live in a specific geographical area (8)
población un grupo de organismos de la misma especie que viven en un área geográfica específica

potable (POH·tuh·buhl) suitable for drinking (213)
potable que puede beberse

predator (PRED·uh·ter) an organism that kills and eats all or part of another organism (44)
depredador un organismo que mata y se alimenta de otro organismo o de parte de él

prey (PRAY) an organism that is killed and eaten by another organism (44)
presa un organismo al que otro organismo mata para alimentarse de él

producer (pruh·DOO·ser) an organism that can make its own food by using energy from its surroundings (20)
productor un organismo que puede elaborar sus propios alimentos utilizando la energía de su entorno

renewable resource (rih·NOO·uh·buhl REE·sohrs) a natural resource that can be replaced at the same rate at which the resource is consumed (149, 188)
recurso renovable un recurso natural que puede reemplazarse a la misma tasa a la que se consume

reservoir (REZ·er·vwar) an artificial body of water that usually forms behind a dam (215)
represa una masa artificial de agua que normalmente se forma detrás de una presa

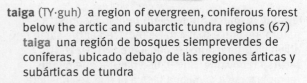

smog (SMAHG) air pollution that forms when ozone and vehicle exhaust react with sunlight (236)
esmog contaminación del aire que se produce cuando el ozono y sustancias químicas como los gases de los escapes de los vehículos reaccionan con la luz solar

solar energy (SOH·ler EN·er·jee) the energy received by Earth from the sun in the form of radiation (176)
energía solar la energía que la Tierra recibe del Sol en forma de radiación

species (SPEE·sheez) a group of organisms that are closely related and can mate to produce fertile offspring (8)
especie un grupo de organismos que tienen un parentesco cercano y que pueden aparearse para producir descendencia fértil

stewardship (STOO·erd·ship) the careful and responsible management of a resource (122, 190, 247)
gestión ambiental responsable el manejo cuidadoso y responsable de un recurso

succession (suhk·SESH·uhn) the replacement of one type of community by another at a single location over a period of time (104)
sucesión el reemplazo de un tipo de comunidad por otro en un mismo lugar a lo largo de un período de tiempo

symbiosis (sim·by·OH·sis) a relationship in which two different organisms live in close association with each other (46)
simbiosis una relación en la que dos organismos diferentes viven estrechamente asociados uno con el otro

T

taiga (TY·guh) a region of evergreen, coniferous forest below the arctic and subarctic tundra regions (67)
taiga una región de bosques siempreverdes de coníferas, ubicado debajo de las regiones árticas y subárticas de tundra

thermal pollution (THER·muhl puh·LOO·shuhn) a temperature increase in a body of water that is caused by human activity and that has a harmful effect on water quality and on the ability of that body of water to support life (210)
contaminación térmica un aumento en la temperatura de una masa de agua, producido por las actividades humanas y que tiene un efecto dañino en la calidad del agua y en la capacidad de esa masa de agua para permitir que se desarrolle la vida

tundra (TUHN·druh) a region found at far northern and far southern latitudes characterized by low-lying plants, a lack of trees, and long winters with very low temperatures (67)
tundra una región que se encuentra en latitudes muy al norte o muy al sur y que se caracteriza por las plantas bajas, la ausencia de árboles, y los inviernos prolongados con temperaturas muy bajas

ultraviolet radiation (uhl·truh·VY·uh·lit ray·dee·AY·shuhn) electromagnetic wave frequencies immediately above the visible range (143)
radiación ultravioleta longitudes de onda electromagnéticas inmediatamente adyacentes al color violeta en el espectro visible

urbanization (er·buh·nih·ZAY·shuhn) an increase in the proportion of a population living in urban areas rather than in rural areas (117, 225)
urbanización un aumento de la proporción de población en las áreas urbanas en lugar de en las áreas rurales

water cycle (WAW·ter SY·kuhl) the continuous movement of water between the atmosphere, the land, the oceans, and living things (94)
ciclo del agua el movimiento continuo del agua entre la atmósfera, la tierra, los océanos, y los seres vivos

water pollution (WAW·ter puh·LOO·shuhn) waste matter or other material that is introduced into water and that is harmful to organisms that live in, drink, or are exposed to the water (210)
contaminación del agua material de desecho u otro material que se introduce en el agua y que daña a los organismos que viven en el agua, la beben o están expuestos a ella

wetland (WET·land) an area of land that is periodically underwater or whose soil contains a great deal of moisture (78)
pantano un área de tierra que está periódicamente bajo el agua o cuyo suelo contiene una gran cantidad de humedad

wind energy (WIND EN·er·jee) the use of the force of moving air to drive an electric generator (174)
energía eólica el uso de la fuerza del aire en movimiento para hacer funcionar un generador eléctrico

Index

Page numbers for definitions are printed in **boldface** type.
Page numbers for illustrations, maps, and charts are printed in *italics*.

Houghton Mifflin Harcourt Publishing Company